An Introduction to Social Entrepreneurship

Voices, Preconditions, Contexts

Edited by

Rafael Ziegler

Co-ordinator, Social Entrepreneurship Research Group GETIDOS, University of Greifswald and Institut für ökologische Wirtschaftsforschung, Berlin, Germany

Edward Elgar
Cheltenham, UK • Northampton, MA, USA

Published by
Edward Elgar Publishing Limited
The Lypiatts
15 Lansdown Road
Cheltenham
Glos GL50 2JA
UK

Edward Elgar Publishing, Inc.
William Pratt House
9 Dewey Court
Northampton
Massachusetts 01060
USA

Paperback edition 2011

A catalogue record for this book
is available from the British Library

Library of Congress Control Number: 2008939771

MIX
Paper from
responsible sources
FSC
www.fsc.org   FSC® C018575

ISBN 978 1 84844 306 8 (cased)
ISBN 978 0 85793 372 0 (paperback)

Typeset by Servis Filmsetting Ltd, Stockport, Cheshire
Printed and bound by MPG Books Group, UK

Contents

PART III CONTEXTS

Figures, tables and boxes

FIGURES

TABLES

BOXES

Contributors

Philipp Albers studied North American studies, philosophy, and cultural studies in Berlin and in Durham, North Carolina. He is a co-founding member of Zentrale Intelligenz Agentur. From 2004 until 2008 he worked as Program Director at the American Academy in Berlin.

Rob Boddice received his PhD in 2005 from the University of York, UK, where he wrote his thesis on blood sports in nineteenth-century Britain. He is currently working on a book concerned with human–animal relations in eighteenth- and nineteenth-century Britain, to be published by Edwin Mellen Press in 2009. Boddice has taught and published in the field of gender history, and maintains a scholarly interest in historiography and historical theory. He was post-doctoral fellow (2006–2008) at the European College of Liberal Arts, Berlin, at the time of the conference on social entrepreneurship which inspired this book.

Holm Friebe, economist and journalist, is one of the chief editors at the award-winning weblog Riesenmaschine.de, co-founder of Zentrale Intelligenz Agentur in Berlin and Professor at the Hochschule der Künste in Zürich. His non-fiction book *Wir nennen es Arbeit – die Digitale Bohème oder intelligentes Leben jenseits der Festanstellung* (co-written with Sascha Lobo, 2006) became an economy bestseller. Together with Kathrin Passig, Friebe writes a monthly trend-column for the *Berliner Zeitung* called 'Das nächste große Ding'. *NEON* magazine listed him among 'the 100 most important young Germans' in 2006.

Paola Grenier gained her doctorate from the London School of Economics and Political Sciences, on the role and significance of social entrepreneurship in UK social policy. She has researched and written on social entrepreneurship in the UK and internationally, as well as on social movements and social capital. Before entering academia she worked for ten years in the non-profit sectors in the UK and in Hungary, specialising in social housing, homelessness, medical self-help and mental health.

Daniel Hjorth is a Professor of Entrepreneurship and Innovation Management, and Research Director (for the Management group) at the Department of Management, Politics and Philosophy, Copenhagen Business School. Hjorth is editor (together with Chris Steyaert) for a series of four books (2003, 2004, 2006 and 2009, Edward Elgar) that represent a so-called new movement in entrepreneurship studies. His work is also published in, for example, *Organization, Human Relations, Journal of Management Inquiry, Journal of Management Education* and *Journal of Business Venturing*. Hjorth is presently focusing on organisational creativity, aesthetics in business competitiveness and a philosophy of entrepreneurship.

Eva Illouz is a Professor of Sociology at the Hebrew University of Jerusalem. She received her PhD from the University of Pennsylvania in 1991. Illouz is the author of *Consuming the Romantic Utopia: Love and the Cultural Contradictions of Capitalism* (which won an award from the American Sociological Association in 2000), *The Culture of Capitalism* (in Hebrew), *Oprah Winfrey and the Glamour of Misery: An Essay on Popular Culture* (Best Book Award, American Sociological Association, 2005); *Cold Intimacies* (Polity Press, 2007), and *Saving the Modern Soul: Therapy, Emotions, and the Culture of Self-Help* (University of California Press, 2008). In 2004 she delivered the Adorno Lectures in Germany. Her work has been translated in nine languages. Illouz was a Visiting Professor at the EHESS in Paris and at Princeton University.

Judy Korn is the founder and Managing Director of the Violence Prevention Network (VPN). She received her diploma in education in 1995 and became a mediator in 1997. She began working on the topic of violence prevention and fighting against right-wing extremism when she was in secondary school, and created her first project: 'Miteinander statt Gegeneinander' ('Together – Not Against Each Other') in 1988. This was the first official recognised project with right-wing-extremist youth in Berlin. After years of social work with adolescents prone to violence, in 1999 she created the first school-mediation programme to receive long-term funding. After nine years in public service, she gave up her permanent position, co-developed the pedagogy of responsibility and in 2005 founded the Violence Prevention Network. In 2007 she was elected an Ashoka Fellow.

Michal Kravcik founded the non-governmental organisation People and Water, and co-authored *Water for the Recovery of the Climate – A New Water Paradigm*. He belongs to the first generation of Slovak Ashoka Fellows, and he is a recipient of the Goldman Environmental Prize. Prior to the foundation of People and Water, Dr Kravcik worked for the Institute of Hydrology and Hydraulics, and the Institute of Ecology of the Slovak Academy of Sciences.

Johanna Mair is Professor of Strategic Management at IESE, the Business School of the University of Navarra in Barcelona, Spain. She teaches corporate strategy and entrepreneurship for social impact in the MBA programme, executive programmes and the PhD programme at IESE. Her current research lies at the intersection of traditional strategy and entrepreneurship. More specifically she is interested in how institutions stifle and enable social and economic progress and the role of entrepreneurial actors in this process. Mair's work has been published in leading academic journals. In 2007, she was recognised as a 'Faculty Pioneer' by the Aspen Institute and received the Ashoka Award for Social Entrepreneurship Education. Mair serves on the editorial board of *Strategic Entrepreneurial Journal and Entrepreneurship: Theory & Practice*. She sits on the advisory board of a number of companies, foundations and social investment funds, and consults with large multinational companies and international organisations such as the World Bank.

Christian Seelos is the Director of the Platform for Strategy and Sustainability at IESE Business School. He is also a Senior Lecturer at the IESE Department of Strategic Management and teaches at a number of business schools in Europe, Africa and the USA. His research focus is on social innovation, sustainable development and innovative business models. His insights in novel corporate strategies in emerging markets (co-authored by Johanna Mair) were recognised by the Strategic Management Society (Best Paper Award for Practice Implications, 2007) and also won him the Gold Prize of the highly contested IFC-FT essay competition on private sector development in 2008.

Krzysztof Stanowski, a historian by training, was an activist in Poland's underground Solidarity movement, the leader of an independent scouting movement during the 1980s and President of the Warsaw-based Foundation for Education for Democracy (2001–2007). Since 2007 he has been serving as a Deputy Minister of Education for the Polish Government. He was elected Ashoka Fellow in 2000, has been awarded the Mongolian Medal of Freedom (2005) and the Order of Polonia Restiuta (2006). He is the author of several handbooks for non-governmental organisation activists.

Richard Swedberg is Professor of Sociology at Cornell University and his two main areas of research are economic sociology and social theory. His books include *The Economic Sociology of Capitalism* (ed. with Victor Nee), *Interest, Principles of Economic Sociology, Entrepreneurship: The Social Science View* (ed.), *Max Weber and the Idea of Economic Sociology, Joseph A. Schumpeter: His Life and Work* and *Joseph A. Schumpeter: The Economics and Sociology of Capitalism* (ed.).

Ion Bogdan Vasi is an Assistant Professor in the School of International and Public Affairs at Columbia University. His research focuses on organisations, social movements, and environmental sociology. He has published research on local actions against global climate change, the adoption of municipal resolutions to protect civil liberties, and the global development of the wind energy industry.

Rafael Ziegler co-ordinates the Social Entrepreneurship Research Group GETIDOS at the University of Greifswald (www.getidos.net) and the Institut für ökologische Wirtschaftsforschung in Berlin. He is also Chercheur associé at the Centre Marc Bloch (Berlin). His research focuses on philosophical dimensions of sustainable development: justice and development, the epistemology of sustainability science and on education for sustainable development.

Acknowledgements

In this anthology, historian Rob Boddice urges social entrepreneurs to ask themselves why they do what they do. But editors also should ask themselves this question (as well as what makes their 'good works' possible). Interaction, especially with those I would like to thank here first and last, would be a big part of my response to this question.

First, I would like to thank students. Undergraduates I first met in an elective on sustainable development, in particular Pranab Singh, proposed social entrepreneurship as a topic of discussion, and as a result we worked together on a week-long social entrepreneurship conference on social entrepreneurship in May 2007. Later, in the fall of 2007, discussions with students during a seminar on social entrepreneurship have influenced the way things are presented and put together here. Lena Schulze-Gabrechten, for instance, wrote her final assignment on social entrepreneur Judy Korn's work.

These teaching experiences were made possible by the European College of Liberal Arts in Berlin. I would also like to acknowledge the support of the college in enabling me to start working on the book in summer 2007. Many members of the faculty contributed ideas and questions, especially Catherine Toal. She helped organise the social entrepreneurship conference, co-designed and co-taught a social entrepreneurship seminar with me, wrote one of the commentaries for the chapter drafts of the anthology and put together most parts of the book proposal for the publisher. For all these contributions I would like to thank her very much.

As for the contributors, I would like to specially thank the contributors to Part I for their efforts to bring together this unusual part of the anthology. It required a lot of back and forth, but it was worth it. Michal Kravcik's colleague, Juraj Kohutiar, read a draft of Chapter 2 and made very helpful comments and suggestions. Thanks to Birger Hartnuß and Judy Korn for permission to use a part of their work as boxes for Chapter 3. The support staff of the Polish Ministry of Education were very patient in dealing with the difficult task of efficient communication flows with a politician.

The University of California's permission for using a modified version of Eva Illouz's Chapter 3 of her *Saving the Modern Soul* (UCP, 2008) is gratefully acknowledged.

My new work environment at the University of Greifswald and at the Institut für ökologische Wirtschaftsforschung has from the beginning provided a welcoming and co-operative environment, and the social-ecological research programme of the German Ministry of Education and Research the means to do this kind of work. Thanks to Christian Bartholomäus from Greifswald for help with the references, to Grisha Damke for professional advice on the book proposal, to Laurin Federlein for designing the book cover and to Lars Bußmann for his help in compiling the index. I am also very grateful to all of the collaborators at Edward Elgar Publishing for their continuous and kind support.

My greatest thanks are to my editor: Anne-Marie Reynaud, whose support ranged from technical advice and proofreading of various chapters to in-depth questions and comments. I am very thankful to have had the luxury of an editor's editor.

Rafael Ziegler
Berlin, 12 August 2008

1. Introduction: voices, preconditions, contexts

Rafael Ziegler

> The danger of an uncritical and exclusive promotion of a free and market-based (social) system is evident. There are domains where the state has a duty to take action and to ensure the basic security of its citizens. But without a permanent input to the state system of new ideas from outside, even this legitimate domain can do more harm than good. (Judy Korn, Chapter 3 in this volume, p. 51)

Social entrepreneurship has become a source of hope, but we are like water-tap users who know little about the origin of the source. Social entrepreneurship is said to be made of ideas that are tried out rather than proclaimed, ideas that are pushed through by initiatives belonging to individuals rather than multinational mega-organisations, ideas that are proposed in languages that are culturally diverse and not necessarily professionally polished, ideas that speak of pervasive social inequalities and exclusions, of ecological problems and risks, and ideas that do not speak of these issues as inevitable predicaments but as challenges that call for societal transformations. Who or what makes all this possible? Social entrepreneurs are said to have innovative solutions to pressing social problems; they are characterised as ambitious and persistent; they are said not to rely on business and government for the realisation of their ideas, and to aim at wide-scale, systemic change.[1] These social entrepreneurs are promoted by support organisations, the media, companies and policy-makers. They have become increasingly familiar, branded and politicised actors. How has this happened? What kind of impact do social entrepreneurs seek? What impact do social entrepreneurs have? And, is it possible not only to learn about social entrepreneurs, but also to become one?

This anthology offers extended discussions of these questions – except for the last one. Oscar Wilde quipped that 'the best things in life cannot be taught'. Whether social entrepreneurship belongs to the 'best things in life' is no doubt a question of individual judgment. But the obstacle to 'teaching' social entrepreneurship is not this question of taste: the frequent claim that people are 'born' as social entrepreneurs is. Social entrepreneur Orlando Rincón Bonilla says: 'It's genetic. You can walk into a room full of people, and pick the entrepreneurs out in seconds. It's something about the look in their eyes.'[2] Is it therefore only possible to 'pick' and 'support' people who already *are* social entrepreneurs, but impossible to teach social entrepreneurship in a vocational sense? The question points to a paradox: 'social entrepreneurs' are presented as special people, as the contemporary heroes and leaders, and at the same time social entrepreneurship indicates a universal ideal: 'everyone a changemaker' (Drayton, 2006). The paradox points to tensions between an elite and a democratic ideal of equality, between an exclusive network and an inclusive vision. These tensions resonate widely, and they call for a consideration of the contexts and presuppositions of social entrepreneurship. Why is social change conceptualised in these individualist terms? Could there be alternative conceptualisations? What is the cultural significance of this phenomenon?

Even if it would be accepted that some people are 'born' as social entrepreneurs, there remains the question: what preconditions are conducive or even necessary for them to act as social entrepreneurs? On the one hand, if Mozart had been born into a family with no musical instruments, no money and no interest in a classic music education for children but with much love for Viennese bakery, would he have lived the life of a 'conceptual entrepreneur'[3] (be it in music, or in bakery)? On the other hand, did his contemporaries call him an 'entrepreneur'? In short, what are the cultural, social and economic preconditions of social entrepreneurship? Social entrepreneurs may embody the power of ideas, but ideas also have power over social entrepreneurs.

In a sense it does not matter whether we think of social entrepreneurs as 'born' social entrepreneurs or as 'becoming' ones – either way they will have to act in specific contexts of local and global norms that they fight for or struggle against; and that they will face terminology choices that may foster one cause better than another; for example, rhetoric that primarily focuses on the individual, on the social entrepreneur as 'hero', even though social entrepreneurship requires organisation and participation. These contexts are worthy objects of study, even if one is not a social entrepreneur or does not want to become one, for they concern basic contexts of the organisation of work today.

Accordingly, this anthology proposes in depth studies of the preconditions (Part II) and contexts (Part III) of social entrepreneurship. Neither the study of preconditions nor the study of contexts will answer the question whether it is possible to ignite this 'look', this 'sense of excitement' and of 'boundless fascination' in everyone's eyes. However, this anthology offers contributions written by social entrepreneurs (Part I): reflections on their work, on social entrepreneurship and on the relation of social entrepreneurship to the state. Taken together, the three parts will help to better understand what the 'looks' are all about, what social entrepreneurs get 'excited' about, and consequently whether one would even want (everyone) to be excited in this way.

In music, an 'introduction' usually sets the 'tone' for a piece of music. The 'piece' here is the real world of social entrepreneurship. Let me explain the choice of perspectives selected for this introduction.

A CONTRIBUTION TO THE SOUND OF INNOVATION

The discussion of social entrepreneurship flows together from a number of quite different types of texts coming from different positions and practices. At least six prominent perspectives can be distinguished.[4] These distinctions help explain the choice of texts in this anthology – and they help listen to the 'sound of innovation' as the interplay of different voices rather than just as the confusing 'noise' of a field (under)mined by multiple definitions.

1. *Social entrepreneurs*: some discussions of social entrepreneurship are written by social entrepreneurs. In comparison to the other perspectives listed below, such texts are relatively rare (see also the section on Part I below).[5]
2. *Social entrepreneurship support organisations*: a large number of texts on social entrepreneurship, including some of the most widely read ones, come from (or are strongly influenced by) the organisations that select and support social entrepreneurs.[6] These texts tend to promote social entrepreneurship, not least because organisations such as Ashoka and the Schwab Foundation have an institutional interest to attract funds and other means of support. Catchy tunes are needed, and the promotion ranges from case studies of (typically successful) social entrepreneurs to manifestos. Here is one example from William Drayton, the founder of Ashoka, who has probably done more than anyone else to promote social entrepreneurship:

> The most important contribution any of us can make now is not to solve any particular problem, no matter how urgent energy or environment or financial regulation is. What we must do now is increase the proportion of humans who know that they can cause change. And who, like smart white blood cells coursing through society, will stop with pleasure whenever they see that something is stuck or that an opportunity is ripe to be seized. Multiplying society's capacity to adapt and change intelligently and constructively and building the necessary underlying collaborative architecture, is the world's most critical opportunity now. Pattern-changing leading social entrepreneurs are the most critical single factor in catalysing and engineering this transformation. (Drayton, 2006: 7)

3.   *Journalism*: book-length studies of social entrepreneurs have been written by journalists,[7] well-known daily newspapers such as the *New York Times* or the *Frankfurter Allgemeine Zeitung* have published 'faces' and features; on television the Public Broadcast Service has aired a 'New Heroes' series that tells 'the dramatic stories of 14 daring people'.[8] These are texts (and films) that feature successful entrepreneurs, and they are often written and produced in close co-operation with the social entrepreneurship support organisations.

4.   *Academia*: management studies, but increasingly also researchers from other disciplines, including economics, sociology and political science, have made social entrepreneurship an emerging field of research. Social entrepreneurship has been examined *inter alia* via the lenses of strategic management, social movement theory and democratic theory.[9] Inevitably, the tone is more sceptical. Social entrepreneurship reverberates from theories of agency, value, democracy and so forth. Historical comparisons and conceptual contrasts are drawn, theoretical analyses of the phenomenon are made.

5.   *Business*: successful entrepreneurs have shown interest in social entrepreneurship. For example Jeff Skoll, first president of eBay, founded in 1999 the Oxford-based Skoll Foundation with a mission to 'advance systemic change to benefit communities around the world by investing in, connecting and celebrating social entrepreneurs'.[10] Many companies support social entrepreneurship support organisations, financially but also via *pro bono* consultancy and other means.

6.   *Fiction*: fiction, written or filmed, offers rich descriptions and very comprehensive perspectives. Consider how William Dean Howells, in his *The Rise of Silas Lapham*, lets his entrepreneur speak. 'I believe in my paint', says Silas Lapham,

> I believe it's a blessing to the world. When folks come in, and kind of smell round, and ask me what I mix it with, I always say, 'Well, in the first place, I mix it with Faith, and after that I grind it up with the best quality of boiled linseed oil that money will buy'. (Howells, 1884–85 [1982]: 16)

Fiction humbles academics and journalists by revealing just how little they have been considering so far, and how many other factors they might still have to consider. In fiction, the characters belong to families – something they would not seem to belong to for anyone who just read the accounts of (most) academics and journalists. They have social aspirations and meet social pressures, and these familial-social ties stand in a complex relation to their work. The 'faith' in his 'paint' is situated in Howells' novel in a larger 'economy of pain' that exhibits a dynamic between family life and economic life. Apart from novels, biographies and autobiographies should also be mentioned. Along with novels and films, they play a (largely unacknowledged role) for the way in which people in 1–4 preconceive the 'story of a life'.

The point of drawing these distinctions is not to say that any perspective is better than the others. And in practice these distinctions are blurred. But the distinctions help explain the choices made when producing this book, as well as offer a trivial, yet important consideration for thinking about social entrepreneurship.

This anthology draws on source one (social entrepreneurs) and source three (academics). The texts by social entrepreneurship organisations, journalists and business are readily available via the Internet and other mass media. But as noted above, thinking about social entrepreneurship calls in particular for exploring the tension between social entrepreneurs, and the preconditions and contexts of social entrepreneurship; between individual (and group) agency and social structure. Accordingly, this anthology has been organised to include a part with contributions by social entrepreneurs, and parts that discuss preconditions and contexts drawing on the work of academic research.

There is therefore no fiction in this anthology; partly for the same reason that novels are easily available from libraries and bookstores, but also because their comprehensive theorising of the life of entrepreneurs – of work and family, reality and faith, individual story-telling and novel structure – does not come in 'chapters'. Still, a more systematic discussion of fiction in relation to social entrepreneurship ought to be a challenge for future research on social entrepreneurship. The same holds for an account of the business perspective. Neither a big business entrepreneur nor a corporation has been invited to contribute to this anthology. These actors are able to effectively communicate their views and fund research, and in this sense are sure to play a role in the way all of us already understand social entrepreneurship. More interesting therefore, and there seems to be a real gap in literature, would be an analysis of the influence of business on social entrepreneurs and the social entrepreneurship organisation – a task for academics and journalists.[11] The chapter by Daniel Hjorth in this anthology is a step in this direction.

Keeping these distinct perspectives in mind does not only explain the choices made for this anthology and how it seeks to contribute to the already existing 'sound of innovation', but it also helps with the study of social entrepreneurship. Consider this passage from Drayton:

By 1700, however, a new, more open architecture was beginning to develop in northern Europe: entrepreneurial/competitive business facilitated by more tolerant, open politics . . . the West broke out from 1,200 years of stagnation and soon soared past anything the world had seen before . . . However, until 1980, this transformation bypassed the social half of the world's operations. Society taxed the new wealth created by business to pay for its roads and canals, schools and welfare systems. There was no need to change . . . the social sector had felt little need to change and a paymaster that actively discouraged it. Hence, the squalor of the social sector. Relative performance declining at an accelerating rate. And consequent low repute, dismal pay, and poor self-esteem and élan. (Drayton, 2006: 5f)

Taken as the statement of a historian, this would seem to be a bold generalisation, and it would surely infuriate all other historians. But taken as a manifesto promoting social entrepreneurship – 'everyone a changemaker' – bold generalisation will be expected, and the focus turns to the political position proclaimed, and to the metaphors and allusions animating the text rather than its historical accuracy. But of course historical accuracy may then well play an important role for examining the position taken in the manifesto (see the chapter by Boddice in this volume). Trivially but certainly not always observed, learning about social entrepreneurship requires taking into account the position and interests of the various voices animating the debate, including one's own. The 'sound of innovation' is one in which we all participate.

PART I: VOICES

But some participate more than others. In Part I of this anthology, people who accept being called 'social entrepreneurs' speak about what they do and what this designation means for them. And people with a social mission, who are entrepreneurial, but who do not accept this title, speak about what they do and what this title means for them.

The contributors, men and women, work on social and environmental issues in Eastern and Western Europe. Judy Korn from Berlin, Germany, co-directs the Violence Prevention Network that seeks to reduce the rate of racially and religiously motivated youth crime. Michal Kravcik belongs to the first generation of Slovak social entrepreneurs. For more than a decade, he and his non-governmental organisation (NGO) People and Water have worked towards an integrated, decentralised and ecologically sound water management in Slovakia. Krzyzstof Stanowski is Deputy Minister of Education in Poland – he was offered this work in no small part due to his prior work, supported by an Ashoka fellowship, as programme director and then president of the Warsaw-based Education for Democracy Foundation operating in Eastern Europe and Central Asia. By contrast,

Philipp Albers and Holm Friebe from the Zentrale Intelligenz Agentur in Berlin are not 'fellows' of any social entrepreneurship organisation (and do not seem to be eager to become 'fellows' of any larger organisation). However, they have set up their own organisation motivated by a vision of large-scale change in the labour world from permanent employment to flexible networks of self-employed people. They seek to co-design and contribute to this social change with new forms of collaboration.

What is it like to be a 'social entrepreneur'? All contributors to this part have been invited to contribute to the anthology, and were asked to write about (a) their initiatives, (b) their biography, (c) social entrepreneurship and (d) how they view their work in relation to the state. Their contributions follow this four-part structure. Korn and Kravcik have written texts; Albers and Friebe, and Stanowski preferred to conduct conversations on these themes, on the basis of which we together produced an edited protocol.

Accordingly, this part seeks to contribute to the understanding of social entrepreneurship in three ways:

1. Often the sound of innovation is presented as a concert for orchestra and soloists – but the soloists are missing. As noted, texts written by social entrepreneurs are relatively rare whereas there is an abundance of texts written 'about' them. Part I offers one way to ask how these 'persistent' and 'ambitious' creatures correspond to the accounts and definitions of support organisations and academics.
2. Unlike the profiles available from social entrepreneurship support organisations, the contributions in Part I include a reflection on social entrepreneurship as well as on the relation between social entrepreneurship and the state.
3. Finally, this part also points to a domain of co-operation between social entrepreneurs and universities, research institutes and so forth. On one level, there is the study of social entrepreneurship as a phenomenon in its own right, on another level, there are the specific ideas put forward by specific social entrepreneurs. Kravcik and his collaborators offer a bold new water paradigm. Korn and her collaborators propose a pedagogy of responsibility. Albers and Friebe argue that we are about to enter a new regime of social hygiene that will force companies and each of us to rethink and re-organise work-life. The innovations proposed in these environmental, social and economic dimensions are necessarily as important as the study of social entrepreneurship on the general level. These specific innovations are at the core of whatever change this actor achieves, and why others would like to learn about it, support it and so forth. But how are 'powerful' ideas made? Part I

suggests an important dialogue with universities and research centres (see also below).

Social Entrepreneurship as a Contested Concept

The approach taken in this first part, notwithstanding one dissenting voice (Albers and Friebe), implicitly endorses the Ashoka approach to social entrepreneurship already cited in the first paragraph of this introduction. This organisation is an example of widely recognised best practice in the field: whatever social entrepreneurship is or ought to be, accredited Ashoka fellows should be considered.

If no 'definition' of 'social entrepreneurship' has been offered so far, it is certainly not because there is a lack of proposals. To the contrary, 'social entrepreneurship' almost inevitably attracts concerns about 'definition'.

Social entrepreneur Muhammed Yunnus speaks of a new type of person,

> who is not interested in profit maximisation. He is totally committed to make a difference to the world. He is socially-objective driven. He wants to give a better chance in life to other people. He wants to achieve his objective through creating and supporting sustainable business enterprises. Such businesses may or may not earn profit, but like any other business they must not incur losses.[12]

The social entrepreneurship support organisation Schwab describes the social entrepreneur as 'a pragmatic visionary who achieves large scale, systemic and sustainable social change through a new invention, a different approach, a more rigorous application of known technologies or strategies, or a combination of these'; social entrepreneurs, the foundation adds, 'combine the characteristics represented by Richard Branson and Mother Teresa'[13] (social entrepreneurs, then, are also a challenge to the imagination). Professor Johanna Mair, a contributor to this volume, and Ernesto Noboa define social entrepreneurship as 'the innovative use of resource combinations to pursue opportunities aiming at the creation of organisations and/or practices that yield and sustain social benefits' (Mair and Noboa, 2006: 122).

The definition by Mair and Noboa is taken from an anthology of recent social entrepreneurship scholarship. It was not the only choice available from this anthology: ten definitions are respectively used by its contributors (Mair et al., 2006: 4f). A large number of proposed definitions are a familiar phenomenon from other concepts that are not only novel, but also important for a number of diverse actors. 'Sustainable development' is a well-known example. They are 'contested concepts' (Jacobs, 1999) in that they function as the 'common currency' of quite different actors from government, civil society, social movements and business. Their use is possible, because contested concepts have two levels of meaning. One level is unitary and vague; it contains core ideas that are substantive and non-redundant. On a second level, definitions are precise and contested.

The first level brings together concepts that have not been related before in this way, but whose combination is compelling. For 'sustainable development' this is the need to integrate 'environmental' and 'economic' concerns; for 'social entrepreneurship' it is the integration of 'social objectives' with an 'entrepreneurial approach'. No doubt, this is 'vague', but the point is that none of the actors could discuss 'social entrepreneurship' focusing exclusively on 'social mission', nor would it be vice versa plausible to focus exclusively on business and earned income. An exclusive focus on social mission will lead to questions on how these actors are different from social service, charity, and social activism; an exclusive focus on 'entrepreneurship' is likely to produce the response that social entrepreneurship is really just a new form of business to promote itself and to enhance its public image. In short, all actors are forced to address both aspects. Judging from the various discussion of social entrepreneurship, this 'vague' level moreover includes the demand that the initiatives be 'sustainable', that they are 'innovative', that they aim at 'systemic change', that they address issues of 'equity' (at least at the level of needs) and/or 'environmental protection', that profit is not the priority and that those supported by the initiative are participants rather than 'mere victims' or 'objects'. To be sure, none of these demands are 'novel'. What makes 'social entrepreneurship' unique is that they must be discussed together.

At the second level, where the definition of social entrepreneurship is related to specific actions – a governmental grant programme, a fellow selection process or an academic research programme – more precise definitions of social entrepreneurship can be found, as well as their contestation. One example from academia is Francesco Perrini's distinction of 'two different schools of thought that have been developing regarding the SE definition' (Perrini, 2006: 6ff). What he calls the 'limited view' considers social entrepreneurship as belonging to theories pertinent to non-profits, what he calls the 'extended view' considers social entrepreneurship as a 'totally new, inter-sectoral field of study' (ibid.). But while there is then a 'contestation' between 'schools', both schools will have to address and interpret one way or the other the core concepts included on the 'vague level'. Disagreements over the 'meaning' of social entrepreneurship on this second level reveal the central arguments that the concept calls forth, and that unites people in contestation.

The specification offered on this second level issues from specific actions; different 'definitions' of social entrepreneurship must be seen in relation to the respective uses – the selection of fellows, a sociological research programme and so forth. If these different uses are noted, a diversity of 'definitions' is less surprising and maybe also less 'threatening' (considering the 'one-definition'-anxiety that preoccupies some in the field). However, this is certainly not to say that 'any' definition is as 'good' as any other (just as any 'social' mission is not necessarily 'good'). Rather, the claim is that these contestations over the approach are an essential part of the political arguments social entrepreneurship attracts. As Rob Boddice notes in this volume, much remains to be done to clarify these arguments.

PART II: PRECONDITIONS

That management and entrepreneurship are clearly distinguished today is not least due to one of the greatest and most influential twentieth-century economists, Joseph Schumpeter. He proposed an economic theory, which in stark contrast to neoclassical equilibrium theory puts a fundamental emphasis on historical change. Unlike Marx, he did not describe this change in terms of class struggles (and their relation to the conditions of production). Instead, Schumpeter put key emphasis on the role of the entrepreneurs and the entrepreneurial function for *economic* development.

This focus made him 'the' theorist of entrepreneurship and later of 'business' innovation studies, widely read, and often only partially read. In his chapter, Richard Swedberg carefully sets out the elements of Schumpeter's full model of entrepreneurship: the motivation of entrepreneurs, innovation, resistance, profit and the structural effect of the innovation on the business cycle.

Swedberg then updates the model, and generalises it to non-economic entrepreneurship, including social entrepreneurship. On this Schumpeterian account social entrepreneurship is defined 'as the pushing through or the successful introduction of social change through a new combination of elements that make up some way of doing things' (see Figure 6.6 in Swedberg's chapter). He reconsiders the elements of the full model of entrepreneurship in this new context and thereby offers a method for a systematic approach to the study of social entrepreneurship initiatives.

Schumpeter wrote the first edition of his famous *Theory of Economic Development* in 1811, that is, towards the end of the so-called 'golden age of capitalism' (the period roughly from 1880 to 1920). During this period entrepreneurs entered the stage, and were given literary monuments as in William Dean Howells' *The Rise of Silas Lapham* from 1885. But *The Rise of Silas Lapham* begins with the 'economic' rise of the entrepreneur – and it ends with his economic decline, outcompeted by a new corporation and financial capital (and in Schumpeter's account, the large-scale corporation and its administrative system is a mortal threat to the entrepreneur, see especially Schumpeter, 1942 [1977]).

In her chapter, Eva Illouz tells a story of this 'other' economic history, not that of entrepreneurship, but of management and the corporation. She notes that during the 'golden age of capitalism' production was increasingly standardised, organisation bureaucratised and the labour forces incorporated into large corporations with thousands of employees. She invites us to think deeply about the culture of management coming about with the corporation, and the role of empathy that has evolved within it.

Rather than juxtaposing management and entrepreneurship, this chapter invites us to study the culture of management as a profound and influential source for the 'empathy' stressed in the social entrepreneurship literature. Indeed, it describes the rise of a 'feminine' model of emotional control and empathy in the modern corporation that even in 'translation' is likely to have a strong effect on social entrepreneurs. Her account of the emerging 'corporate' self leads her to a final paradox: the suspension of emotions as a condition of co-operation and communication.

If the work of cultural sociologist Eva Illouz raises deep questions about the antecedents of currents social entrepreneurship discussion in the twentieth-century American culture of management, historian Rob Boddice invites readers to directly question a number of prominent features of social entrepreneurship: its claim to novelty, the precise meaning of the 'social' and 'ethical' in social entrepreneurship as well as the motivation of social entrepreneurs.

Boddice offers case studies of the British industrialist and visionary Robert Owen, the French social Catholic Léon Harmel, the American tycoon-philanthropist Henry Ford and the American high-tech computer entrepreneur William Norris in support of his argument that social entrepreneurship has its roots in a variety of movements stretching back to the industrial revolution. Reconsidering this history, he argues, sensitises us to the ideological forces that moulded social entrepreneurship. In particular, the historical perspective shows that a mere attributing of 'ethical' motives and justifications to these past actors conceals the variety of religious, utilitarian, authoritarian and communitarian motives and values that inspired or 'called' forth these actors. But if in retrospect these past entrepreneurs with a 'social' vision do not appear straightforwardly good, what then, by analogy, about the 'social' and 'ethical' claims of contemporary social entrepreneurs? Boddice urges social entrepreneurs and those supporting them to reflect on the sources of their values, and how they are held accountable for the values they promote.

His spirited, historically informed attack on some aspects of the presentation and self-understanding of (some) social entrepreneurs and the organisations supporting them is likely to meet some likely equally spirited responses on questions that no doubt are important for a deeper understanding of social entrepreneurship: can 'value neutrality' be assumed or even achieved as a possible goal? Do tycoon philanthropists such as Henry Ford, who got an entire society 'moving' (Boddice), not meet all the criteria of social entrepreneurship, and if so what does this imply for current 'corporate social responsibility' and 'corporate citizenship'? Finally, as a basic question of precondition, is social entrepreneurship an epilogue to what Max Weber called the 'spirit of Capitalism'?

PART III: CONTEXTS

Joseph Schumpeter places his analysis of entrepreneurship in a theory of (economic) *development*. The choice is conspicuous; it points to an important context of social entrepreneurship, that is, the role of social entrepreneurs in so-called 'developing' countries (see the chapter by Seelos and Mair), and in so-called 'developed' ones (see the chapters by Grenier, and by Hjorth). Is 'social entrepreneurship' an alternative to more traditional development 'aid' in the former? Does it advance sustainable development there? And does social entrepreneurship 'also' have a place in 'developed countries'? If so, what kind of place is this?

Before social entrepreneurship is put into this developing/developed context, a chapter (by Ion Bogdan Vasi) re-asks, for the purposes of this anthology, the methodological question that Schumpeter had already put forward with so much methodological sensitivity: how to study (social) entrepreneurship? He develops his answer drawing on the sociology of entrepreneurship (issuing from Weber and Schumpeter) and the theory of social movements. His chapter 'New heroes, old theories? Toward a sociological perspective on social entrepreneurship' notes the tendency to frame social issues in terms of individuals in the post-Thatcher/Reagan welfare states. The focus on individuals as the primary source of (their respective) responsibility for unemployment, is the focus on individuals as 'heroes' taking responsibility for social change. But from a sociological perspective such a focus is inadequate, Vasi argues, and leads to a futile search for the 'entrepreneurial personality'.

According to Vasi, social movement research and the sociology of entrepreneurship offer tools for a deeper analysis of the phenomenon. The study of social entrepreneurs – of 'success stories', but also the 'failures' of unsung 'heroes' – should take into account social entrepreneurs' perception of political and discursive opportunities, their mobilisation of organisational resources, and their interpretative work.

Consider Victoria Hale, founder of the Institute for One World Health that develops safe and affordable medicines for people with infectious diseases.[14] On the 'hero perspective', we should focus on the inspiration, creativity and courage of Victoria Hale. However, Vasi argues, in order to explain the success of the institute so far we have to focus on how it overcame distrust from government and business: collaboration with the National Institute of Allergy and the World Health Organization provided moral and financial resources.

But these tools from social movement research are not only important for the analysis of success and failure of social movements, Vasi argues, they also sensitise for the difficult task of assessing the 'success' of social entrepreneurs. The work of social entrepreneurs cannot be measured simply in terms of the growth of the respective organisation, and its products and services. Rather social entrepreneurs' success in meeting social goals can depend on successful administrative and organisational reforms that make social entrepreneurship akin to social activism rather than business entrepreneurship.

'Sustainable development' is not only a well-known contested concept, it also offers an important context for locating social entrepreneurship as Christian Seelos and Johanna Mair show in their contribution 'Hope for sustainable development: how social entrepreneurs make it happen'. They analyse sustainable development in terms of three clusters of goals: (1) satisfying basic needs, (2) creating communities to establish norms, rights and collaborative behaviour as a prerequisite for participating in social and economic development, and (3) translating the more abstract needs of future generations into action today. These goals have become (at least partly) internationally agreed on goals via the Millennium Development Goals adopted by the United Nations.[15] However, they argue that traditional efforts to achieve such goals, roughly speaking the respective national governmental implantation of internationally agreed on and internationally financed plans, have failed. More financial aid to the central administrations can be insufficient as these are already overwhelmed by the existing programmes. In particular in poor countries, there are problems with effective government and market structures. Finally, they point out that sustainable development is a complex challenge that makes internationally agreed on plans and related top-down efforts difficult to implement. However, they argue that there is also (some) hope. They find that the social entrepreneurs contribute to all of the basic elements of sustainable development.

The complement to Mair and Seelos's focus on sustainable development in 'poor' countries of the 'developing world' is a focus on the 'rich' countries of the 'developed' world. The slowdown of post-World War II economic growths rates along with persistent, high unemployment offered arguments for restructuring governmental administrations, for the privatisation of goods and services, and for changes to the social insurance system. Needless to say, this restructuring did not meet all social needs (and moreover created new ones). But efforts to privatise goods and services, and to restructure social services with a 'neo-liberal' twist, provided fertile soil for the emergence of social entrepreneurs in the 'developed' world.

In her chapter, Paola Grenier traces the rhetoric of social entrepreneurship in the UK, where the 'enterprise culture' of Thatcherism was followed by policy prominence given to social entrepreneurship with the election of the New Labour Government in 1997. Prime Minister Tony Blair announced: 'We will be backing thousands of social entrepreneurs – those people who bring to social problems the same enterprise and imagination that business entrepreneurs bring to wealth creation' (cited by Grenier, section 10.1 of her contribution to this volume). The rhetoric of social entrepreneurship in the UK, as elsewhere, is one of sweeping change. But Grenier also examines the *practice* of social entrepreneurship in the UK: the policy interventions of the UK government (through the Active Communities Unit, the Millennium Awards Scheme, the Community Champions Fund, and the granting of a £100 million endowment to the foundation for social entrepreneurs, UnLtd), and actions of social entrepreneurship support organisations such as Ashoka, the School for Social Entrepreneurs and the Community Action Network. She concludes that in the UK context, the understanding of social entrepreneurship based on innovative individuals (as pioneered by Ashoka) has been marginalised. The charismatic social entrepreneur seeking transformative change was not so appealing to policy-makers keen on 'modernisation' and 'reform'. They were more attracted by 'social enterprise' as a balance of social and economic goals, and in 'social entrepreneurship' as a mechanism for local community development.

Her analysis of the rhetoric and practice of social entrepreneurship therefore leads Grenier to the conclusion that, in the UK, social entrepreneurship has not given rise to the wide-ranging innovations announced in the 1990s, nor to coherent social entrepreneurship policy interventions. In practice, social entrepreneurship took place on the community level, involving the labelling and support of several thousand 'social entrepreneurs' who carried out small-scale social initiatives. Surprisingly then, even if the general discourse context is initially shaped by neo-liberal, Thatcherite, ideas the 'practice' of 'social entrepreneurship' in the UK is much informed by a small-scale communitarian tendency in policy discourse.

Daniel Hjorth, in his chapter 'Entrepreneurship, sociality and art: re-imagining the public', analyses 'social entrepreneurship' more generally in terms of the enterprise discourse. For him, 'social entrepreneurship' stands for a tamed version of entrepreneurship that promises solutions to social problems, and that simultaneously re-describes these problems as economic problems subject to management knowledge.

Do we have to move beyond social entrepreneurship? At stake, according to Hjorth, is the possibility of a public that offers ways of living based on principles of equity and abundance, a public that does not unite only for reasons of self-interest and scarcity. Such a future public, he argues, requires creative and playful actors that break with contemporary economic routines and that invent new forms of living together. Hjorth calls these actors 'public entrepreneurs'.

But are there, and will there be public entrepreneurs? Hjorth suggests that art with its destabilising function could provide the space for public entrepreneurship. Art, Hjorth proposes, has a democratic force that addresses anyone, a force that can stop each one of us, make us re-think, and thereby prepare a space for re-imagining the public.

EDUCATION

This anthology originates in a student proposal to discuss social entrepreneurship at the university level;[16] it led first to a week-long conference on social entrepreneurship, then to a social entrepreneurship seminar and, finally, to this anthology. More than half of the contributors gathered in this volume attended the week and/or the seminar.

Among those participating were three of the contributors to Part I (and the fourth one indirectly[17]). There is not only an interest from students to learn about social entrepreneurship, social entrepreneurs also have a strong interest in education. Stanowski's focus is primarily on a specific approach to education for democracy, for Korn political education is a basic component of her programme to reduce recidivism among right-wing extremist and religiously motivated offenders, and Kravick has organised a water university in an effort to disseminate and implement his approach (and as Boddice's chapter shows 'antecedent' figures such as Robert Owen and Léon Harmel also had strong views on education: Harmel considered religious education a condition of industrial development, Owen's projects included schools meant to build the character of the community members). These are all examples of a mission-oriented approach to education (although the mission varies from Christian views, to human rights to a New Water Paradigm). And the interest to learn about social entrepreneurship is no doubt partly due to this mission orientation.

Social entrepreneurship has become a source of hope – sources are the place where ground water flows off the ground, the spring of brooks that form the rivers flowing to the sea. But it is the sea that has provided perhaps 'the' image of science in the twentieth-century. Philosopher of Science Otto Neurath speaks of sailors on the open sea who must reconstruct their ship, but are never able to start afresh with the best materials on a dock (Neurath, 1932–33: 206). The metaphor of science at sea is one of survival and discovery – and one of independence from the land and its concerns. The metaphor suggests, therefore, that science and science education is at odds with the social mission based education.

However, in keeping with the image, there is no reason why the ships and their science-sailors could not return to ports, at least from time to time; likewise there is no reason why those with strong missions on the land could not come to the coast, at least from time to time. In this light, social entrepreneurship education at the university level is a natural meeting point of 'land' and 'water'. It is the 'wetland' that is known as a source of life, and as an often treacherous ground with foul smells. This anthology is a hybrid that brings together social entrepreneurs and academics, that begins with Michal Kravick's call 'to return the lost water to the continents', includes discussions of the paths and of the dead ends of social entrepreneurship and ends with a chapter on 'hope for sustainable development'.

I think that social entrepreneurship is one interesting possibility within education for sustainable development, and that the collaboration of social entrepreneurs with academic researchers on thematic issues could be extended much further – but of course only under the watchful, synthesising eyes of students.

NOTES

1. See www.ashoka.org/social_entrepreneur, last accessed 10 July 2008.
2. Cited in Elkington and Hartigan (2008: 10). David Bornstein introduces the founder of Ashoka in this way: 'Bill Drayton might be someone you might expect to find in a library on a Saturday night. He is inordinately thin. He wears out-of-fashion suits, thick glasses, and wallabies. His hair is limp, his skin a little pale, his tie is generally askew. Yet, his eyes convey a sense of excitement about life, a seemingly boundless fascination with the world that is reminiscent of a young child's curiosity' (Bornstein, 2004: 12). See also the comments by Krzyzstof Stanwoski in this volume.
3. I take this term from Elkington and Hartigan (2008: 13f).
4. This list is not exhaustive; consider for example policy-makers, and think tanks close to them. As Paola Grenier's chapter (in this volume) shows, these actors played an important role in the UK's 'history of social entrepreneurship', and what is so labelled, but I am not sure to what extent, at this point in time at any rate, the importance of policy-makers and think tanks in UK history can be generalised to other countries. See also the discussion of social entrepreneurship as a contested concept below. A further perspective would be that of other civil society actors.
5. See for example Yunnus (2006).

6. These organisations include Ashoka (1472 entrepreneurs in 48 countries); Echoing Green (371 fellows in 30 countries); LEAD (1402 Fellows in 70 countries); Avina (324 partners in 20 countries) and the Schwab Foundation (78 members in 30 countries). Numbers from Grenier (2006: 128). For lists of social entrepreneurship support organisations also see Perrini (2006: 13) and Nicholls (2006: 10).
7. A pioneer publication is Bornstein (2004). It stands at the beginning of what appears to be almost a distinct genre. See for example Stefanska and Hafenmayer (2007), Koch (2007), Elkington and Hartigan (2008). Of course these books vary considerably in terms of the depth of analytical framework for presenting social entrepreneurs. Still, already by their titles all of them invite to learn something about special people: unreasonable people, future-makers, change-makers, social capitalists.
8. www.pbs.org/opb/thenewheroes/index.html, last accessed 10 July 2008.
9. For lists of university centres devoted to social entrepreneurship see Perrini (2006: 12) and Nicholls (2006: 8), as well as the online university network (www.universitynetwork. org/node/310, last accessed 10 July 2008).
10. See www.skollfoundation.org, last accessed 10 July 2008.
11. However, there is research on corporate social entrepreneurship. See Austin et al. (2006).
12. www.grameen.com/bank/socialbusinessentrepreneurs.htm, last accessed 10 July 2008.
13. www.schwabfound.org/whatis.htm, last accessed 10 July 2008. Prior to their clarification of the term 'social entrepreneur' the foundation writes: 'Social entrepreneurship is 1) about applying practical, innovative and sustainable approaches to benefit society in general, with an emphasis on those who are marginalised and poor, 2) a term that captures a unique approach to economic and social problems, an approach that cuts across sectors and disciplines, 3) grounded in certain values and processes that are common to each social entrepreneur, independent of whether his/ her area of focus has been education, health, welfare reform, human rights, workers' rights, environment, economic development, agriculture, etc., or whether the organisations they set up are non-profit or for-profit entities.'
14. See www.oneworldhealth.org/, last accessed 10 July 2008.
15. 1. Eradicate extreme poverty and hunger (*inter alia*: reduce by half the proportion of people living on less than one US dollar a day; reduce by half the proportion of people who suffer from hunger). 2. Achieve universal primary education (*inter alia*: ensure that all boys and girls complete a full course of primary schooling). 3. Promote gender equality and empower women (eliminate gender disparity in primary and secondary education preferably by 2005, and at all levels by 2015). 4. Reduce child mortality (reduce the mortality rate among children under 5 by two-thirds). 5. Improve maternal health (reduce by three-quarters the maternal mortality ratio). 6. Combat HIV/AIDS, malaria, and other diseases 7. Ensure environmental sustainability (*inter alia*: reduce by half the proportion of people without sustainable access to safe drinking water. 8. Develop a global partnership for development. See www.un.org/millenniumgoals/, last accessed 10 July 2008.
16. See State of the World Week 2007 at the European College of Liberal Arts in Berlin: http://swwe.ecla.de/, last accessed 4 August 2008.
17. One student wrote her final essay on Judy Korn and the Violence Prevention Network.

REFERENCES

Austin, J., H.B. Leonard, E. Reficco and J. Wei-Skillern (2006), 'Social entrepreneurship: it is for corporations, too', in A. Nicholls (ed.), *Social Entrepreneurship*, Oxford: Oxford University Press, pp. 169–80.

Bornstein, D. (2004), *How to Change the World. Social Entrepreneurs and the Power of New Ideas*, Oxford: Oxford University Press.

Drayton, W. (2006), 'Everyone a changemaker: social entrepreneurship's ultimate goal', *Innovations – Technology, Governance, Globalization*, Winter, 1–32.

Elkington, J. and P. Hartigan (2008), *The Power of Unreasonable People – How Social Entrepreneurs Create Markets that Change the World*, Boston, MA: Harvard Business School Publishing.

Grenier, P. (2006), 'Social entrepreneurship: agency in a globalizing world', in A. Nicholls (ed.), *Social Entrepreneurship: New Models of Sustainable Social Change*, Oxford: Oxford University Press, pp. 119–43.

Howells, W.D. (1884–85 [1982]), *The Rise of Silas Lapham. Edited by D.L. Cook*, New York: W.W. Norton.

Jacobs, M. (1999), 'Sustainable development as a contested concept', in A. Dobson (ed.), *Fairness and Futurity*, Oxford: Oxford University Press, pp. 21–45.

Koch, H. (2007), *Soziale Kapitalisten. Vorbilder für eine gerechte Wirtschaft*, Berlin: Rotbuch.

Mair, J. and E. Noba (2006), 'Social entrepreneurship: how intentions to create a social venture are formed', in J. Mair, J. Robinson and K. Hockerts (eds), *Social Entrepreneurship*, London: Palgrave Macmillan, pp. 121–36.

Mair, J., J. Robinson and K. Hockerts (eds) (2006), *Social Entrepreneurship*, London: Palgrave Macmillan.

Neurath, O. (1932–33), ,Protokollsätze', *Erkenntnis*, **3**, 204–214.

Nicholls, A. (ed.) (2006), *Social Entrepreneurship: New Models of Sustainable Change*, Oxford: Oxford University Press.

Perrini, F. (ed.) (2006), *The New Social Entrepreneurship*, Cheltenham, UK and Northampton, MA, USA: Edward Elgar.

Schumpeter, J.A. (1942 [1977]), *Capitalism, Socialism and Democracy*, New York: Harper & Row.

Stefanska, J. and W. Hafenmayer (2007), *Die Zukunftsmacher. Eine Reise zu Menschen, die die Welt verändern – und was Sie von ihnen lernen können*, München: oekom.

Yunnus, M. (2006), 'Social business entrepreneurs are the solution', in A. Nicholls (ed.), *Social Entrepreneurship: New Models of Sustainable Social Change*, Oxford: Oxford University Press, pp. 39–44.

PART I

Voices

2. Return the lost water back to the continents

Michal Kravcik

2.1 PEOPLE AND WATER

Whether we like it or not, giving birth to a new idea always brings about certain conflicts, as it clashes with old, obsolete stereotypes. Following the Velvet Revolution and the fall of communism in 1989, I found that I could not wait until somebody came to me and offered me some perspective. I had to act. I started to mobilise people, to convince them, to hold hearings, meetings and lectures. I was one of the founders of the Slovak River Network, and then, when I found that the way money was dealt with in this network was wrong, I established the non-governmental organisation People and Water.

People and Water was launched in August 1993 in Slovakia. The mission of our organisation is to promote an alternative, integrated water management. It was created in response to the new Slovakian state water management policy. The alternative approach we created was called 'Water for the Third Millennium' (People and Water, 1994). This alternative was elaborated by People and Water at the cost of US$1500; other non-governmental organisations like the Slovak River Network and the Slovak Union of Conservationists also joined the initiative. It was presented to, and then accepted by the Slovak Parliament. Since 2 June 1994, the government is obliged to incorporate principles of 'Water for the Third Millennium' into the official water management policy of Slovakia.

However, authoritarian Prime Minister Vladimir Meciar, after his return to power in 1994, ignored the Parliament decree and, in support of the old water management concept, he provided a government guarantee for the construction of outdated and costly water projects to be implemented by the state-owned Water Management Company. With the help of JPMorgan loans, guaranteed by the government, the Water Management Company stopped the institutional reform that aimed to give Slovakia a modern water policy.

With the help of a media campaign and lobbying, we managed to get our water programme back to the Parliament. The government was again obliged to incorporate the decree in Slovakia's water policy, nevertheless it was ignored. Prime Minister Meciar granted the Water Management Company a US$500 million governmental guarantee. Slovakia has paid dearly for this political decision. If our approach would have been accepted, we estimate that the state would have saved 18 billion Slovak korunas (or the equivalent of US$500 million in 1994), and Slovakia would have had a much more effective water policy system.

This alternative proposal was People and Water's first serious activity. However, we realised that in essence we had no chance to win against the interventions of state enterprises, politicians and budding markets. We therefore focused more on the local activities. The mid-1990s saw a dramatic conflict of interests concerning the villages threatened by the plan for a dam in Tichy Potok (Silent Stream) area, which is located in the Levoca Mountains and in the watershed of the Torysa river. The plan included the highest dam wall in Slovakia (64 metres). From an ecological perspective, the construction would have meant the flooding of approximately 123 hectares of the Upper Torysa River Valley area. The wall of the dam would separate the upper part of the watershed from the downstream portion (Kravcik, 1996). From a social perspective, the plan for the dam included a 'hygienic protection zone' that would have radically limited the existing agricultural and economic lifestyles of four villages, and 144 houses directly neighbouring the streams would have to be 'moved' (ibid.).

We got involved in the conflict and prepared an alternative for Tichy Potok. The Blue Alternative proposed a solution approximately ten times cheaper than the proposed government plan. Volunteers with scholarly background elaborated the proposal Blue Alternative at the cost of US$ 2000. Instead of a big dam, the Blue Alternative proposed the fixing of rapids, steps and weirs on the stream, the construction of some 45 small dams (water level height of up to 5 metres, and an area of up to one hectare), the construction of depression areas (water holdings) for the accumulation of rain water, water-supply pumps at the mouth of selected catchments and the construction of water-supply collectors. The goal of this alternative was the prevention of big floods, as well as securing a sufficient water supply for the needs of villages and of the nearby cities of Kosice and Presov.

Unfortunately, the Blue Alternative was not accepted, and we were ridiculed. Water experts told the media that it was impossible to solve water problems more cheaply than proposed by the government plan. The expert community had firmly supported the dam construction, and we had no chance to defend our view. Even though various forums had been held by the state in the budding Slovak democracy, these were made in such a manner that democratic principles were only seemingly accepted, while in fact it was not possible to access the process. For example, when there was an expert evaluation of the Blue Alternative by ten experts in 1996, we were not invited.

This political situation lead to a radical change in our campaign: orientation to work with the public via public meetings, lectures, and discussions and showing practical concrete examples directly in the field, while improving the dissemination of information through the media. We organised the Blue Alternative camps for young people and media campaigns. It was not without failures. We made our first experiment in a small dry valley, but we underestimated some things and lacked experience. We started with a small brook, but a flood came and water destroyed our work. But this also enlightened us, and we restarted in the upper areas, from the springs where the drops start and concentrate. We managed to increase the public interest in protection of disadvantaged communities threatened by the Tichy Potok dam construction. The general public learned about the Tichy Potok case – that there was an alternative to it, that it was possible to get more water for less money and that the threatened communities could thrive thanks to the alternative.

Due to the campaign, we gained many supporters. Even a group of US citizens, who have their ancestry in the Tichy Potok area, organised a petition and gathered over 300 signatures against the Tichy Potok dam construction, and officially – through the Slovak Embassy – asked the Slovak government to stop any attempts to build the dam. Patient work with the public bore fruits. The citizens of the disadvantaged villages grasped very quickly that they also had allies, and their self-confidence grew. They learned how to present their views publicly; they could lead sound and assertive discussions. At the final public meetings held in the affected villages, the situation was such that the state officials and investors' deputies could not answer the citizens' well-compiled and well-founded questions.

The arrogant stance of government and state-owned water industry with respect to ordinary people and common sense had always frustrated us, but it also taught us that it is necessary to pay more attention to rural citizens and that they deserve better education. Common villagers could give very competent answers, while often the lords could not answer adequately. So this was a particularly positive process, and we managed to make it known across the whole of Slovakia. In the end, the Ministry of the Environment issued an assessment of the environmental impacts of this investment, and advised not to build the Tichy Potok dam.

Following the successful campaign, a big meeting was held on 5 April 1997 in a Torysky village, home to 400 inhabitants. Over 1200 people participated. The investors got so angry that they obstructed many activities in the Tichy Potok area. For example, they imposed fines for the small dams that had been built (without building permission) during the Blue Alternative camps (in 1995 and 1996), and they enacted a ban that no trees could be planted during the 5 April celebration. The pressure to stop the Blue Alternative project was very strong, but despite this, further (small) initiatives kept arising. In Torysa village, *circa* 15 km distant from the Tichy Potok area, a small flood-protection project was constructed in 1999 that serves the flood-protection needs to this day. In Obisovce village, 45 km from Tichy Potok, another Blue Alternative project was implemented as part of the village's flood-protection measures: waterholdings for the recharge of groundwater and small wooden dams with a maximum height of 1 metre.

Following the successful campaign against the dam, People and Water decided to continue their activities in the region via development projects. Due to the plan, still from the communist era, to build a large dam on the site, investments to the affected area were diminished and citizens of declining villages felt they were living in a forgotten country. In 1997, we launched the Village of the Third Millennium Project (education, dissemination of information, encouragement of traditional local crafts, training on small projects, entrepreneurship, and so on). We launched the *Blue Alternative* magazine, publishing 1500 copies (27 issues were published altogether).

We organised workshops, trainings, excursions and discussion fora, and helped launch non-governmental organisations; we launched a community foundation, implemented several pilot projects (a waste water plant in Repase, restoration of a school in the Tichy Potok area, restoration of a historic stone mill in Krivany, a Roma community centre in Lipany and an information centre in Repase). Since 1998, we have been building capacities for regional development. During the whole period, the activities have spread from four to over eighty villages. On the basis of our skills gained through the Tichy Potok campaign, our activities have extended up to the whole Svinka river watershed where over 25 000 residents live in 35 communities, and later also to other regions like Kecerovce, Kosice and High Tatras.

People and Water carried out this project, and all its other projects with basically the same staff. It has not changed much for 15 years. We have a permanent staff of five people. I am the chairman and co-ordinate projects for integrated management of water sources and regional development, Jaroslava Pajtinkova takes care of the financial management, Jan Hronsky is a project manager for regional development and technical assistance for water management, Juraj Kohutiar is a further project manager and responsible for publications, Eugen Toth manages water projects and Pavol Varga works as an assistant for ecological restoration of watersheds.

For our work we also draw on a group of external experts: Michal Pjecha is an assistant for geographic information systems, Peter Straka is an advisor for integrated water management of river basins, Peter Pacaj is our media advisor, Rudolf Soltes is our research advisor for water projects, Matian Rusnák is our assistant for the implementation of projects in the countryside, Anton Bednár advises on issues of landscape and mapping and Stanislav Stasko co-operates with us as a photographer. Finally, we draw on a group of 78 volunteers (as of 2007). We attempt to create new projects, and seek means for their implementation; our income is not ensured and nobody finances us. We keep on trying to get some financial support from various grants and funds. This is very energy demanding, and we are tired of it. It is very difficult, and also increasingly complex.

Our engagement provided us with deeper insight into water management. Of course, some of our knowledge was theoretically underpinned by our studies, and by previous work of some staff members at the Hydrological Institute of the Slovak Academy of Sciences. But the most important driver of deeper understanding was the work on alternative proposals, and the conflicts and arguments around these proposals. We realised that the only chance for the future is a design of landscape and ecosystem that can cope with climate-related water extremes. Any system – be it a farmland or a forest, village or urban zone – has to keep the capacity to conserve as much water as possible during the rainfalls. This water stored in surface water bodies, underground water, soil and vegetation should be allowed to evaporate into the atmosphere and provide important cooling effect in favour of recovery of the climate. As we came to realise, we had discovered a New Water Paradigm. But before I turn to the paradigm, let me say something about my biography.

2.2   AUTOBIOGRAPHICAL OBSERVATIONS

I was fired for the first time in 1986, from the Institute of Hydrology and Hydraulics of the Slovak Academy of Science, a second time in 1988 from the Landscape Ecology Institute of the Academy, and then I was unemployed for three months during the socialist regime. That means that I had permanent conflicts even before People and Water. But let me start with the beginning.

I was born in February 1956 under the sign of Aquarius and as it looks now, I was predestined to deal with water most of my life. I graduated from grammar school, and my love for fine arts made me wish to continue with art school. However, I did not dare to do so. I applied to the Faculty of Architecture, but I was not accepted. Finally, I studied water management in Bratislava in 1975–80 – that is, my way to water management studies was involuntary. I finished my studies with a thesis on computer methods for the filling of locks of the Gabcikovo Dam.

For the first three months after my studies, I worked with the Engineering Constructions Company at the Starina Dam. I worked for this company because they financed three years of my studies. But I was drawn to research, and left the company after the 'trial period'. Then, for six years I had to repay the money they had given me during my studies. I felt that I should know more about the mathematics, so that I could solve water problems better. I applied to Charles University in Prague. They only ridiculed me there: why do you need a second university degree?

In 1981, I began to work at the Institute of Hydrology of the Slovak Academy of Sciences. It was ill-fated for me. For six years I worked at the East-Slovak Lowland basin. It was almost an official claim that the East-Slovak Plane is flat as a table, and that it has zero surface run-off. But there were still some tiny elevation differences and water accumulated in depressions without run-off. It took me about six years to understand the trivial fact that in some (lower) places the balance of water column equals 3 metres per year, and in other (higher) places it may be only 40 centimetres per year. This fact pointed to the possibility of using a wetland model, and a strategy different from the official strategy for the fertilisation. I only gradually realised that the entire (official) research on ecological optimisation in the East Slovakia Lowlands was meant to confirm and approve the research done on a very different Danube river lowland close to Bratislava. As a young man with scientific ambitions I did not understand that political context.

In connection with that I remember my publication problems. I could not publish my first articles in Slovakia – but the Czech Water Management magazine published them. One of my articles was even praised as one of the best in the 1986 volume of the Prague-edited *Vodní hospdá stvi* (Water Management). I realised that in professional circles we often schematically follow ways of thinking, and there is little interest in going deeper to the root of a problem. We do things only superficially. I remember one of my colleagues, who was about to retire, asking me why I nag so much. He told me that everything had already been explored in this field. So I asked myself, why did they appoint me to my position? Just to transcribe their opinions? This was the time, when I started to understand the opposition my studies provoked. My bosses hired a politically correct comrade from Michalovce and made it clear to me that I should leave.

Then I switched to the Institute of Land Ecology of the Slovak Academy of Sciences, where I had another conflict. I wrote a research study on the hydrology of East Slovakia Lowlands and its influence on the agricultural productive potential (Kravcik, 1988). I published my conclusions in *Mlady Svet* (Young World), which was then the most popular youth magazine on the wave of Gorbachov's policy of glasnost (openness). Our group of young ecologists was encouraged by this policy and we were not afraid to speak out. The magazine organised a national award for the best projects from youngsters. My study assessed the impacts of government directed investments on the water regime and on the agricultural potential of the East Slovak Plane. It showed that a project to drain 100 000 hectares of agricultural land did not make it more fertile but, rather, devastated it. My article won the main prize of the journal.

During the communist period it was very difficult to publish this sad result. The people behind this agricultural project also had a very strong impact on research programmes, and even today alternative, innovative solutions are marginalised. If you open such sore points, and if you confront people who worked for decades in a research programme, then it is difficult to achieve change – especially, if you are a young man telling them that they forgot this and that. Quite logically, there were conflicts. I even sent a letter to Rudolf Schuster, then the Chairman of the East-Slovak Regional Committee. In the letter, sent in good faith, I wrote: Comrade Chairman of the Regional Committee, here we have such and such results, which show that something is wrong with the East-Slovak lowlands, and something should be done with it. But sadly this water management engineer (later to become Slovak President, despite his communist past) did not appreciate my critical voice. I got fired again.

After a short period of unemployment I started to work at the Soil Management Institute. I completed the project I worked on, and even five times cheaper – the planned investment amounted to 10 million koruna, while my solution cost only 1.8 million koruna. My bosses, however, did not like that. They said that such a solution would not bring any money for the institute. So, they transferred me to work on another problem, and finished the previous work without me. However, I did not satisfy them in the other project either. My task was to design a river adjustment at the Poprad Basin, where they planned investments. There was an amazing wetland in the planned area, and my heart would have broken, if I had to let it dry out. So, I secretly informed the conservationists how to save the wetland. Fortunately, it was saved.

After many work experiences and conflicts, I finally, as noted above, co-founded People and Water in 1993. When I look back, I can say it was hard and complicated, but beneficial. I am often asking myself, why do I need all this? I come up with new ideas, but when I see what trifling things are financed in the world, I lose my appetite completely. I am convinced that everybody should do what he or she loves, knows or understands. I wish that everyone's wishes are fulfilled. The world now, however, is built on a completely different, materialist basis, as I realised while working with water. I will return to this theme below, but let me first continue the story chronologically with my work for People and Water and its relationship to the social entrepreneurship organisation Ashoka in the 1990s.

2.3   SOCIAL ENTREPRENEURSHIP

Ashoka Central Europe was launched in the mid-1990s. It included Poland, Czech Republic, Hungary and Slovakia. I belonged to the first people from Slovakia to become an Ashoka Fellow in 1996. As the last section might have already indicated, professional life in Slovakia is very dependent on money; people with a mind of their own have only a few professional avenues. Dissenters and innovators very often lose their professional positions. Being open to new ideas and proposing cheaper and more effective solutions can be dangerous. Therefore, a three-year Ashoka stipend created a precious time of independence for me. I became totally independent, and for the first time in my life I felt secure. I could say what I wanted, and I did not need to beg any longer. It was the start of a period of key importance for me. Without this support I would have not been able to fully devote my time to these ideas. I would have had to take a job so as to feed my family.

Independence is fundamental to new ideas. In the news I read that the participants of an international conference in Berlin observed a lack of leaders around the globe. Ashoka offers a unique support for the independence of creative people around the globe, at a time when professional dependence is the rule.

From my perspective, most international grant schemes and programmes are too narrow-minded and promote too materialist an outlook, which I associate with Marxism – more spiritless stuff than sense, as I would put it. The world now, as I perceive it, is built on a materialist basis. I realised this while working with water. A look at water legislations worldwide shows legislation to be focused almost solely on the protection of the freshwater that we can see. But much more water is in the atmosphere, hidden in the soil, flowing underground to come out as springs again. Without paying attention to the full phenomenon, it is hard to understand all feedback and its integrity. Only a very little part of water has been protected by law. The law ignores a substantial part of the water cycle. This is a great pity, because a holistic and integrated view brings about amazing knowledge and new connections that we had not seen or perceived, or perhaps that we did not want to see or to perceive. We only protect what we can see;

and what we cannot see does not exist for us. But we must protect what we cannot see, and then there will be great possibilities of repairing the previous harms that have been done worldwide.

However, while I value very highly the independence created by the stipend, I also would like to add that it can be dangerous. After three years, you get used to this independence, and there is a problem of professional sustainability, because Slovak society has little space for supporting creative and innovative people. After three years you suffer an 'independence stomach-ache'. To cure it you need soberness and courage.

There have been attempts to buy me. I was offered 5 million koruna, if I would stop the Tichy Potok campaign. I pretended I did not understand. When I was awarded the Goldman Environmental Prize in 1999, everybody was disconcerted. Not only had I been awarded the EU-US Democracy and Civil Society Award in 1998, but now also the Goldman Prize! Both prizes included financial support, so I could say we have obtained honestly earned money. This international recognition helped us to open doors and eyes.

I have been to many Ashoka meetings – most recently in Argentina in 2007 – and I have got to know many people. Occasionally, we Ashoka Fellows plan some common activities. They are not always successful. I would say that my contacts and relationships with the rest of the world are better than those in Slovakia. People and Water and I personally always acknowledge the support from Ashoka, and Ashoka is still involved in our activities. Along with the Ashoka work many things arose, of which Ashoka even now could profit. It is impossible to predict the further developments of Ashoka, but I would be happy to co-operate with the organisation, and have proposed the New Water Paradigm as an idea that might be of interest to Ashoka Fellows worldwide. So let me finally turn to the New Water Paradigm.

2.4 SOCIAL ENTREPRENEURSHIP AND THE STATE: TECHNOCRACY AND THE NEW WATER PARADIGM

After the Velvet Revolution I longed to return to science, but as mentioned above, I encountered many obstacles and opposition. So I created my own space. After the successful completion of the Tichy Potok campaign, we submitted a holistic integrated model of regional development to public debate with established sectional teams, business, state administration, experts and NGOs. The conference 'Regions Help Themselves', held in Levoca in February 2002, created space for new ideas, and a quite interesting methodology resulted from it. When I compared this methodology in 2002 with what was done elsewhere in the world, I found that they did the same as we had done during the last years. United States and British universities promoted principles that we had been discussing here. For me this means that we have created something that is brilliant, new, primordial and provocative.

As we conducted research to get more information and better arguments, we discovered things that have not been clear to us until now, for example the transformation and distribution of rainfalls in time and space. In the rainforest, precipitation is constant throughout the whole year. There was a regular water cycle in our country in the past, because the small water cycle was saturated, supplemented, balanced and stabilised by water from the landscape. But if the forest is changed into agricultural land, then the pattern of rainfalls changes too. Up until now, we understood the decline of the water cycle as 'given' or 'irreversible'. But if there is a negative trend and we understand it, then there can also be a positive trend and we can promote it.

We discovered a new paradigm of water management (Kravcik et al., 2008[1]). Briefly summarised, the presence or absence of water is the key factor of the destiny of solar energy coming to the land. If water is present on the land, the solar energy is consumed in evaporation and it does not cause increase of temperature; vice versa, water vapour moderates temperature differences. On the other hand, if the land is dry, huge amounts of heat are produced and temperature gradients trigger weather instabilities. That is why a key principle of the paradigm is to secure affluence of water in the land by rainwater harvesting and infiltration (instead of run-off to the sea), which would stabilise the climate through evaporation (via vegetation which acts as a valve between soil and atmosphere). Modern state policy has for too long drained wetlands, straightened rivers and removed dead-end tributaries so that water could be sluiced away as fast as possible; now is the time to return the lost water to the continents. In the New Water Paradigm, we elaborate the theoretical background of the water-cycle mechanism, as well as the measures to be taken to get the benefits of plentiful good quality water, anti-flood and anti-erosion protection, increase of biodiversity, and so on. Nevertheless, our New Water Paradigm still needs to be tested further, as is the case for any pioneering, eco-systemic, holistic approach.

Following a violent storm in High Tatras mountains in November 2004, the forest in and around Stary Smokovec was destroyed, and not much later a fire burnt many of the fallen trees. At the site of this 'black forest' we started a 'blue forest'. The Water Forest is a big project of around 80 hectares. People and Water together with volunteers built a few thousand small dikes to slow down run-off from the slopes, increase soil moisture and create conditions for the forest to return. Our approach was met with strong resistance from environmentalists who argued that nature should be left to itself. We responded that people are part of the ecological system, and ought to co-operate with nature; if they degrade part of the ecosystem, they are also responsible to look for new solutions. Not to do so, is in our view just a further instance of the sectional approach dominant in modern societies. We need a holistic approach. Today, researchers monitor the Water Forest and they are surprised, because they did not expect such a growth of biodiversity as is happening there. If you leave water in the land, it will immediately use it.

The New Water Paradigm, just as the alternative proposals that gave rise to it, is to some extent ahead of its time. Water for the Third Millennium was developed against strong opposition in 1993–94. The EU Water Framework Directive in 2000 brought the same philosophy. The Blue Alternative was developed around 1995–1996. In 2003, the World Bank together with the World Wildlife Fund (WWF) Alliance for Forest Conservation and Sustainable Use issued a report with recommendations for the best, cheapest and most effective eco-systemic water conservation that is conceptually equal to that of the Blue Alternative (Dudley and Stolton, 2003).

Finally, as far as Tichy Potok is concerned, the same institutions and structures that had proposed the dam and that had been in power before our intervention, are now toying with the idea of constructing a dam in this area again. Personally, I do not see it so tragically – you cannot step in the same river twice. After all, the world has now taken a step forward. Water managers have begun to communicate with us, colleagues from the Hydrology Institute approach us, as do even people close to Julius Binder, then the general director of the State Water Management Company responsible for the investment mentioned above. The philosophy of water management has shifted somewhere else. I suppose that it was the recognition we received internationally that contributed to this significant change. Looking back I can say that all these conflicts forced me to get a deeper understanding. I realised some things that others did not. The New Water Paradigm is a summary of our ideas about water management principles. It is a new systemic view of water, a new view of reality that suggests a feasible way for addressing water issues from micro-structures up to the global level.

Technocracy now rules all over the planet. We can see it clearly in the domain of water. Water is a treasure with a spiritual dimension. It offers creation of new life. Water allows us to grasp many things. A whole philosophy can be made about water. Historic trends of the development of civilisations can be understood in relation to water. If you understand this development in the last hundred years, then you can see back into history, and around the next corner.[2]

I met a priest recently, who claimed that some themes are the privilege of God. I asked him whether he said that because he did not understand them, or only because he does not want to understand. We people like to rid ourselves of responsibility very quickly, and say that something is in God's hands. Humans should have ambitions to influence the passing of times and events. If humans believe they influence them negatively, they should also think of influencing them positively, and take responsibility either way.

NOTES

1. See www.waterparadigm.org/, last accessed 1 August 2008, and Kravcik et al. (2008).
2. In hydrology, of course, many people will be sceptical about such claims. Why? I think because the dominant methodology in science is statistics, which serves as a black box that figures are thrown into and extracted from regardless of chronology.

REFERENCES

Dudley, N. and S. Stolton (2003), *Running Pure: The Importance of Forest Protected Areas to Drinking Water. A Research Report for the World Bank/ WWF Alliance for Forest Conservation and Sustainable Use*, Gland, Switzerland: WWF International.

Kravcik, M. (1988), 'Hydrology of East Slovakia Lowlands and its influence on the agricultural productive potential', research study, Institute of Ecology of Slovak Academy of Science.

Kravcik, M. (1996), 'The truth about Tichy Potok', edited by the Slovak Union of Nature and Landscape Protectors and the NGO People and Water, Kosice, April.

Kravcik, M., J. Pokorny, J. Kohutiar, M. Kovác and E. Tóth (2008), *Water for the Recovery of the Climate. A New Water Paradigm*, Kosice: Municipali and TORY Consulting.

People and Water (1994), 'Water for the Third Millennium', Kosice.

3. Taking responsibility: breaking away from hate and violence

Judy Korn

3.1 VIOLENCE PREVENTION NETWORK

The Violence Prevention Network (VPN), founded in 2005 in Germany, has developed a novel pedagogy of responsibility that lowers recidivism among juvenile offenders motivated by racist and religious prejudice. The target group of the VPN programme, Verantwortung übernehmen – Abschied von Hass und Gewalt (Taking responsibility – breaking away from hate and violence), are male offenders[1] who have been put in prison due to aggravated acts of violence, and who justify these acts by drawing on extreme right, ethnocentric or cultural-religious[2] patterns of justification.

The VPN approach combines political education and anti-violence pedagogy in a comprehensive training programme. The in-prison training programme is followed by a 'real-life test' out of prison, during which the participants are accompanied by their trainers for up to a year. Moreover, the adolescents' relatives are integrated into the programme so as to secure a social network after release from prison.

The VPN asks adolescents to question not only their acts of violence, but also their justifications of these acts; they have to examine how their justifications draw on political, ideological and religious convictions and the social ties usually coming with these convictions. Only when they examine in detail their offence are juvenile offenders able to search for alternatives. After examination, the usual excuses and patterns of justification lose their validity.

The pedagogy of responsibility is based on humanistic principles. The philosophy of the programme is to establish dialogue and to ask questions. Rather than asking for direct and total 'conversion', the programme proposes a development by steps. For example, an intermediary goal for a juvenile delinquent might be to always kick a wall or object rather than beating a person when getting angry. The pedagogy of responsibility takes the available resources into account and offers support to the individual in his or her place. Adolescents have to make up for the missing elements of their socialisation, but without being humiliated in the process, that is, on the basis of respect and recognition.

BOX 3.1   THE ONE-ON-ONE DISCUSSION

T. is going to take part. He's ready to talk to the group about the offences he's committed, his opinions, and his life. Talking about himself, however, is unusual and it's clear he's having some difficulty. Today he's going to have the one-on-one discussion with the trainer. After that, the first training session with the group will take place. T. thinks he immediately has to talk about his offence today, has to defend himself, be reasonable. That's why he's so surprised they're not even talking about what happened on that day at all. The trainer takes his time. He asks T. how he's doing. He asks him to talk about himself, about his childhood and growing up. Talking about feelings is also allowed. T. is suspicious, but he begins to talk; carefully, without going into detail. He talks about the village where he was born, about the father who was hardly ever there, about his mother whom he praises above all. The trainer listens and asks questions. He doesn't judge. T. keeps talking, about his crowd, about his right-wing extremist mates to whom he feels he belongs. He talks about his hatred of foreigners, his belief in the National Socialists, and about excessive violence. His hatred is profound, as is his distrust. And it becomes clear just how much it influenced his everyday life outside the prison. T. is used to reacting to everything and everyone with suspicion. He sees every remark someone else makes as a potential attack that he only has one answer to: defence and violence. The trainer shows understanding for T.'s distrust, his resistance and his fears. But while he understands his resistance, he has no understanding of what happened. At the end of the session T. is shocked at how much he has talked about his life. He notices that someone is interested in him and not just in what he has done. The trainer makes it clear what the goal of training is: what do you need to get by on the outside without resorting to violence, without becoming a repeat offender? That's what it's all about, about him and his future. The trainer is able to make an assessment about T. after this talk. The foundation for the work to come in the next weeks and months has been laid.

The VPN seeks to achieve its basic goals, that is, the prevention of recidivism and a conduct of life that is self-responsible, free from felony and independent from inhuman ideologies and acts, via the establishment and promotion of the following capabilities:

- to engage in meaningful relationships
- to have empathy
- to have a sense of self-worth
- to have a sense of responsibility
- to be able to analyse.

These capabilities, according to the VPN approach, enable a life free from violence. As every human can acquire these capabilities in a process of learning, even the most violent criminals can change their conduct. The VPN achieves its learning goals in a group process that complements the scrutiny and critical examination of patterns of thought and behaviour with esteem for the person and her or his potentials and resources. After the release from prison, the trainers also accompany the transfer of learning experiences from the group-work in prison to real-life groups.

From 2001 to 2007, 317 youths participated in the programme. Of these youths, 80 per cent have been released already, less than 5 per cent have been imprisoned again and only 1 per cent due to a criminal act of violence. By comparison the average rate of recidivism in Germany is currently at around 78 per cent and half of all youth return to prison after their release. It is also noteworthy that only 3 per cent, that is, nine participants have dropped out of our programme so far.

BOX 3.2   THE FIRST SESSION

Eight young men, inmates at the youth prison, sit in a circle. The two trainers who are in charge of the course sit in the middle. It's the first session. The situation is unfamiliar. They slowly get to know each other better by playing relaxed communication games. No one is driven too hard. Nothing happens that the youths find embarrassing. The ice is broken. The goal today is to clarify what they expect from the course. More still: they have to say what they want to learn here. Everyone has a different objective: to be in control of themselves and not fight anymore; to be able to control oneself even when provoked; to understand why one completely 'flips out' and how to get things back under control; to avoid becoming a repeat offender and ending up in jail again; how to keep from slipping up and being lead astray by 'old mates' again; to stop talking 'rubbish' and doing 'stupid' things; to prepare for life after prison. Everyone has their own story and everyone has something different to learn. They are not all just lumped together, but rather viewed as individuals and accepted. The aim of the first session is to decide on the rules they want to work on together in the course. They have to decide on these rules themselves. This is also the time to clarify what they expect from the trainers. Agreement is first reached in small groups and then as a whole. No one here is in the mood for advice, and especially not for any 'brainwashing'. The talk is of respect and acceptance. The trainers ask what they mean by this. 'Well, that when I speak my opinion that no one here says it's wrong.' It's amazing. The group decides upon its own demo-cratic rules. The first step is taken to develop feelings of respect for others and to experience what it means to be taken seriously, to have a say and thus be able to have an effect on things.

The programme, Verantwortung übernehmen – Abschied von Hass und Gewalt, rests on three columns (also see Figure 3.1):

- Column 1: in a training course, lasting approximately five months, eight participants work on key themes such as biography, assault, political and religious-cultural strategies of justification, conse-quences for the victims, 'mates' and 'cliques'. They also prepare for their release and the new start 'out there'. Relatives and friends, who have a positive significance for the adolescents, are included for approximately the last two-thirds of the programme.
- Column 2: all participants have the option of a mentor for a maximum of one year following their release from prison. This option is con-ditional on a contract that stipulates concrete rules of conduct and developmental goals. These goals are, first and foremost, the stable re-inclusion into a social environment and no recidivism. The rules of conduct include the active work on personal conduct (for example, the participants are expected to immediately contact their mentors in the case of a conflict), and the will to reflect and to share information with the mentor. Failure to observe these rules of conduct results in exclusion from the programme. By contrast recidivism is not an eliminating criterion. The mentor is the same person as the prison trainer in column 1. The goal is to offer a continuous relationship and to thereby foster the capability to engage in relationships, a crucial condition if recidivism is to be prevented.

- Column 3: the VPN offers information and further-education events as well as certified further training for prison staff. The goal is to thereby promote the VPN approach locally and to win competent collaborators.

Column 1 and 2 are practically two phases as shown in Figure 3.1.

A network of experts, long active in the domains of violence prevention and political education, founded the VPN in 2005. The network seeks to reduce the number of juvenile delinquents motivated by prejudice. To this end, it develops and refines methods and procedures for pedagogy and political education aimed at the prevention of violence, xenophobia, extremism and fundamentalism. Concretely this means:

- Working directly with adolescents who exhibit an evident willingness for prejudice-motivated, spontaneous aggression and aggravated acts of violence.
- Developing methods for political education for adolescents from groups with an anti-democratic structure. These methods include the pedagogy of responsibility, as well as the pedagogy of subversive insecurity proposed by Eckart Osborg (Osborg, 2006), which the VPN has further developed and refined.
- Offering pedagogues, who work with this target group, as well as further education and direct local, conceptual support.
- Promoting structures of co-operation via a network of further education in this domain.
- Making available (digitalised) up-to-date information and publication to stakeholders. For political education with right-wing offenders, trainers need to draw on historical material that is often not publicly available without restrictions. For this reason the VPN homepage contains a password protected domain where this educational material is made available.

The VPN is directed by three experts who have been active in the field for many years. Helmut Heitmann, born in 1956, holds a diploma in education and supervision and has long been working against xenophobia and violence in sport. He is a co-founder of the fan-project movement and has developed a concept against violence in soccer stadiums together with the German Soccer Association (DFB) and the German Association of Cities and Towns ('Deutscher Städtetag'). After the fall of the Berlin wall, he made a central contribution to the implementation of the federal programme against violence (headed by Angela Merkel, then Minister of Youth).

Phase 1: Voluntary group training in prison*

Method
- Length of training: 4–6 months (115h)
- Group size: 8 participants
- Format: Group sessions accompanied by one-on-one interviews
- Inclusion of relatives in preparation of time after prison

Set-up
- Pedagogy of responsibility
- Reliable work on relationships
- Critical coming to terms with the offence
- Political education
- Biographical work
- Questioning patterns of justification
- Appreciation of the person

Phase 2: Targeted, individual coaching after prison ('real-life test')

Method
- Coaching length: 6–12 months
- Continuity: Coaching by group trainers from prison training sessions
- Regular meetings
- Continuous telephone counsel
- Inclusion of relatives

Set-up
- Learning-transfer
- Return into a social environment (build-up of a new surroundings)
- Establishment of stable relationships
- Structuring everyday life
- Integration into a workplace

Note: *For all training groups there are more applications than places. The drop-out rate is below 3 per cent.

Figure 3.1 The VPN two-phase programme

Thomas Mücke, born in 1958, holds diplomas in pedagogy and politics and has devoted his professional life to projects dealing with especially vulnerable adolescents. As a teacher, consultant and coach, he works on methods of anti-violence and conflict management, as well as in the domains of youth work, street social work and right-wing extremism. Of highest importance for him is an interaction with adolescents that is based on esteem and that is free from humiliation. His attitude offers him access to especially vulnerable adolescents, a crucial condition of success for this work.

I, Judy Korn, was born in 1971 and hold diplomas in education and mediation. As I will describe in more detail below, I have been politically active and have grappled with extremist violence since my school days. After a number of years in public administration, I gave up my 'position for life' (life tenure) and created with the VPN the possibility to implement my ideals and to co-shape social life in an important way. In 2007, I was selected as a social entrepreneur and Ashoka Fellow.

The leadership is complemented by a team of 13 experienced experts from anthropology, history and political science, pedagogy, therapy, management and administration. They are united in their commitment to further the VPN's goals with the help of their different qualifications, resources and competences.

BOX 3.3   COMING TO TERMS WITH RIGHT-WING EXTREMIST IDEOLOGY

The discussion in the group revolves around social problems in Germany: unemployment, welfare, economic crime, corruption. 'What are the causes of this? Who is responsible?' One youth has an immediate answer: 'It's the Jewish financial capital! They have the money. They're pulling the strings and are driving Germany into the ground.' The trainer pauses and then gets involved in the debate. 'OK, so where is the financial capital concentrated in Germany? Right, the banks. So, Josef Ackermann from the Deutsche Bank is a Jew? No? So he's not. I see.' The trainer goes through the list of large banks in Germany and their chairmen. One after the other. He is well informed, he knows exactly what he's talking about. This makes an impression on the youths. They don't find any Jews on the executive level at the banks. The youths are irritated. Then the trainer tries a different angle. 'And what about Frank Schwerdt (a member of the NPD's executive committee and head of the NPD party headquarters in Berlin)? Is he a Jew?' The group is horrified. 'What are you doing? Are you

> trying to provoke us?' 'No, I'm just taking your type of argumenta-
> tion a bit further. Mr Schwerdt has a lot of money. He's a big deal
> in the real estate business, speculates on the stock exchange. He
> has power due to his capital and uses it for political purposes. Isn't
> he actually a Jew according to your definition?' The youths are
> confused. The discussion has a lasting effect. That's the purpose.
> They've been given some food for thought. That's not the end of
> the issue, though. The trainers pick up this topic at a later date
> and continue the discussion.

The VPN co-operates with numerous institutions in Germany and elsewhere, and promotes interdisciplinary and trans-boundary expert dialogue. The VPN network consists of numerous national and international co-operation partners, who respect and support the work of the VPN: Ashoka Germany, the German ministries of the Interior (BMI), of Law (BMJ), of Family Affairs, Senior Citizens, Women and Youth (BMFSFJ), for Labour and Social Affairs (BMAS), the Federal Agency for Civic Education (Bundeszentrale für politische Bildung), numerous ministries of the Länder, the Centre for Research on Antisemitism at the Technical University Berlin, the universities of Bremen, of Cologne, and of Potsdam, the Central Council of Muslims in Germany (Zentralrat der Muslime in Deutschland), the University of Kent in the UK, as well as the UK National Offender Management Services, the Northern Ireland Association for the Care and Resettlement of Offenders, the US Human Rights Advocates and the US Human Rights Watch.

The VPN finances its work largely with public funds, and to a smaller degree also with private donations and income. It aims to increase the part of private donations, revenue from training qualifications and sponsors within five years to 20 per cent so as to sustainably secure the funding of the VPN, that is, to secure funding not only on a short-term basis of only one year. The VPN seeks to create more independence from the ministries currently funding it, and a more active performance in the market. The ministries have a reduced structural interest in lowering the rate of recidivism to the extent that this would imply a reduction in public staff. Some independence from this source of funding is therefore desirable, and requires a stake in a market so far dominated by the big charities with their established lobbies and networks.

Within only a few years, VPN has emerged as a serious competitor to the mainstream approach of the pedagogy of confrontation (Weidner und Kilb, 2006). The goal of this pedagogy is to condition delinquents to stop reacting violently. To this end, this approach uses confrontational means.

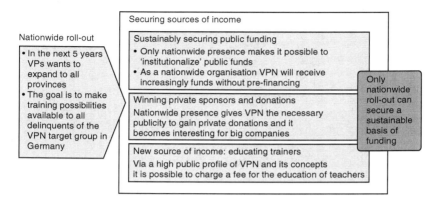

Figure 3.2   VPN next steps

By contrast, the pedagogy of responsibility eschews confrontation; it does not transgress the boundaries set by its humanist principles. As a result, the VPN's co-operation partners consider it to be not only a reliable and competent partner, but also a very innovative one. In the landscape of German support organizations – essentially the big charities, trade unions and provincially owned/university institutes and foundations – such recognition is a notable achievement.

By 2008, the VPN approach has been introduced and used in seven provinces (Berlin, Brandenburg, Bremen, Hamburg, Mecklenburg-Vorpommern, Niedersachsen and Sachsen-Anhalt). The VPN seeks to become within the next five years the leading body for work with delinquents and educational work with extremists based on the pedagogy of responsibility. This goal is to be achieved via a countrywide rollout in the domain of tertiary prevention (prevention of recidivism), as well as the conceptual extension of the approach to include the time prior to imprisonment (secondary prevention[3]).

The strategy is tailored for a continuous spatial extension of the VPN approach. The conceptual extension of the approach as well as its international dissemination will be co-tracked as a secondary goal from 2009 onwards and successively extended. The targets of this process will be the provinces that still need to be won as partners and funders.

3.2   AUTOBIOGRAPHICAL OBSERVATIONS

I had the idea to develop an approach for the fight against extremism, ethnocentrism and violence, and to thereby support people in their change

BOX 3.4   COMING TO TERMS WITH PROBLEMS OF VIOLENCE

Today the session is devoted to the subject of violence. It's not yet time to deal with the actual offences the youths committed, but rather to have an intellectual dialogue about the advantages and disadvantages of violent actions. The trainer first splits the group into two smaller groups. Group A should describe why violence is so 'great'. Group B has the task of describing the disadvantages. The participants in group A quickly come up with a whole list of advantages: I get noticed when I use violence; I have a feeling of power and superiority; it's like a buzz that numbs your feelings; when I use power I can get more money, for example, when I rob someone. Meanwhile, the boys in group B are having a much harder time. 'Yes, of course, there are the consequences, when I get called to account for the violent acts.' Slowly, they start remembering it's because of violence that they are now in jail. And it's only when questioned that they seem to realise this deed will stick with them after prison. They have a record and have to come to grips with the fact that they will face prejudice, rejection, and problems getting training and a job later in life. The discussion shows that behind the supposed advantages and disadvantages of violence there are a variety of basic needs for recognition and respect which have to be accepted. What cannot be accepted, however, is the way they have satisfied these needs. It becomes clear over and over again that recognition and respect have always been missing in the lives of these young men. As they did not have these experiences, they never came to terms with themselves as a person.

The discussion about the pros and cons leads to a sort of appraisal. Of course the youths' basic attitude towards violence doesn't change completely. The acceptance of violence is deep-rooted and is part of their right-wing extremist beliefs. And yet, the discussion has sparked a feeling of insecurity in the group. The myth of violence and its fascination has lost some of its appeal. The trainers continuously change perspectives during the discussion. They switch from the group debate to an individual level and then ask, 'What's it like for you?' The goal is a search for possibilities of breaking through this vicious circle in the future. The danger of using violence in everyday situations occurs extremely fast. There's no time for a careful weighing of consequences and risks. The trainers ask the youths about the worst possible consequences of a return to violence. T., for example says, 'that my mother would cry again. I don't want my mother crying because of me anymore.' The trainers suggest that T. should store this image in his head. He should use it as his personal 'stop-card'. In every day life, after prison, there will always be situations where he will be tempted to react violently. Pulling the 'stop-card', the memory of this one image, can help him to lower his fists instead of striking.

of conduct, long before the start of the VPN. I had worked on this during secondary school.

In reaction to the considerable support the right-wing extremist Republican Party gained during my teenage school years, in 1988 I joined the very active anti-fascist movement in Berlin. The movement organised demonstrations and boycotted screenings of election-spots of the German (right-wing) Republican Party in the large cinemas of the city. When putting up posters against the candidacy of Republicans for the House of Representatives Election in 1989, I got detained by the police. In order to prevent a second detainment, my mother continued the distribution of the posters. At the same time I remember that my father was also very active in the peace and anti-nuclear movements, and that I spent quite some time on his shoulders protesting against 'something'. I also remember that my companion was astonished when entering my parents' house during the early US invasion of Afghanistan. In the entrance corridor there was a big poster, 'Auch Afghanen lieben ihre Kinder' (Afghans also love their children). My mother had made this poster for a demonstration. This parental support of my political activism and their (often emotional) example still gives me strength to stand up for my interests.

I should also mention my history teacher, who supported my activism and made it a topic of discussion in class. He also persuaded me that even though my actions were an important civic protest, they would have little influence on the right-wing oriented teenagers that were causing trouble in my part of town. I came to doubt the approach of the so-called 'left', which fights right-wing extremism by seeking to exclude wherever possible.

BOX 3.5 THE VIOLENCE SESSION

This session focuses on T.'s offence. At first there is the usual 'flash' round: the youths can talk about what has happened this week in jail, current political events and anything that might be on their minds right now. K. has had some stress with his girlfriend and expresses his thoughts about this. Then the group is ready and the focus is on T. The trainers prepare the other youths for the roles they're to play in today's session. They should listen to T., ask questions about his story, comment on it and criticize him, but most of all they should support him as he comes to terms with his offence.

The interview about his offence begins. One trainer concentrates on T., the other on the group. T. was sentenced because of a jointly committed murder and was 18 years old at the time. He is asked to speak about what occurred on that day. What happened exactly? What happened before he acted? How did the offence occur? Who else was there?

T. tells his story. The victim owed him money. He went to his house with three mates. Then the bloke got the beating he deserved. T. only hit him at the beginning. The other three were the ones who really beat him up, the ones who were responsible for the victim's death. T. didn't even really know what was going on. His whole story takes about a minute to tell.

The trainer confronts T. about his view of the murder he and his friends committed together. Are you to blame? Are you the murderer? No, answers T., without hesitating. At first, T.'s description is not commented on, evaluated or scrutinized in a critical way. A slow-motion reconstruction of the order of events on that day is made. The trainers proceed like Columbo, the inspector in a famous American detective series. The questions deal with concrete details and observations that don't appear to have anything to do with the murder. T. can't yet see any connection to the actual murder. On that day he was under way with three mates and his girlfriend. One of his mates was 14, two were 15. When they got to the victim's house T. broke down the door and knocked his victim down with a hard punch. Then he demolished the furniture. Together they gave the victim a 'working over'. T. then retired to the kitchen with his girlfriend while the others continued to beat-up the victim with kicks and heavy objects. The trainer asks about seemingly minor details. What did he and his girlfriend talk about? What was on the table? T. can remember exactly that they talked about – pubs in the neighbourhood. There was a bottle of beer and an ashtray on the table. After a while he told his mates that it was enough. Then they left, leaving their blood-covered victim behind. A short while later he died from serious injury.

The trainers open the discussion to the group. Who was the instigator? The youths have listened closely and analysed the situation. T. provoked the action. He and his mates went to the victim's home as a result of T.'s initiative. He was the oldest and led the group. He took the first step, kicked in the door, knocked down the victim and finally put an end to the whole thing. The group is united: T. was the instigator. Can it really be that T. remembers details about the conversation he had with his girlfriend in the kitchen but didn't realise that a few metres away a person was being beaten to death? The group's questions and those of the trainer come to a head. T. can't shirk things anymore. He can't pass on the blame any longer. His lips are trembling. He has to take responsibility for his actions.

To my mind, adolescent right-wing extremism was more an attitude of protest than a closed political ideology. There were massive conflicts due to violent assaults by a group of right-wing adolescents in my neighbourhood. Together with another pupil, and with the support of a youth institution, I dared to seek a dialogue with this group rather than support the counter-violence organized by the Antifa.

Out of this dialogue, and with the support of the Senator of Youth and the responsible town councillor, the first project emerged in Berlin that actively worked with adolescents who identified themselves as right-wing extremists. Due to this project, named Miteinander statt Gegeneinander (Together instead of against each other), I changed my initial plan to study natural science and started a diploma in education. The project was guided by a maxim that I still follow today: do not talk about delinquents, but with them.

Briefly after the start of my university studies, the situation escalated in the 'new provinces', that is, the former German Democratic Republic (GDR), and Angela Merkel, as noted, then Federal Minister of Youth, started the Aktionsprogramm gegen Aggression und Gewalt (The Action Programme against Aggression and Violence). Within the framework of this programme I worked as a teacher sharing my work experience regarding right-wing adolescents with others, and further developing my qualifications in adult education and university education.

During my university time, and for many years that followed, I worked as a social worker with adolescents prone to violence. Then, in 1999, I changed focus and developed the first mediation programme for schools in Germany that would receive funding on a regular basis. I particularly focused on students prone to violence, using their 'conflict experience' as a positive resource for turning them into mediators. After nine years in public service, I gave up my permanent position for the challenge of developing the pedagogical approach described above.

Today, as founder and managing director of the VPN, I have much less contact with adolescents. But my entire entrepreneurial commitment is guided by the conviction that all human beings are capable of positive change if only they receive sufficient support. No human being is prone to violence or right-wing extremism by birth, born a fundamentalist or in other ways excluding and devaluing others. Such views and actions are the result of social structures and social environments, that is, they are the result of learing processes and as such always contain possibilities for change. This knowledge and conviction was and is the mainspring of my professional work.

BOX 3.6   FAMILY DAY

The youths have visitors, but it's not like normal visiting hours. They sit in a room at a table, each one of them with their family. They're supposed to talk about things, about what happened, but also about the future. The trainers go from table to table, listen and ask questions. Uncomfortable questions are asked as well. 'What did you do when you noticed your son had gotten involved with the right-wing extremist scene?' T.'s trainer asks the parents. They hesitate, and think things over. 'We were horrified. And in the beginning we fought against it.' Then the trainer asks T. how he experienced the situation at that time. Right-wing extremism was never a theme that the parents discussed, according to T. He wished it would have been. Instead, his parents punished him by disregarding him, calling him names, and threatening him. T. felt like he had been rejected as a person. At some point they just didn't bother anymore, his parents say. His right-wing extremist orientation, his belonging to the right-wing extremist scene simply became taboo.

'How could it go this far; why is T. in prison today?' The trainer continues to ask questions. The parents have already thought about the reasons: he had the wrong friends, after the wall came down everything went wrong, the judges at the hearing 'had it in for him'. It never occurs to them that something was wrong with the family.

'What are your son's strengths? What is he especially good at?' The mother looks incredulous, shrugs her shoulders and looks questioningly at the father. No answer. They don't know. The parents are irritated. Perhaps the idea of reflecting about T.'s development and their role in all this has been set in motion.

Perhaps. The trainer encourages the parents, 'Find out about your child's strengths, praise him when he does something well, show him that you respect and acknowledge him! He's going to need it when he's outside again.' The trainer warns them too, 'Don't expect a 180-degree transformation. Your son is going through a change. We can clearly see that at training here. But for the time being, a completely different person won't be coming home to you.'

3.3 SOCIAL ENTREPRENEURSHIP

I had never heard of Ashoka prior to my nomination by a sponsor of the VPN. This might also be owed to the fact that following its foundation in the 1980s, Ashoka had been mainly active in South America and Asia. The social entrepreneurship support organisation only became active in Germany in 2005.

Ashoka made inquiries about me via the VPN homepage as well as via VPN sponsors, and then invited me to participate in the selection process for Ashoka Fellows. This process includes a comprehensive description of the work of the candidate, numerous interviews with the candidate and his or her co-workers, clients and other individuals who might provide information. Ashoka examines very comprehensively and elaborately who to choose and support as a Fellow.

As a result, the selection process forced me to work on the precision and structure of my ideas, and to define my goals. This alone was already valuable for the VPN. Since then the goal and the implementation path have become a lot clearer. The selection process helped me to define my role, and to find an answer to the question: what have I been up to all these years? Prior to the selection process, I had not been familiar with the concept 'social entrepreneur'. Prior to meeting Ashoka, I would not even have defined myself as an 'entrepreneur'. This new definition, and the security such a role definition brings along, altered my entire way of relating to and presenting myself to clients and partners. This change is a result of the selection process.

Unlike other foundations and institutions, Ashoka supports social entrepreneurs on their path to success. This support means that fellows receive all sorts of support for the implementation of their project, the dissemination of the idea, and the expansion of the enterprise. A three-year stipend gives the financial security for expanding the idea. But just as decisive is the support in the form of contacts, *pro bono* services from well-known companies as well as the support from a worldwide network of human beings with a similar bent and enthusiasm. Every entrepreneur knows that a functioning network and the right contacts are worth much more than financial support for an idea.

For example, the Ashoka network made possible the free support of two McKinsey consultants. While I disagree with much of this company's[4] work, I happily acknowledge the support of these two consultants in 'translating' the work of the VPN in such a way that business people would understand it. Learning the language of business is a precondition for obtaining funds from the private sector. There is also a comic element to such 'translations', and at a recent VPN presentation a member of the audience stood up, pointed to my slide and the use of 'roll-out' and said that the colour of these graphs and their language looked very familiar to him from somewhere else . . .

Ashoka's fixation on the person of the entrepreneur rather than on the enterprise can lead to difficulties with organisations like the VPN, which are based on the idea of a network. I am not the sole founder of the VPN, rather there is, as described above, a team of founders, which has led and further developed the network. However, for the VPN the selection of one founding member as an Ashoka Fellow had very positive consequences. The role of the (social) entrepreneur within the VPN became very distinct as compared to the scientific work and educational-practical activities of the VPN. The leadership of the VPN comprises very different individuals with different competences. The Ashoka Fellow is the person with the entrepreneurial abilities, not the chief trainer and not the scientist in the team. The art is to use this group in such a way that the different competences are mutually recognised and appreciated.

Ashoka supports the project implementations of individuals, who have ideas that can change and improve society. The organisation bases its support on the assumption that human beings, who are so inspired by an idea that they seek to implement it in spite of all resistance, ultimately will have the staying power and energy to bring their idea to reality. This 'entrepreneurial spirit' is so far associated more with the business sector than with the social sector. However, in the end it does not matter whether it is the social sector or the economic sector. Development always draws on ideas. But pressing ahead with an idea requires stamina and audacity. The difference between an entrepreneur in a profit-oriented business and in the social sector is his or her personal motivation. To be a social entrepreneur means that monetary maximisation of gain does not have priority – or is often not even a goal at all. The 'gain' of the social entrepreneur is the solution of a societal problem. Ashoka promotes this struggle via the support of individuals, who in spite of all obstacles, stick to an idea until it has been implemented. This type of support is difficult to implement with 'group social entrepreneurship'.

Ashoka needs people with empathy, meaning the capacity to (quickly) grasp other people's intentions and outlook. For example, if you work with prison staff and administrators from the ministries, you must be able to understand how staff think and what their fears are, otherwise they are unlikely to co-operate. However, empathy is insufficient. Social entrepreneurs first and foremost must have moral integrity. As we have experienced first hand at the VPN, any new and promising approach will sooner or later face 'dilemmas' and 'indecent proposals' that social entrepreneurs must be able to deal with and turn down respectively.

BOX 3.7   COUNSELLING UPON BEING RELEASED

The trainer's telephone rings. It's P., he seems nervous and upset. 'I've really made a mess of things. I need your help.' Ten months ago P. was let out of prison. The training programme in prison was good for him and he gladly took up the counselling offer upon release from prison. The first days and weeks outside were hard. During this period P. and his trainers saw a lot of each other. They were there and helped him get back on track with the everyday things in life. He wanted to live where he had lived before, but he didn't want to move in with his parents again. The trainers helped him find his own apartment and furnish it with the things he needed most. Together, they went countless times to diverse public officials, to the housing authorities and public utilities. A thousand things of varying importance needed to be taken care of, but it was worth the effort. P. is standing on his own two feet, even if he's a bit unsteady at times. He has a flat and a construction job that he takes very seriously. He doesn't earn a lot of money but it's enough to get by. It would be much easier if he didn't have the old debts to pay as well. Together with the trainer and a local debt adviser he's come up with a plan to slowly lessen this burden.

He keeps his distance from his old mates in the right-wing extremist scene. Once in a while they cross each others' paths. Right after he got out of prison they used to come around regularly, call him up and want to go on a 'tour' with him. But P. turned them down. He knows how quickly something can happen again when he's under way with that crowd and the beer starts to flow. The word is out in the scene that he's not up to much. And this annoys him a bit.

He gets along much better with his parents since he doesn't live with them anymore. His mother is especially important. The trainer talks to her at regular intervals and gives her hints about how she can support P. By now P. has learned to talk about his feelings, even with his parents. They've talked about the past a lot, also about all the things that went wrong. P. now has a much better understanding of the context of things and can explain things better as well. He's also learned to deal with criticism and not see it as a personal attack.

But there are still times when he is disheartened. When he lost his first job after a short time, he had to go to the social welfare office and didn't have any idea how things were going to go from there, he often resorted to the bottle. Even though he didn't get back in touch with the right-wing extremist crowd, P. still looked for friends who liked to 'have a ball' and would never avoid a fight. At such times it was especially important that someone was available to help him get his everyday life under control. The trainer served as a kind of living memory who reminded him to avoid resorting to violence, because at times P. was really itching to do something.

Everything has gone quite well for the last few months. At work, with the family; he even has a girlfriend now. The trainer doesn't see him as often anymore, but they regularly talk on the telephone. But nevertheless, last weekend something happened again. It was completely unexpected, even for P. himself. He was with his girlfriend at a nightclub. They had had a lot to drink, and then this bloke got in his way. P. freaked out and beat him up. Now he wants to speak with his trainer about this setback. His insecurity on the phone is clearly perceptible.

They meet a couple of days later and go through the incident. P. wants to understand what happened. Just as he did in the past, he's trying to blame it on someone else. Step by step, as they reconstruct the evening, the trainer is able to make P. see that he is responsible for the fight. P. understands and is reasonable. It's a big setback for him; he's dejected and disappointed in himself. As much as the trainer condemns this new violent behaviour, she tries very hard to encourage P. as well. It's a good sign that he came to her on his own and wanted to reflect on the incident. But it is also clear just how difficult it is to change one's behaviour permanently and lead a life without violence. To keep working on this remains the task.

3.4 SOCIAL ENTREPRENEURSHIP AND THE STATE

In comparison to the 'market leaders' in the domain of penal systems, and considered only within the federal republic of Germany, the VPN is a very small supplier. Surely the VPN approach could be developed more quickly and comprehensively for the entire juvenile justice system, if the VPN was to become a part of the penal system. However, unfortunately the structure of this system contradicts the basic philosophy of the VPN. It is not yet possible to offer the VPN approach to young delinquents – and to comply with the reporting commitment. Due to the public staff's duty to report, young delinquents permanently fear that details of what they say will be passed on to the judge. This fear in turn blocks the possibility of working on past errors and leads to instrumental actions and adaptations.

The VPN pedagogy of responsibility relies on relationships between participants and the trainer that are based on trust and stability. Only in such circumstances can the trainers be both critical and supportive, and accompany the process of change. If they could not assure professional secrecy, their attempt to question patterns of behaviour and thought would be perceived as uncovering things that might influence the length of the detention or conditions after release from prison. For this reason, the programme Verantwortung übernehmen – Abschied von Hass und Gewalt cannot be run by public service staff, only by external trainers.

A structural change of the penal system aimed at releasing certain professional groups in prisons from the reporting commitment could certainly remove this hurdle and clear the way for an implementation of the approach within the regular penal system. But there are no indications for such a change; the work of the VPN at least exposes this problem.

The danger of an uncritical and exclusive promotion of a free and market-based (social) system is evident. There are domains where the state has a duty to take action and to ensure the basic security of its citizens. But without a permanent input to the state system of new ideas from outside, even this legitimate domain can do more harm than good. The public service of the Federal Republic of Germany has mutated in the 45 years since its foundation to such a rigid, large and expensive apparatus that since the 1990s we have been drudgingly trying to reform it.

A healthy mixture of public and private approaches can provoke the necessary new ideas that a permanently changing society requires for its strategies to deal with problems. Put concretely and for the purpose of the VPN, the state if left alone to itself will hardly create the necessary novelties, but the system will be forced to deal with necessary changes if there are external suppliers – and this might in turn improve the state system.

NOTES

1. The large majority of offenders are male, and the VPN only works with male offenders. However, the VPN has male and female trainers. We have not noted any difference in the work results between male or female trainers; not least, I think, because the work primarily depends on trainers' personality and their idea of human beings and gender is secondary – so to speak. Still, we would not work with women-only trainer teams, because the young men especially have to work on their definition of masculinity; this work has an enormous impact on their propensity to act violently.
2. I use the term 'cultural-religious', because youth in diaspora usually draw on a mixture of old cultural values and the respective religious perspective, even though they might think that it is an exclusively religious heritage.
3. Primary prevention takes place in early childhood education.
4. My co-operation with McKinsey also follows the maxim not to talk about people, but with them. I had to revise many of my prejudices during my work with the consultants. This is only possible, if you engage in a dialogue – rather than reading only news stories.

REFERENCES

Osborg, E. (2006), 'Der konfrontative Ansatz der subversiven Verunsicherungs-pädagogik in der Präventionsarbeit mit rechten und rechtsorientierten Jugendlichen', in J. Weidner and R. Kilb (eds), *Konfrontative Pädagogik. Konfliktbearbeitung in sozialer Arbeit und Erziehung*, Wiesbaden: VS Verlag für Sozialwissenschaften, pp. 191–206.

Weidner, J. and R. Kilb (eds) (2006), *Konfrontative Pädagogik. Konfliktbearbeitung in sozialer Arbeit und Erziehung*, Wiesbaden: VS Verlag für Sozialwissenschaften.

4. Not about the number of seats in parliament: education for democracy and its places

Krzysztof Stanowski

This is the edited protocol of a conversation with Krzysztof Stanowski, Deputy Minister of Education in Poland, which took place on 31 July 2008. Prior to his work for the government, Stanowski was a programme director and President of the Education for Democracy Foundation. The Foundation seeks to improve the understanding of rights and responsibility that come with democracy and a free market. Stanowski was elected an Ashoka Fellow in 2000.

4.1 FUNDACJA EDUKACJA DLA DEMOKRACJI – EDUCATION FOR DEMOCRACY FOUNDATION (FED)

Rafael Ziegler: In your view, education for democracy is, above all, indirect education; it consists not so much in passing on knowledge about parliamentary systems or about voting in presidential elections as in the experience of social interaction. Please explain, and how this pedagogy informs the FED approach.

Krzysztof Stanowski: In the region FED works, that is, in the former Communist countries, the main issue with respect to human rights and civil society is not 'the law' or 'legal status'. The Soviet Union had the constitution with the longest list of human rights – the only problem: it was just a joke. Unlike in post-Apartheid South Africa, the 'division of power', the 'constitution', 'human rights' are well known by people in the post-communist countries of Eastern Europe and Central Asia, but the reality for them is such that they do not understand these concepts as something to be taken seriously. So the main issue to change the situation is to help people to believe in these concepts, and to given them the chance to exercise democracy in real life.

A good example of bad practice is the traditional school. School is very important, it is the first public institution the young future citizens encounter – and quite often the school is the institution where basic human rights are violated, where people don't understand the law, where people don't feel that the procedures are fair. This is the first message a young person and their parents are getting from the system; this is their first contact with the state. Very typical in this respect are student councils that are merely puppet bodies controlled by the teachers. The biggest danger is that teachers encourage students to have elections and to vote. Let's decide, but then there is nothing to decide.

The crucial issue is to empower people to take real decisions and to help them put these decisions into practice. Currently our approach is implemented in Crimea, Ukraine. Adver Seitosmanov, who completed the FED train-the-trainer programme several years ago and is now employed by the Crimea Integration and Development Programme, developed the project Increase Tolerance and Social Cohesion.[1] It has a very simple structure. He approaches a multicultural village with the following proposal: if we can meet together, 80 per cent of the time, in the school community, and if we will decide what kind of action, what kind of investment will be good for the future and the development of our school, then I will pay for 50 per cent of the costs. They decide together. This is the first time that the community of parents is really taking decisions and developing a structure. This is a very poor area; so they build school gyms, computer classrooms and so on.

For our approach two things are crucial. First, the question of legitimacy: that the decisions really represent all the parents. Second, I talked to parents in one such village. I asked them: 'Did you do something on tolerance?' The head of the parent council answered: 'Tolerance? No, we haven't had time yet. Last year we built the sport room.' But they were working together: Russians, Crimean-Tatars, Ukrainians, Jews . . . They were not talking about tolerance, but exercising it. The results of a UNDP survey conducted with students of this village showed this project to have changed the relations in the village. People started to be interested in other cultures and in people from other nations. It was not 'talking', it was not 'the law', empowering people to do something else produced this change.

The Foundation

The FED was founded in 1989, and I will say more below about the tradition of independent civic education it carries on. The FED's mission is to improve understanding of the rights and responsibilities that go with democracy and a free market. Through its training and publications programmes in Poland, Eastern Europe, and the New Independent States (NIS) of the former Soviet Union, the Foundation promotes the skills necessary to perform civic duties in a democratic society among teachers, students, and democratic activists. Small groups, comprising volunteer educators and emerging community leaders, collaborate to solve local problems, restore civic awareness and participation, and implement training efforts to bolster basic citizen skills. These local, community-focused efforts provide the basis for democratic societies by establishing lasting patterns of cross-cultural co-operation and tolerance.

The FED was founded as a non-governmental organisation based in Warsaw by Polish and American educators. Among the founders were Americans from the American Foundation of Teachers, including Albert Shanker, the President of the American Foundation of Teachers; and well-known Polish educators from the underground, that is, people who were preparing educational reform during the martial law in Poland:[2] Wiktor Kulerski (former deputy minister of education), Janusz Onyszkiewicz (former minister of defence), Edward Wieczorek (vice chairman of the European Parliament) and Jacek Woznikowski.

The FED has organised hundreds of workshop (of three to six days in length) in Poland, Latvia, Lithuania, Belarus, Russia, Ukraine, Kyrgyzstan, Uzbekistan, Kazakhstan, Tajikistan, Azerbaijan, Georgia and Mongolia; it has educated thousands of participants including teachers, journalists, students, and activists from non-governmental organizations (NGOs); and it has produced, translated and adapted numerous publications of training materials for workshop participants in Polish, Russian, English, Latvian, Lithuanian, Belarusian, Ukrainian, Crimean-Tatar, Albanian, Azeri, Farsi, Kyrgyz, Uzbek and Mongolian.[3]

Finance

Our approach is based on developing local trainers and local educators, who are not full-time trainers but teachers, headmasters, engineers and doctors. They work together to change the community. Therefore the cost of these educational activities is really minimal. In the above example of the village, 50 per cent of the resources were bought from the local community. I also remember one of the first student newspapers published in Crimea. After a few days of workshops with trainers and basic materials (provided by us), the students set up an editorial team. However, there was no computer in this village. The mother of the head editor baked some sweets. Her son went with them to the market, sold them, and with this money he purchased a bus ticket. Then he went to another town, to

Bakchisaray, the former capital of Crimean-Tatars. There he stayed with a family, used the computer of an NGO, put together all the articles the students had written, and after two days went back with printed materials. In short, we are not really talking about money; at the start money is not the main issue. We should empower people to act. Later, when money is needed we link people directly with sponsors, that is, we do not finance them through us.

To fund the FED staff needed for developing and implementing the various programmes, we initially obtained funding from the US-American National Endowment for Democracy and from the US-American Federation of Teachers. Gradually we started to find local resources in Poland; first from local governments, then European Union funds arrived. In the last few years, the Foundation also received money from the Polish Ministry of Foreign Affairs for several development projects in Eastern Europe and in the Global South, including Africa. The FED is also the grant operator for the Regions in Transition Programme, sponsored by the Polish-American Freedom Foundation, and aimed at promoting co-operation between Polish NGOs and NGOs from other former Eastern Block countries. Today, the FED budget is somewhere around US$ 10 million.

Scale

Today, of course I speak as the Polish Deputy Minister of Education. But when you start from bottom-up it just takes some time to influence the higher structures. And this is different in every region. Please remember that in many totalitarian countries you should remain relatively invisible and unimportant if you want to do something. If you are too important and visible, there will be no way that you can operate there. Our experience is that when you start in the local community on the school level, then in the second year headmasters and local education authorities will approach you and ask for some help. In Uzbekistan, it took eight years from the local start to the introduction of the first handbook written by a non-governmental organisation into the educational system. Unfortunately, the political situation in Uzbekistan has become really very bad, but still it is an example of how you can influence the big scale. After six years of re-granting experience in the region, FED experts developed the grant procedures for the Polish Ministry of Foreign Affairs, and these procedures are used to this day. So if you have real knowledge, and if you know how to implement your ideas in the system, then you can really achieve big-scale change. I have become Deputy Minister of Education as a result of my experience in the non-governmental sector. I have never been a member of a political party.

4.2 AUTOBIOGRAPHICAL OBSERVATIONS

Rafael Ziegler: You mentioned above the tradition of independent civic education in Poland. How has it informed your work?

Krzysztof Stanowski: As a young boy I was a boy scout in a relatively independent boy scout troop Puszca (Jungle). Scouting started in Poland just before World War I as a youth movement struggling for the freedom of Poland. Scouting was really a way for young people to become citizens. For a long time I was just working in the local scouts community.

I would also like to mention that I studied history at the only non-state university between Warsaw and West Berlin: the Catholic University of Lublin. In Lublin, there was a professor of Ethics named Karel Woytila; my professor of history was Władysław Bartoszewski. Lublin was a place gathering very interesting scholars and scientists, and it attracted many interesting students.

My father was in the Youth Catholic Group during World War II, and he was fighting in the Warsaw uprising in 1944. In the 1950s, he was the leader of a religious organisation. He was sent to jail by communists, sentenced for seven years because he tried to change the political system by force using false argument. So for me the contact with the democratic tradition was something very natural.

Finally, I would also like to mention Jean Goss from the non-violence movement. I met him personally in the mid-1970s, and understood that the non-violent way can be effective.

These traditions inspired me. I became first one of the regional leaders of the scouts, and then the national leader of the first independent scout organisation in Poland, the Independent Scouting Movement (since 1989, Scouting Association of the Republic). But I also understood something important while working with deaf scouts in my first years. My first group of scouts were deaf students. I said that education for democracy is not about the number of seats in Parliament. When scouting with deaf students you cannot sit around a bonfire with the guitar and sing songs or something like that. You have to ask yourself what you would like to accomplish. Tradition is not enough.

Deputy Minister

For a long-time I criticised the Ministry of Education and the State for failing to develop important relations such as the Polish-Ukrainian Youth Co-operation Programme, and that there was no way for non-governmental organisations to effectively co-operate with the school on the local level. But then I was offered to take responsibility for this issue, and to bring a change.

I usually say that being a minister is similar to being pregnant: on the first day you know that it will end some time. This is not a permanent position. The real question is, what will be the result? At this moment I am working on several important projects: Polish-Israeli Youth Exchange, Polish-Ukrainian Youth Exchange, non-governmental organisations' co-operation with schools, and the development of a system of education for Polish students abroad. If these projects succeed, then I would say it was worth doing it.

Family

I could not imagine doing all this without my family. For me family is extremely important. I have a wife, and we have four children together. We got married at the time when there was no future, during the time of the early martial law. It was sure that at some point I would 'move' to jail. But all this time there has been a giant involvement. We are supporting each other. My family visits the places where I work, and they are directly involved in some activities.

Just two weeks ago we married one of 'our' Crimean-Tatar students. He had arrived as a boy in Poland for studies, completed his education, obtained a master's degree, and went back to the Crimea, where he works at a university. It is all a family issue. Otherwise it will never work, at least in my case.

4.3 SOCIAL ENTREPRENEURSHIP

Rafael Ziegler: According to Ashoka 'social entrepreneurs are individuals with innovative solutions to society's most pressing social problems. They are ambitious and persistent, tackling major social issues and offering new ideas for wide-scale change'.[4] Please comment.

Krzysztof Stanowski: For a long time I did not like to use the word 'social entrepreneurship', especially as it sounds really strange in Polish. Obviously, social entrepreneurs are people who are entrepreneurs in the 'social' sense. But there were times when people called them 'leaders'. Somehow social entrepreneurs are a specific kind of leader, one who brings innovation. But it is difficult to specify this innovation as it is also always some kind of adaptation, and it always relies on the experience of others. And yet, it brings the innovative element of design from zero.

Social Entrepreneurs and Organisation

It is very important to keep a balance between the innovators and those who share the experience. In some areas I would say that they are needed on an equal basis. The experience of social entrepreneurs shows that without effective organisation, without people around you, and without an understanding of the mechanisms of implementation you cannot be effective. Even if you are innovative, you will not be entrepreneurial.

I would like to say that what I am proud of the most in the last year, that is, the year I left the FED to work for the government, is the realisation that the FED is established. They don't need me on an everyday basis. After a long period, during which I was leading this initiative in the very direct sense that it could collapse without me, we have succeeded in building a group of innovative, well-organised people. Not people who follow patterns like students who repeat some design, but people who design new ideas, new programmes and approaches. I am very, very proud to see this.

How did we do it? First, we really believe in democratic structure. That means that we have a strong council of people who are not directly involved in the activities. These people are not paid by us; they are people who really watch what is going on, and we keep very good contact with them. Second, we try to find strong people, strong independent people with their own views. We try to find a common way: we do not try to employ; we do not try to force people to do something for us. The ideal situation is when you find people who are independent from you but hold similar views, and will be glad to do something together with you. Then there is common value and joint ownership. The people involved understand that this is something they can influence, and that it gives them a chance to do what they want to do.

We talked about family. When I talked to a lady who really wanted to be involved in our activities, I asked her: 'Why do you so much want to be with us?' The answer really surprised me. She said: 'You all have families.' I had never thought about that. That means that the FED is in the majority not about singles, but about family people who understand the limits which family life brings with it, but also the importance of family life. It has not been designed this way, but at this moment I understood: yes, this is true, we are family people.

Ashoka

One Ashoka Fellow tried to involve me in Ashoka, and for a long time I responded: 'I have no time.' But then support from Ashoka became important for me in three ways. First, for sure there was the stipend, which allowed me not to take any job just to make my family survive. Second, there was the process of recruitment. During this process, you really better understand what you are doing. It was very helpful for me to go through this process of discussion – even if I would not have been elected. This experience was really very important. Finally, some Ashoka Fellows are really very interesting and great people. I have collaborated with some of the other Fellows for seven years now. Dealing with such people and co-operating with them is really very fascinating.

But might there also be some contradiction between Ashoka Fellows and Ashoka staff? Ashoka staff are paid to design new activities and so on, and the Fellows are doing what they are doing. Are Ashoka staff sometimes designing new ways of involving people which are not needed?

Empathy

I work in extremely delicate areas. When you deal with democracy issues in non-democratic societies, then there are direct risks. When I was in the underground, I knew that mistakes done by others, for example, by supporters from abroad, can put me to jail. Therefore the first thing that I would like to say is that you don't have a right to provoke people. You can show them something, you can suggest something, but in the end it is about their lives. I often say this: 'I don't plan to live in your village. I will not send my son to this school. This is your life.' It is very important not to overuse people. Not to pull them, not to bring them to a situation which somehow seems positive *for you*. That means simply that if you work in the area of democracy you should follow democratic standards.

Second, I would like to point out that one of the important pillars on which we are building our programmes is using the local language, drawing on the local culture, tradition, and history. Therefore you need empathy, and you should do everything to understand what is going on. When you are coming to a community, and you believe that 10 per cent is OK, but 90 per cent is wrong, and you will come to fix things, then you should leave this place as quickly as possible.

Building communities and working with communities is most effective if you can find a traditional fundament to build on. Let me give an example. When you try to build a community foundation in Central Asia, you are not talking about the tradition of the UK, of the US or the great Polish tradition. You ask: 'Do you remember the times when your grandfathers where sending talented students from poor families to town for education, at the costs of the whole village? Let's do the same. The only difference is that it is not obligatory to be a boy.' So you bring this small difference, but you really re-establish something that was very democratic. You just 'fix' this one element. In the majority of the communities you can do something like this.

Finally, I would like to add that as an educator you cannot teach something that you are not yourself. If you really believe that people can take decisions, that they can be responsible and that they can bring a change, if you exercise these beliefs, then you can do it. But quite often you can see educators who are not democratic, but who talk about democracy. Quite often you can meet in the Global South people from the West who say how great it is to be a volunteer, but who never volunteered in their own life. It will never work.

Social Entrepreneurship Education

Some people speak of 'schools for social entrepreneurs': forget it! There are courses on 'leadership', but are leaders created in this way? Take it easy. Of course these courses are useful and helpful. But leadership is not just to be completed as a university class – the same holds for social entrepreneurship.

There is a really strong push to develop your CV. This is something I observe here in Poland, and in the East and West more generally. It really means that youth has no time; they don't have time for long-term investments. They have to complete courses, collect diplomas, and so on. If you would compare my CV to that of a 25-year-old person, then my CV will be poorer! They collect everything that is possible, they designed all these activities to facelift their CV.

4.4 SOCIAL ENTREPRENEURSHIP AND THE STATE

Rafael Ziegler: How do you understand the relation between the state and social entrepreneurship?

Krzysztof Stanowski: I am really afraid of too much intervention of the state in civil society (including social entrepreneurship). Poland is a place where traditionally society does not trust the state very much. Partly the reason is a historical one: we could not trust the state for many decades. We cannot give up to the state too many responsibilities, and we do not want to. The language survived not thanks to the state, but thanks to the families. Some democratic education survived through the NGOs. It is very dangerous when the state starts to control and finance civil society, including social entrepreneurs. I very strongly support the 1 per cent mechanism in place in Poland. The state allows citizens to send 1 per cent of their taxes not to the state but to selected NGOs. It is a big danger if the state over-supports civil society. It should rather happen via mechanisms that enable community funding, that support private donors and that support tax deduction allowing citizens to support the NGOs they believe in.

Public Goods

Consider education: do you believe that the state is responsible for education, that it should provide education? In the US it is more the responsibility of the local community, in Germany it is more the responsibility of the state. Our beliefs on such matters depend on our specific positions.

In the last two decades in Poland, the system of education, under the influence of the civil society, has been decentralised. The schools are run by the communities or by NGOs, the schools are not state owned, the state is not publishing handbooks, it is not even providing curricula. The state only provides a general policy and standards so that we know what we would like to learn (that is, the skills and knowledge needed to live in society); and the state controls through exams the results and intervenes in situations were something is going wrong. The Polish education system is getting better and better. I am not saying this as a Deputy Minister of Education, I would have said exactly the same thing six months ago.

Promoting Innovation

First, there are the very young people. Ashoka understood that it is not about innovation in the mid-30s. This is really about lifestyle, about a way of thinking. And you can really influence this, somewhere around the age of 11. So in the long term this is about activities which support interest in the world at a very early age, and dealing with students at this age.

Then there is the need to give experience to university students, to do something practical, to implement something, to make a change, any kind of change, to make something of one's own. When you build something, then you can fail and you can grow.

Finally, there is the Ashoka approach of investing in Fellows. This way they can do what they need to do. This is a very effective tool.

East and West

Are these questions of education and innovation different in East and West? In the end, I am not really sure whether there is such a big difference.

If you do not compare with the poorest areas, where people simply try to survive, then it is really not so obvious for me. The key issue is really simply that of responsibility. If the state takes responsibility out of citizens, builds insurance relations between citizens and the state, then this destroys social entrepreneurial activity.

I believe that people should have a right to make decisions and to make mistakes. Otherwise people get frustrated – and you get exclusion of people when they understand that their vote counts for nothing. To be sure, there are some issues that cannot be delegated from the national level, but a lot more is possible on the local level. This is what I really believe.

NOTES

1. See also the film UNDP CIDP School Project for Tolerance Education (Crimea), available from YouTube, last accessed 13 August 2008.
2. 'Martial law in Poland' refers to the period in the early 1980s when the Polish (military) government attempted to crush political opposition against the community rules. General Jaruzelski declared a 'state of war' in December 1981. People from the pro-democracy movements were arrested (including Lech Walesa from Solidarity), and some people were killed.
3. For a discussion of various FTD programmes see Stanowski (1998); also see the FTD homepage www.edudemo.org.pl/, last accessed 30 July 2008.
4. See www.ashoka.org/social_entrepreneur, last accessed 10 July 2008.

REFERENCE

Stanowski, K. (1998), 'Teaching democracy in postcommunist countries', *Journal of Democracy*, **3** (9), 57–65.

5. We call it work

Philipp Albers and Holm Friebe

This is the edited protocol of a conversation with Philipp Albers and Holm Friebe from the Zentrale Intelligenz Agentur (ZIA – Central Intelligence Agency), which took place in Berlin, on 17 June 2008. The ZIA is a virtual firm with projects in the commercial domain (mainly advertisement and marketing), and in the arts. A key development for the ZIA is the transformation of work, in particular from permanent employment to flexible networks of self-employed people. Its mission is to co-design and contribute to this social change with new forms of collaboration.

5.1   ZENTRALE INTELLIGENZ AGENTUR (ZIA)

Rafael Ziegler: The opening citation of your book manifesto, *We Call it Work* (Friebe and Lobo, 2006), is taken from Brecht's Three-Penny Opera: 'What is the murder of a man to the employment of a man?' Please comment.

The Employment of a Man and Self-Employment

Holm Friebe: I am convinced now more than ever that the new generation, not least due to Web 2.0 and related developments, has learned how to take things into its own hands; its members can structure their days and their activities for themselves.

Therefore this generation will neither understand nor appreciate the still dominating way in which work is constituted in Europe and in North America, and in all bigger economic organisations: for example, showing 'face-time' from nine to five, behaving opportunistically all the time and so on. There will be a very interesting conflict as soon as this generation enters the workforce and is expected to 'make a career', because this 'career' is at odds with this generation's self-understanding. In terms of so-called 'social hygiene', this will be a major source of conflict comparable to earlier struggles for a secure workplace. The demands for self-determination, for free spaces of action and for time autonomy hold a huge potential for conflict, and it is an open question whether companies will be able to respond to these demands, or whether there will be a mass exodus, because the jobs they offer simply will not remain sufficiently attractive.

Viewed from the perspective of the individual, self-organisation in loose and flexible networks becomes increasingly visible and tangible. There are, more and more, examples of such work in everyday life. It is no longer possible to defame such work as second-best. Rather, as we can already see with those working in the advertisement sector, the true professional end-goal will be self-employment, whereas being permanently employed by somebody else becomes an intermediary step towards this goal.

However, many people still do not understand that the Web is not only a medium of communication, but also a medium of economic co-ordination. On the one hand, the Web gives people the possibility to organise work on a very large scale. Wikipedia manifests the spontaneous emergence of large groups that produce meaningful results. The Web lowers what Coase called transaction costs, that is, the costs associated with the co-ordination of economic exchange; these costs can even entirely disappear. On the other hand, many utopian movements of the past foundered, because their projected exodus from the factory and the alternative creation of small-scale organisations came up against distribution problems. These organisations faced unsurmountable problems to get their products and services distributed. Consider for example the distribution of independent music. The Internet really disburdened this movement. As a result, the channels of distribution are no longer a necessary obstacle.

Structure and Hierarchy

Philipp Albers: The ZIA gives priority to self-employment and self-organised work, but without falling into the cliché of the self-employed, small-scale creative person who bungles things up and cannot take on larger projects because these require partners. We tried to establish a network structure that does not repeat these problems. We did not start a firm in expensive rooms, with two secretaries, many interns and a huge overhead that requires a large income before one earns anything. Instead, we started a network of self-employed people, a 'virtual firm' that has no fixed place, no office and no regular nine to five work hours. We established forms of communication that allow co-operative work, online and offline.

As far as 'being a firm' is concerned, you really only need to keep a profile, have a website and a business card (with name, email, website, mobile phone number and skypename), and you can right away stage a public appearance.

How the firm is organised internally is an entirely different matter. For our 'internal' politics it is important that there are only roughly defined task areas, but no fixed positions in relation to these tasks. Everyone can become the leader of a project, and choose the people he or she wants to work with. There is no classic division of labour in the sense that one person is the manager, another works on content, and someone else does the accounting and so forth. To be sure, there is a distribution of tasks, but everyone can say: 'Hello, I have acquired this project, I would like to co-ordinate it, build up a team and take responsibility for the work.'

Holm Friebe: We are a society of partners, but without subaltern employees and secretaries. There are responsibilities, but there are no authorities that issue directives. Responsibilities change and shift. There is no one boss who directs everything, and there is no sweeper in the penalty area that has to clean up the mess. Instead, everyone's tasks change with each constellation. This requires a legal structure that is as simple as possible to allow maximum flexibility.

When we started the ZIA all of us had gathered some experience as employees, and as seemingly self-employed (that is, only formally self-employed, but de facto employed by somebody). We then tried to avoid the worst from both of these worlds. We noted that the firm structure is a very useful infrastructure as long as one really cuts away all the cumbersome elements of the classic firm; if one really does without all that is not urgently needed – really just a homepage and some cards. We worked very hard against conventions and structures said to have always been like this and to always remain so ('somebody always has to be the boss'). Instead of simply accepting them, we tried to do things differently. For example, we worked a lot on the possibility of working together digitally without sitting in the same room; everything is on a server and can be accessed from anywhere. That means that there is no such thing as a 'centre' of the company and no 'top'. Rather than relying on hierarchies we rely on shifting responsibilities.

An important structural feature is our two-column model. In column one, we do professional marketing work for clients, adopt their perspective and in this way think through situations that can be quite demanding and complex. We get jobs done to the satisfaction of even large corporations. It is a school of routines for working together. Yet, this work is not the ultimate goal, and therefore has to be deliberately limited in order to create space for column two: our own projects; projects that we think ought to exist and that perhaps in some sense even improve the world. These projects have to be worked on with the same professional sense and with an equal sense of priority, that is, not as something secondary.

Philipp Albers: To give two examples: in 2007 we organised a three-day festival camp in Berlin. Under the title '9 to 5 – We Call it Work' we created an event for those who feel – as we do – that working should be more like living and not the other way around. The basic idea was to turn the 9 a.m. to 5 p.m. routine of the regular office worker upside down: discussions, workshops, entertainment shows and so on ran from 9 p.m. in the evening until 5 a.m. in the morning. During the day people could hang out at the festival site and network or work on projects. A second example is the blog Riesenmaschine (http://riesenmaschine.de). It is a collective blog in the format of an ironic feuilleton. A group of about 30 writers fills it with observations on all things new and interesting – from gadgets and digital innovations to consumer products, rodents and scientific discoveries.

There is a feedback loop between our commercial jobs and these projects. Those 'other' projects that we simply do because we like to can become a reason for companies to approach us, because they want exactly the style they see in our own projects.

Holm Friebe: As our work is project based, the income from these projects is divided in terms of the respective project immediately after its completion. To be sure, there can be some struggle regarding the shares, but the struggle is at this point and not at the end of the year. Ten per cent of the project revenue is kept as a resource for new manoeuvre, for pre-financing new projects, or for supporting somebody who does not have enough project work, though this has not happened for a while.

Growth and Employee Mentality

Holm Friebe: A question that we now face concerns growth bottlenecks. At the moment we very much experience the classic growth crisis of an enterprise, when informal structures no longer work, when informal hierarchies are replaced by formal hierarchies. So where are the bottlenecks? One challenge is clearly the overhead, that is, the administration has to be organised in such away that it can grow without turning into an obstacle for decentralised work.

Philipp Albers: Another bottleneck is project management, because the number of people involved as well as the number of projects we do simultaneously grows. We would like to keep the structure as lightweight, non-hierarchical and flexible as possible. So we try to develop our own resource and project management tools, which reflect this attitude, rather than to rely on off-the-shelf solutions.

Holm Friebe: One distinguishing feature of the ZIA is a filter that differs from the classic entry filter of staff divisions. We ask: does this person take responsibility for herself or himself? Does this person have ideas? Does this person fit in? In this respect, we do not necessarily handle people with care. As soon as there is only a whiff of 'let's wait' 'let's wait for directives from outside', then this employee mentality is mercilessly pecked at. There is self-observation of the organisation, and of the person in the organisation. Positively put, this is a form of mutual coaching.

5.2 AUTOBIOGRAPHICAL OBSERVATIONS

Rafael Ziegler: ZIA proclaims 'intelligent life beyond permanent employment'. How are we to imagine this new form of life?

Doing and Managing

Holm Friebe: I would not like to speak only of myself here, but rather of us, and here I believe that we are people who have something in common, perhaps it is an anthropological constant . . . perhaps I should not go that far, let me talk about myself after all. I have always enjoyed bringing people together, to see how something emerges, and to design social processes, though without seeing myself as an 'entrepreneur'. Perhaps, my degree in business administration has given me a thorough prejudice not to use this concept too positively and emphatically.

But no matter, it has always given me a kick to produce something that, as a market product, mirrors back that it is socially useful in the sense that somebody is willing to pay money for it. I think this joy of producing and implementing can be found very widely in our firm. Internally we call it Fippfappismus. It is also known among programmers as 'extreme programming': simply start, see how far you can get, adapt along the way.

Philipp Albers: No classic roadmaps, milestones . . . simply getting started and getting people involved in the process of feedback – no beta-version, but directly on the market and in public.

Holm Friebe: This approach of course is not taught in start-up seminars offered by chambers of commerce, to the contrary, there it is considered a risk. You are supposed to make an orderly plan and not just to throw yourself into projects. But to throw oneself has the advantage that one works, and really works a lot, directly with the material. Gratification is not postponed but instant, it is an experience of flow and all that comes with it. This joy of creating and of getting something done functions like a drug, once you have experienced it.

Philipp Albers: This is also the difference to the classic manager (or established entrepreneur): that 'doing' comes before 'managing'.

Heroes and Hedonism

Holm Friebe: Biographies of social entrepreneurs often read like classic hero tales. For a long time you run in the wrong direction, but you gather a lot of important material, then there is an epiphany – this is my vocation, and so on. Such a story has not happened to me, and not to us.

Our motivation is more down-to-earth and hedonistic. How can we work together – with maximum comfort and taking into account our hedonistic defects – how can we have a good livelihood? How can we prevent the feeling that we only fabricate nonsense or even that we make the world worse off?

Empathy and Karma

Holm Friebe: Empathy is important in the immediate surroundings. If you choose the people you work with and if they are friends, then a lot is at stake. The interest to take advantage of others is not so strongly articulated at the ZIA; I would even claim that competition within the firm cannot really be felt. This means an increase in life quality, and in work quality.

But empathy also goes beyond these narrow bounds to the extent that we do not want to make the world worse off. At the end of the year, we do not publish a business report, but a Karma report with which we hold our projects during the year accountable to ourselves and to the readers of our newsletter. If there are no entries, then the karma report is bad.

Philipp Albers: Instead of the numbers of a corporate annual balance sheet, the karma report lists and evaluates our activities in light of the question, whether we have tried (and hopefully succeeded) to make the world a little better – according to our own standards, but also according to a more general code of ethics.

5.3 SOCIAL ENTREPRENEURSHIP

Rafael Ziegler: According to Ashoka 'social entrepreneurs are individuals with innovative solutions to society's most pressing social problems. They are ambitious and persistent, tackling major social issues and offering new ideas for wide-scale change'.[1] Please comment.

Self-Adulation and Development

Holm Friebe: When I hear this I immediately have a heretical, critical impulse. This is so luminous and heroic – and one encounters this heroism all the time in self-descriptions – that there is a question how much self-adulation is at play, how much staging of oneself as a model human being; a phenomenon that one also encounters in charity.

This being said, I am convinced that social entrepreneurship is important for the domain of development politics, where the effective approaches are those that tease out solutions that are built already into the human being and that support these solutions and create a framework in which they can become active.

But I do not wish to go from there to the neo-liberal 'short-cut' that this individual, entrepreneurial action is all that matters, and that there is no role for the state. I do not share a deep suspicion against big organisations and the state, but rather believe that there is a role for the state. Entrepreneurship is not a cure-all. And just because we find the entrepreneurial spirit congenial and fruitful for us, it does not follow that it is a general panacea for the improvement of the world that can be prescribed to all.

Philipp Albers: On my reading of this Ashoka definition, society and community are in the end only the 'object' of social entrepreneurs, who are the heroes that take care of the big questions. Yet what about the small and local action, does it also count as social entrepreneurship, or is this something different? What is the relation of these people to their local environment?

Holm Friebe: There is a sociological question regarding the mechanisms of exclusion and inclusion in this field where social entrepreneurship decorations are bestowed. Who gets accredited, what are the insider deals and what are the networks? Do the members of a new elite lend each other a hand? I have a slight suspicion in this direction, but I cannot really prove it. Perhaps, it could be analysed with the instruments of Pierre Bourdieu.

Support Organisations

Holm Friebe: The domain that we work in is not very formalised, and there is little enthusiasm for 'club life' and the life of associations with their rituals of nomination, events and semi-official ways of doing things. What matters to us are truly spontaneous, emergent networks, and the complicity of coalition partners from quite different places: that there are people in newspaper who are favourably inclined towards our work, or who even from a distance feel like-minded; and that there are playgrounds on the Internet where you can let off steam, negotiate private matters and start a conversation.

Social Entrepreneurship and Brands

Holm Friebe: What I find remarkable about this whole domain of social entrepreneurship is that domains such as politics and arts that used to rely on quite different means of articulation increasingly emphasise entrepreneurial means for their rather different goals. 'Business art' is one example, professionally managed NGOs are another one.

I believe that the *brand* is a driving force behind this development, especially the mechanism of brands. It took me a long time to understand, perhaps due to a mixture of disgust and fascination, that the fundamental mechanism of brands – visibility, the poignancy of an idea, recognition and trust – are meaningful and effective in totally new contexts.

5.4 ZIA AND THE STATE

Rafael Ziegler: What are the values motivating the call 'beyond permanent employment'? Are they perhaps grounded in, and in reaction to, a cultural German concern for security and a strong social welfare state?

Security and Freedom

Holm Friebe: In the classic dualism this value is freedom. Sovereignty over one's own day is appreciated very highly by all self-employed, with the qualification that this only pertains to those who have chosen to become self-employed and not to those who have become self-employed because they had to.

I think self-employment is also becoming more attractive because security can no longer be taken for granted and hence the deal of loyalty in exchange for a secure course of life (and the possibility of a life-plan) has come to an end unilaterally due to globalisation and the end of the Rhenish-paternalist capitalist model. In this situation, the other model, even if it does not offer more security – which it does not – still becomes more attractive simply because the alternative becomes increasingly less attractive.

Philipp Albers: Security as a high value in German culture would explain the strong opposition between the employee and the self-employed. My impression is that this opposition might not be so strong in other cultures, especially not in the Anglo-Saxon world, because the people there simply do not have the expectation that they will live in the same place for 30 years – if there is no work, or if the work is dull, then you move from the East Coast to the West Coast.

Culture, Business and the State

Holm Friebe: The beauty of an organisation that prances at the boundary between cultural enterprise and business enterprise is its double irritation. Business people are always surprised to learn that we are discussed in the feuilleton. Inversely, the culture industry is irritated that we work for money and the dirty industry. We quite enjoy this situation.

For culture producers it has something very liberating not to depend on governmental funds and the 'prose' of its funding applications. In this case we prefer to be paid by business.

Philipp Albers: Here again the advantage of the two column model can be seen.

Holm Friebe: We have tried to obtain state funds, and we do not have any fear to get in touch. But still there are good reasons not to do it. If you work for a business, they do not want to see every single cab receipt. They will take the final product or they will not take the final product; they will pay or they will not pay. If you work for the state, it is not sufficient to simply deliver a final product that costs X-amount of money. There are good reasons for these demands, but still you feel as if you have to itemise everything and to declare what you have done with your pocket money at the end of the month.

Still it is good to have this choice of options. The good thing about options, as Gerhard Schröder once said, is that one has them. It might be most comfortable to decide case by case whether to look for a sponsor or whether to make an application for government funding – or even whether to make one's own business plan.

I believe that governmental chicanery does not benefit the state and that it is a result of ignorance. The people in the ministries still have in view the medium-sized business as the smallest economic unit. They do not see the individual human being who has to somehow get by. If this person decides to start a business, which is difficult enough, then it will be exposed to all kinds of chicanery that I could go on about forever. Usually clamour against bureaucratism is only a disguised big business demand for total freedom from governmental control, no more taxes and so on. But much red tape especially hits those people who have to do everything for themselves.

I am not anti-government, and I am very much in favour of the state getting engaged in many domains, taking things into its hands, not privatising everything and keeping public matters in focus. But to repeat the point, it seems to me that private initiative is often the victim of ignorance and of a misunderstanding of the needs and the impositions of self-employed life.

Philipp Albers: This situation might also have something to do with the fact that the group of self-employed people does not have a lobby that brings forward its demands, be it in tax law or in other bureaucratic questions. Could there be new forms of organisations that take on this task, does this new form of work require its lobby? I am very unsure with respect to these questions, and I do not know what the answers might be, but I am convinced that the growing number of a new generation of self-employed people will find new and effective ways to voice their concerns and their vision of self-determined life.

NOTE

1. See www.ashoka.org/social_entrepreneur, last accessed 10 July 2008.

REFERENCE

Friebe, H. and S. Lobo (2006), *Wir nennen es Arbeit* (*We Call it Work*), München: Heyne.

PART II

Preconditions

6. Schumpeter's full model of entrepreneurship: economic, non-economic and social entrepreneurship

Richard Swedberg

6.1 INTRODUCTION

The reality of social entrepreneurship is by now well established thanks to a wealth of books, articles and other testimonies. To understand what exactly constitutes social entrepreneurship, and how to explain it, however, represents still something of a challenge (for example, Martin and Osberg, 2007). Since social entrepreneurship is also increasingly being taught as a skill, a better understanding of this phenomenon is needed.

In an earlier paper I suggested that one can use Joseph Schumpeter's ideas to get a better theoretical handle on social entrepreneurship (Swedberg, 2006). I emphasised that the work of the young Schumpeter is especially useful in this context. The first and little known edition of *The Theory of Economic Development* from 1911 contains, for example, a much more dynamic version of Schumpeter's theory of entrepreneurship than his later work (Schumpeter, 1911). It is also only in his early work that Schumpeter says that one can apply his theory of entrepreneurship to non-economic activities. Social entrepreneurship, I suggested, can be seen as belonging to the category of non-economic entrepreneurship; and making this suggestion opens up the prospect of applying Schumpeter's theory of entrepreneurship to the phenomenon of social entrepreneurship. This is where my article 'Social entrepreneurship: the view of the young Schumpeter' ended.

This chapter picks up where the earlier paper left off, and contains an effort to work out in detail the idea that we may use Schumpeter's theory of entrepreneurship for a better understanding of social entrepreneurship. I have given it the title 'Schumpeter's full model of entrepreneurship: economic, non-economic and social entrepreneurship' because what I suggest is to apply Schumpeter's *full model* to social entrepreneurship.

By the expression 'full model' I mean that all the essential elements in Schumpeter's theory of entrepreneurship will be applied. Schumpeter's theory of entrepreneurship is often shrunk to what is only one of its elements – *innovation* (and sometimes to only one version of this, *technological innovation*). That one may proceed in this way, and nonetheless accomplish interesting things, can be exemplified by, say, the important work of William Baumol (2002). Still, this is not how I proceed in this chapter. I instead try to show that one can get considerably more out of Schumpeter by expanding one's scope to include *all* of the key elements in his theory.

One important task in looking at the full model of Schumpeter's entrepreneurship is to tie all of its elements together, and in this way see how they are linked to each other and operate together. Another and equally important task, I suggest, is to try to generalise as well as update Schumpeter's model. It is useful, I argue, to try to raise Schumpeter's model to a level of generality beyond some of its particularities (and peculiarities). More precisely, we want to be in a position where we begin to play around with the parts of the model, while being true to its overall original intuition.

We also need to update Schumpeter's model on a few points. It is, for example, often pointed out that Schumpeter failed to see that one can innovate by changing the form of the firm. Also on a few other points updates may be necessary – again, while being true to Schumpeter's original intuition of what constitutes the core of entrepreneurship.

Before getting starting, however, a few words need perhaps to be said about Schumpeter's general status as a theoretician of entrepreneurship and the context within which his ideas emerged. Joseph Schumpeter (1883–1950) was born, raised and educated in the Austro-Hungarian Empire, and he shared the conservative views of its ruling elite (for example, Swedberg, 1991). As an intellectual and economist he early developed a taste for bold and original ideas. He enjoyed playing around with ideas from all perspectives, including those of Marx and the Austro-Marxists.

Schumpeter is generally seen as the first major economist who developed a major theory of entrepreneurship. He did this primarily through the work I referred to earlier, from 1911. Schumpeter later produced a second edition (1926), which also appeared (with some slight changes) in English translation as *The Theory of Economic Development* (1934). Schumpeter was naturally not the first economist to write about entrepreneurship, something that he himself often had occasion to point out since he was also the first person to write the history of the study of entrepreneurship. He especially emphasised the contribution of various French economists to entrepreneurship, such as Richard Cantillon and Jean-Baptiste Say (see, for example Schumpeter, 1928 [2003]; 1954: 554–7, 893–8).

But even if many other economists (before and after Schumpeter) have tried to understand and theorise entrepreneurship, Schumpeter's analysis is very special. While Schumpeter approved of and wanted to work within what we today call neoclassical economics, he always argued that entrepreneurship means the breakup of an equilibrium. His theory of entrepreneurship, in all brevity, deviated from mainstream economics on crucial points. The early Schumpeter liked to highlight these differences, while the mature Schumpeter tended to underplay them.

6.2   STEP 1: SCHUMPETER'S FULL MODEL OF ENTREPRENEURSHIP

The task of reconstituting how Schumpeter himself viewed his full model of entrepreneurship is straightforward; and for this task one may rely exclusively on the second (and final) edition of *The Theory of Economic Development*. Once you start playing around with Schumpeter's model, in contrast, it is also helpful to draw on other writings, such as the first edition of *The Theory of Economic Development*, the article 'Entrepreneur' (1928), and so on.

First, then, we need to present and draw attention to Schumpeter's own definition of entrepreneurship. Entrepreneurship, we read in *The Theory of Economic Development*, can be defined as a new combination of already existing elements in the economy. '*Development [or entrepreneurship] is then defined by the carrying out of new combinations [of productive means or materials and forces]*' (Schumpeter, 1934, 65–6; emphasis added).[1]

Of the separate elements that make up Schumpeter's model, the first has to do with the motivation of the entrepreneur. What I am referring to is Schumpeter's well-known statement that the entrepreneur has a 'non-hedonistic character' and is driven by three main motives:

> First of all, there is the dream and the will to found a private kingdom, usually, though not necessarily, also a dynasty . . . Then there is the will to conquer: the impulse to fight, to prove oneself superior to others, to succeed for the sake, not of the fruits, but of success itself . . . Finally, there is the joy of creating, of getting things done, or simply of exercising one's energy and ingenuity. (Schumpeter, 1934: 93).

The central reason for Schumpeter's ideas about motivation is that we need somehow to get the entrepreneur going. The issue, at this stage, is not whether the individual somehow 'causes' entrepreneurship, by the power of his or her will, or if entrepreneurship is collective in nature. The individual, to repeat, simply has to get going in an entrepreneurial direction.

For Schumpeter, it may also be added, the entrepreneur is always assumed to be a male. I will, however, refer to the Schumpeterian entrepreneur in this chapter as he or she.

The second key element in Schumpeter's full model of entrepreneurship consists of *innovations* or, as he also calls them, 'new combinations' (Schumpeter, 1934: 66). From Schumpeter's definition of entrepreneurship, it is clear that this element constitutes its very heart. More precisely, it is the actual pushing through of an innovation that constitutes its core element (*'the carrying out of new combinations'*).

An innovation, as Schumpeter clarifies in a well-known argument, differs from an invention. While the latter can also be part of an innovation, it does not constitute an innovation by itself (Schumpeter, 1934: 88–9). The reason for this is that an invention constitutes a discovery, with or without a potential for economic exploitation, while an innovation represents a successful attempt at economic exploitation.

Schumpeter outlines what he regards as the five major types of innovations in a famous passage in *The Theory of Economic Development*:

1. 'the introduction a new good'
2. 'the introduction of a new method of production'
3. 'the introduction of a new market'
4. 'the conquest of a new source of raw materials or half-manufactured goods'
5. 'the carrying out of a new organisation of any industry' (Schumpeter, 1934: 66).

For similar enumerations, see also Schumpeter (1911: 159; 1928 [2003]: 250).

The third key element in Schumpeter's model can be summarised as *overcoming resistance* to innovations. Economists typically ignore this element, which is central to Schumpeter's theory of entrepreneurship. One reason they do so may well be that resistance is social and not economic in nature. In the current division of labour in the social sciences, it falls in sociology and not in economics.

What role should resistance to entrepreneurship play in Schumpeter's model? Or, to phrase it differently, can it be ignored, as the economists do? From Schumpeter's perspective it cannot be ignored, and there are mainly two reasons for this: a new combination is (1) hard to conceive and (2) hard to push through. In short, resistance is closely related to static behaviour. It anchors the existing way of doing things in economic life as effectively as 'a railway embankment [is rooted] in the earth' (Schumpeter, 1934: 84).

That the hostility in the social environment towards an entrepreneur may be extremely strong can be illustrated with an anecdote from Schumpeter's work. In his discussion of early European economic history, Schumpeter says that 'entrepreneurs were not necessarily strangled but they were not infrequently in danger of their lives' (Schumpeter, 1939: 243). To this statement a footnote is added, in which Schumpeter cites a document that tells about an entrepreneur who was strangled to death in 1579 in Danzig. Since the accuracy of the source is unsure, Schumpeter elegantly adds in Italian *se non è vero è ben trovato* (even if it is not true, it is well said).

Schumpeter explicitly uses the term 'resistance' in *The Theory of Economic Development*, and describes it with such terms as 'tradition', 'routine' and 'social habits and conventions' (Schumpeter, 1934: 84, 91–2). Resistance can be found in the entrepreneur's mind as well as in 'the social environment' (Schumpeter, 1934: 86). When linked to an interest, resistance is strengthened.

The fourth key component in Schumpeter's model is *profit* or, in his terminology, 'entrepreneurial profit' (Schumpeter, 1934: 128–56). For the full process of innovation to take place, it is not enough that some good be conceived and produced and so on – it also must be sold at a profit. Making a profit is decisive for the entrepreneur, and it marks off a successful and 'correct' combination from a failed combination. In a capitalist economy an innovation that does not make a profit is not an innovation.

The demand to make a profit as well as the need to overcome resistance represent two aspects of Schumpeter's theory that are often passed over in silence in discussions of his theory of entrepreneurship. This is sometimes also the case with the fifth and final element of his model, namely, its link to the business cycle.

That this link was critical to Schumpeter is clear from the fact that he devotes a full chapter to it in *The Theory of Economic Development*, and two full volumes in *Business Cycles* (Schumpeter, 1934, 212–55; 1939). While it is true that Schumpeter's focus is squarely on the individual, there is also a collective and aggregate part to his theory of entrepreneurship.

Individual acts of entrepreneurship set off wavelike macro changes in the economy, according to Schumpeter. 'The swarm-like appearance of entrepreneurs ... constitutes the only cause of periods of boom [in the business cycle]' (Schumpeter, 1934: 214). Exactly what happens when these swarms of entrepreneurs appear is worked out in great historical detail in *Business Cycles*. Schumpeter argues that three types of cycles are being played out at the same time: one that is short, one that is of medium length and one that is very long. Schumpeter calls the first type of cycles Kitchin cycles (about 40 months); the second, Juglar cycles (about 9–10 years); and the last, Kondratieff cycles (about 40–50 years).

So far the capitalist system has gone through three Kondratieff cycles: that of the Industrial Revolution and what Schumpeter calls the bourgeois

Table 6.1   The three Kondratieff cycles of the capitalist system

The Kondratieff cycle of the Industrial Revolution	
Prosperity	1787–1800
Recession	1801–13
Depression	1814–27
Revival	1828–42
The bourgeois Kondratieff cycle	
Prosperity	1843–57
Recession	1858–69
Depression	1870–84/85
Revival	1886–97
The neo-mercantilist Kondratieff cycle	
Prosperity	1898–1911
Recession	1912–24/25
Depression	1926–38

Kondratieff and the neo-mercantilist Kondratieff (Schumpeter, 1940 [2000]). Their respective phases are shown in Table 6.1.

We may then summarise Schumpeter's full model of entrepreneurship as follows (see Box 6.1). Driven by non-hedonistic motives, the entrepreneur overcomes resistance within himself or herself as well as in the social environment, and succeeds in pushing through, at a profit, an innovation or a new combination of already existing elements. When several entrepreneurs do this, a business cycle is formed which works itself out in a characteristic pattern.[2]

BOX 6.1   SCHUMPETER'S FULL MODEL OF ENTREPRENEURSHIP

The Main Thesis

Entrepreneurship is defined as the successful introduction of a new combination of already existing elements in the economy. '*Development [or entrepreneurship] is then defined by the carrying out of new combinations [of productive means or materials and forces]*' (65–6).

The Five Key Elements

1. Motivation
The entrepreneur has a '*non-hedonistic character*'; and his main

motives are of the following three types: '*the dream to found a private kingdom*', '*the will to conquer*' and '*the joy of creating*' (93–4).

2. Innovation
Innovations are defined as '*new combinations*' (p. 66). There are five major types: (1) '*the introduction of a new good*', (2) '*the introduction of a new method of production*', (3) '*the introduction of a new market*', (4) '*the conquest of a new source of raw materials or half-manufactured goods*' and (5) '*the carrying out of a new organisation of any industry*' (p. 66). An invention is not an innovation, but can be an element in an innovation (88–9).

3. Overcoming resistance
In carrying out innovations entrepreneurs have to overcome '*resistance*' – in themselves as well as in '*the social environment*' (p. 86). Resistance takes many forms, including '*tradition*', '*routine*' and '*social habits or conventions*' (84, 91–2). Some resistance is also anchored in interests (86).

4. Profit
'*Entrepreneurial profit*' is a requirement for the fulfilment of entrepreneurship (ch. 4).

5. Link to the business cycle
Innovations set off wave-like macro changes in the economy. 'The swarm-like appearance of entrepreneurs . . . constitutes the only cause of periods of boom [in the business cycle]' (214).

Comment: In his main work on entrepreneurship, *The Theory of Economic Development* (1934), Schumpeter presents a multi-dimensional model of entrepreneurship in a capitalist economy. While Schumpeter's theory of entrepreneurship is usually equated with innovations (and sometimes exclusively with technological innovations), it also contains other crucial elements: the idea of the need to overcome resistance, to make a profit, to consider the macro-effect of innovations on the economy and that the entrepreneur is driven by special motives.

Source: Joseph Schumpeter (1934), *The Theory of Economic Development*, Cambridge, MA: Harvard University Press, pp. 65, 66, 86–9, 92–3, 128–56, 33, 212–55; emphasis added.

6.3   STEP 2: SCHUMPETER'S FULL MODEL OF ENTREPRENEURSHIP, GENERAL AND UPDATED VERSION

The main purpose of this section is to show that it is possible to develop a more general version of Schumpeter's full model of entrepreneurship, and that such a general model also allows for some updating Schumpeter's ideas (Figure 6.1). Schumpeter's model is finally also flexible enough to allow for some intellectual playing around with. What follows is one way of doing so. I invite others to do the same – and hopefully with a different result.

The core of Schumpeter's full model remains the same, whether generalised or not: *the pushing through and successful introduction of a new combination of already existing elements in the economy*. The concept of *combination* represents, as I will try to show the most suggestive and precious element in Schumpeter's theory.

While Schumpeter speaks of entrepreneurship being 'defined by the carrying out of new combinations', I have chosen a slightly different formulation, 'the pushing through and successful introduction of a new combination'. This is to draw attention to the fact that the entrepreneur makes a strong push and has to keep an eye on the entrepreneurial process from start to finish.

What would a general version of the first element – the motivation of the entrepreneur – be like? First, Schumpeter's three key motives ('the dream to found a private kingdom', 'the will to conquer' and 'the joy of creating') look a bit outmoded and arbitrary today. Add to this the failure of psychologists to isolate some entrepreneurial feature or personality, and we may simply want to say that what characterises the motivation of the entrepreneur is (a) its complexity and (b) that it is not exclusively economic in nature. This way of looking at things also allows us to make sense of Schumpeter's observation that the entrepreneur in a socialist economy may be motivated by status (Schumpeter, 1942 [1977]: 208).

Another way to update Schumpeter is to argue that the entrepreneur does not have to be a single entrepreneur, and especially not a heroic one of the type that Schumpeter talks so much about, particularly in the first edition of *The Theory of Economic Development*. What is at the heart of Schumpeter's theory of entrepreneurship, however, is *not* the individual entrepreneur but that innovations are carried out. Schumpeter also uses the impersonal expression 'the entrepreneurial function' for innovations being carried out ('the entrepreneurial function [is] the carrying out of new combinations' – Schumpeter, 1934: 137).

Now, the entrepreneurial function can in principle be carried out by a single person or by a group or a team of people. This is something that

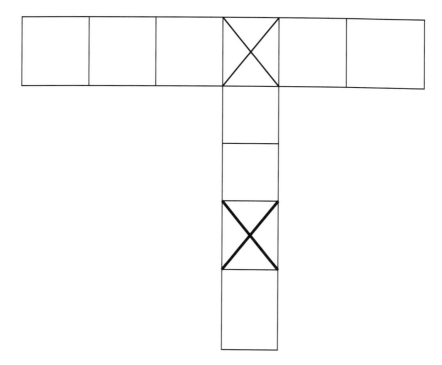

Comments: Schumpeter's statements about innovations as combinations are ambiguous; and one may argue that they point to two different ways of understanding what constitutes an innovation. The consequences of this way of looking at Schumpeter's view of innovations are far reaching for his theory of entrepreneurship.

If there is a change in *one element* in the chain of production (as indicated by the '**X**' in bold style), this element can *in itself* be said to constitute a new combination or an innovation. This is illustrated by the vertical line above; and one example would be 'a new good'.

But Schumpeter also indicates that he regards *the whole production* of some item as a combination. And when one of its elements changes (as indicated by the 'X' in non-bold style), there is consequently also an innovation. This is illustrated by the horizontal line above. One example would be *the full production* of a new good.

Figure 6.1   Schumpeter's two types of innovations[3]

Schumpeter explicitly states in one of his later essays: 'The entrepreneurial function need not be embodied in a physical person and in particular in a single physical person. Every social environment has its own way of filling the entrepreneurial function' (Schumpeter, 1949 [1951]: 255). This means that a collection or a team of persons can be 'the entrepreneur'. 'The entre-preneurial function may be and often is filled co-operatively' (Schumpeter, 1949 [1951]: 256). Even the capitalist state can be an entrepreneur, he states, using the US Department of Agriculture as an example (Schumpeter, 1949 [1951]: 255).

The second element in Schumpeter's model of entrepreneurship is, to repeat, at the very core of his theory of entrepreneurship: *innovation*. First, what is an innovation? Most interpreters of Schumpeter agree that it is something like a new good or some new technology. This goes well with Schumpeter's enumeration of the five basic types of innovations, which includes, as we know, 'a new good', 'a new method of production', and so on.[3]

Schumpeter also defines an innovation as 'a new combination', and this makes sense as well. A new good or a new piece of technology typically consists of a new combination of already existing elements. The entrepreneur, as Schumpeter puts it, 'recombines' (Schumpeter, 1934: 134).

This represents the standard interpretation of innovation, as this concept is to be found in Schumpeter's work, and Schumpeter himself used it many times in this sense. In *Business Cycles*, for example, we find at one point a list of actual 'innovations' from Prussia during the period 1787–1842 that reads as follows: 'Senfelder's lithography in 1785 and 1806; the first beet-sugar factory in 1796; Koenig and Bauer's printing press in 1814; Krupp's cast steel in 1815; first steamboat on the Weser in 1816' (Schumpeter, 1939: 282).

But there also exists *a second, less known meaning of innovation*, as used by Schumpeter. This is that an innovation is something broader than just a new good or a new technology. In *The Theory of Economic Development* Schumpeter talks, for example, of the economic process as a 'combination', and this means that a new combination would be a new way of organising the economic process. He points out, among other things, that the economic process can be organised according to either economic or technological criteria. In the latter case ('a technological combination'), something is produced according to what is technologically the most efficient; and in the former case ('an economic combination'), it is economic logic that is decisive (Schumpeter, 1934: 14–15).

Another indication that Schumpeter at times had something broader in mind when he used the term innovation can be read from his definition of an innovation. It is not just 'a new combination', but 'the carrying out of a new combination'; it is not just 'a new good' but 'the production and carrying out [of a new good]', as he once clarified (Schumpeter, 1934: 65–6; 1928 [2003]: 250). An innovation, in brief, is not just a new good because this new good also has to be produced and marketed. Schumpeter usually emphasises that it is not so much the novelty that is at the heart of the innovation as the pushing through of the whole thing.

Finally, while we can easily conceive of a new good or a new technology as consisting of a new combination of already existing elements, what do we do with, say, the type of innovation that consists of 'a new source of raw material'? This type of innovation does not seem to be made up of some recombination of some already existing elements – but we can easily see how a new source of raw material can be combined with other material, and in this way form part of a new combination.

What all of this indicates is that Schumpeter's concept of innovation contains two very different views of what constitutes an innovation. In one, the innovation itself is a part of the economic process (say a new good or a new method of production); in the other, the innovation is again a novelty but also the larger process of pushing something new through, from beginning to end. The former represents the conventional meaning of innovation, the latter a more intriguing one that Schumpeter often seems to have intuited but never spelled out in clear and unambiguous terms. Nonetheless, it is present in his work and sometimes comes to the fore in surprising ways.

Take, for example, his famous list of the five major types of innovations. These are, to recall: (1) a new good, (2) a new method of production, (3) a new market, (4) a new source of raw material, and (5) a new organisation. If we put these side by side and, so to speak, add them up, something interesting happens. They turn out to cover *the whole spectrum of production*, and represent therefore a full unit of production. The entrepreneur first conceives of the good, puts together an organisation for its production, gets the material that is needed for production, produces the good, and markets it – and *voilà*, a new combination!

One can also proceed in the opposite way. The process of production can be decomposed into five elements – which can then be *recombined*. If the elements remain the same, the end product will also remain the same; but each of the five elements can also be changed in some way, and this means that a new combination will occur. Translated into a visual figure, we can illustrate this argument as in Figure 6.2.

In making this argument I have not only reproduced and interpreted what Schumpeter says, but also updated his theory on one point, namely, his use of 'organisation' (item 5). Schumpeter himself referred to the organisation of an industry (type trust), while I refer more broadly to the organisation of a firm. This represents an obvious update, but what may be less known is that Schumpeter himself suggested this change, even if he was less emphatic in doing so than one may have wished (see especially Schumpeter, 1928 [2003]; 1954, 893–8). It also deserves to be pointed out that only a change in the organisation of the firm that immediately results in a high profit counts as an innovation for Schumpeter, not a change in the organisational form per se.[4]

Another area where Schumpeter's theory of entrepreneurship needs to be updated has to do with his analysis of finance. For one thing, the

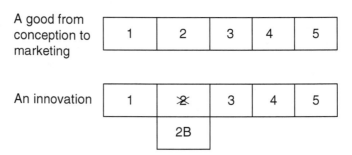

Figure 6.2   A normal good versus an innovation

assumption that the entrepreneur never finances his or her own enterprise does not fit empirical reality (Schumpeter, 1934: 137). Second, the idea that the entrepreneur who borrows money always finances his or her enterprise through a loan from a bank seems old-fashioned today. The modern entrepreneur may not only get loans from a bank but also from business angels, angel-investor groups, venture capital firms, boutique investment bankers and more.

To update Schumpeter when it comes to organisation is simple enough since this element is already part of his original combination of five elements. All we need to do is to change the element that Schumpeter calls 'the organisation of an industry' to something like 'the organisation of the individual enterprise or firm'. The situation is different with finance, since this is not part of Schumpeter's original combination of five elements. The reason for this is presumably that Schumpeter (like some modern theoreticians of entrepreneurship) felt that a person does not need to own capital to be an entrepreneur; instead an entrepreneur is someone who is able to procure access to capital. However that may be, one may still want to add finance as a new and sixth element in the process of production on the ground that there will be no economic process in the first place without capital. It is also clear that the way an enterprise is financed can take the form of an innovation.[5]

This leaves us with six elements in Schumpeter's combinatorial innovation, but one may also ask if other elements are not missing as well. This represents another question that deserves a good discussion among scholars interested in Schumpeter's theory of entrepreneurship. My own sense is that one may possibly want to add at least one more element that can turn into an innovation: *the legal form of the enterprise.*[6]

The reason for making this argument is that the economic process always takes a legal expression; and this expression has to take a certain form, as surely as the economic process has to take a certain technological form. The firm has to have a certain legal form, and so do transactions such as buying and selling as well as other elements that are integral parts of the economic and entrepreneurial process. A legal innovation would consist of some legal act that would result in high profit.[7]

My suggestion then is that we may want to conceive the Schumpeterian combination as consisting of seven elements, with law and finance added to the original five. The number of possible combinations now increases dramatically, which leaves us to discuss questions such as the number of combinations, and why and how the entrepreneur settles on one of these.

With the help of some type of combinatorial mathematics (that takes the order of the elements into account), one should be able to answer the first of these questions. As to the latter – why the entrepreneur picks one particular combination – Schumpeter argued that the entrepreneur neither has the time nor the energy to go through all of the combinations in order to find the right one. Instead the entrepreneur uses his or her intuition:

> Here [in the entrepreneurial process] the success of everything depends upon intuition, the capacity of seeing things in a way which afterwards proves to be true, even though it cannot be established at the moment, and of grasping the essential fact, discarding the unessential, even though one can give no account of the principles by which this is done. (Schumpeter, 1934: 85)

An alternative formulation of Schumpeter's argument would be that when the entrepreneur picks a certain combination, he or she draws on *abduction*, in the sense that philosopher Charles Peirce uses this term (Peirce, 1957).[8]

Also item number 3 in Schumpeter's model – resistance – needs some reworking and updating. While acknowledging Schumpeter's brilliance for realising the importance of resistance in the entrepreneurial process, one should also be aware of the fact that he theorised this element very little. While he provided the reader with a typology of the entrepreneur's motives (3) and the types of innovations (5), we have only scattered and casual references to '*tradition*', '*routine*', '*social habits or conventions*' and the like (Schumpeter, 1934: 84, 91–2; emphasis added). Schumpeter does not, in other words, explain what constitutes, say, a habit, what distinguishes it from a tradition, and so on.

This is where sociologists should come into the picture. Drawing on the works of Max Weber, Emil Durkheim and onwards, sociologists may want to properly theorise and distinguish between norms, customs, habits, tradition and order. Standard definitions of these can be found, for example, in Weber's work, including the less known term 'order' (see Weber, 1978: 29–38). The latter term was introduced by Weber, and in all brevity it means ways of behaving that are viewed as exemplary or obligatory, and to which actors orient themselves.

Some of the insights that sociologists may provide can also be provisionally complemented by recent brain research. I say provisionally because research of this type is still in its infancy. Nonetheless, some interesting ideas have been generated by looking at neural activity patterns and how these are related to habits. One such idea is that once a habit has been forgotten, it takes very little to reawaken it (for example, Delude, 2005). Translated into our concern with entrepreneurship and resistance, we can perhaps draw the following conclusion. Once a habit has been learned, and a similar – but not identical – situation appears, it will tend to be interpreted in terms of the original habit. Or to give a concrete example: when someone has an idea of what, say, a new good might be like, the idea may be reinterpreted in terms of the old conception and locked into the old pattern.

But even if Schumpeter did not give the topic of resistance the attention it deserves, he gave some interesting hints for how to proceed. One of these is to be found in his comments on what constitutes resistance in 'the social environment' (Schumpeter, 1934: 86). Schumpeter mentions the following examples of this type of resistance: resistance among 'customers', among people whose 'necessary cooperation' is needed, and among 'groups threatened by the innovation'. In the last example, what is meant is resistance in the form of norms, customs and so on, *strengthened by an interest*.

Another interesting hint that can be found in Schumpeter's work is his insistence on certain people being particularly vigilant in enforcing existing norms. These are people who in all brevity view it as being their personal task to stop others from breaking norms. Sociologists have a nice term for this type of people: '*restricters*' (for example, White, 1955: 22–3, 39–53). This term, incidentally, was invented by an industrial sociologist to cover behaviour in the economy, so it fits naturally in a discussion of entrepreneurship.

A third suggestive hint in Schumpeter can be found in his reference in *The Theory of Economic Development* not only to custom in general, but to 'economic custom' (Schumpeter, 1934: 61). The implicit idea here is that we should not only look at resistance of norms, customs and so on *in general*, but also at resistance in the form of economic norms, economic customs and so on. Richard Nelson and Sidney Winter (1982), for example, use the term 'routines' for social actions in the firm; while I and my collaborator Thorbjørn Knudsen suggest that economic innovations are successful to the extent that they break up and replace an *economic order* (Knudsen and Swedberg 2007).

As to element number 4 – profit – it should first be repeated that in a capitalist economy profit is part of the cumulative process and that no innovation is complete before it has resulted in profit. Schumpeter himself seems to have been well aware of this. He states, for example, at one point of his discussion, that if the best combination from a technological perspective was selected, it would look very different from the best combination from an economic perspective. An 'economic combination', as he puts it, lets 'economic logic' prevail, while this is not the case when it comes to a 'technological combination' (Schumpeter, 1934: 14). He also notes that entrepreneurship in early and non-capitalist economies differed from entrepreneurship in a capitalist economy (for example, Schumpeter, 1934: 67; 1939: 88; 1942 [1977]: 178, 188).

In terms of updating Schumpeter, one may also raise the question if one should not replace 'entrepreneurial profit' with profit in general. While this would liberate the analysis from Schumpeter's special theoretical construct of 'entrepreneurial profit', it also leads to new problems to address. Exactly how much profit is involved? A common-sense answer would be a sizeable profit, defined as higher than what ordinary ('static') business would bring in.

It is also well understood these days that what constitutes 'profit' is closely dependent on accounting rules; and that it is very difficult to supply some generally accepted definition of profit (for example, Heatherley et al., forthcoming). While it may be stretching things to argue that a novel and creative use of some accounting rule should be regarded as an innovation, this type of question does draw attention to the role that laws and regulations play in the entrepreneurial process.

This brings us to the last key element in Schumpeter's model, the link to the business cycle. My own view is that people have often chosen to ignore this issue because they have found Schumpeter's argument about an overall business cycle consisting of three distinct cycles quite unconvincing. While one may agree that investor overconfidence is often followed by investor panic, Schumpeter's version of business cycle theory is easy to criticise.

What then to do? There exist two other strands of thoughts in Schumpeter's work that relate to this problematic, and both of them are worth bringing up at this point. They also allow us to recast the link between individual entrepreneurship and macro-level tendencies. One is what Schumpeter occasionally refers to as 'capitalist evolution' (and more generally as 'Economic Evolution'); and the basic argument is that entrepreneurship helps shape the general evolution of the capitalist economy (Schumpeter, 1939: 84, 304; 1942 [1977]: 82). At a theoretical level Schumpeter conceived of this evolution as the result of two forces that are in complex interaction with one another, namely, static and innovative economic behaviour. This intuition is also present in Schumpeter's theory of the business cycle, but tends to get lost in the argument about the three cycles. It might nonetheless be worth reworking in some other fashion.

Another concept that comes to mind as a remedy to an exclusive concern with business cycles is 'creative destruction'. This famous expression was introduced in the 1940s in *Capitalism, Socialism and Democracy*, but the idea itself (if not the term) is already present in his first work on entrepreneurship from the early 1910s (Schumpeter, 1911 [2003]: 84–5; 1942 [1977]: 81–6).

What makes creative destruction interesting is, to my mind, especially the following. First, this concept draws attention to the fact that every successful innovation also has another side, namely, the destruction of some other business. Note that this differs from the idea of the business cycle, where destructive effects are not coupled to successful innovations but to investors overshooting, once the first generation of imitators have done their business.

The second quality that makes creative destruction interesting is that it is not exclusively about money and profit but also about social structure. In discussing creative destruction, Schumpeter's focus is on *structures*, and we may therefore want to study these and lay them bare (Schumpeter, 1942 [1977]: 83). Mass unemployment in a small town, for example, may lead to the destruction of families, habits of health, and worse. Here, as with Schumpeter's full model of entrepreneurship more generally, we may therefore want to go beyond his model and update it in various ways (see Box 6.2).

BOX 6.2   SCHUMPETER'S FULL MODEL OF ENTREPRENEURSHIP, GENERAL AND UPDATED VERSION

The Main Thesis

Entrepreneurship is defined as the pushing through or the successful introduction of a new combination of already existing elements in the economy.

The Five Key Elements

1. Motivation
Entrepreneurs have complex motivations.

2. Innovation
Any part of the economic process can be changed through innovation. To the five ones mentioned in *The Theory of Economic*

Development, two may be added (organisation and law). This makes the number seven: (1) the conception of the good or the service; (2) financing the venture; (3) its legal forms; (4) its organisation; (5) resources needed for production; (6) method of production; and (7) marketing of the item. One may visualise the seven elements that make up the whole process or combination as follows:

3. Resistance

Resistance to innovations has to be overcome. It takes many forms, including habits, customs, tradition, norms, routines and orders, and these may also be anchored in economic interests. Some of the obstacles are specific to the economy.

4. Profit

Profit is a requirement for the fulfilment of entrepreneurship.

5. Link to the business cycle

Innovations cause creative destruction; they also contribute to macro changes and the evolution of the capitalist economy.

Comment: In his work on entrepreneurship, Schumpeter presents a model of entrepreneurship in a capitalist economy and describes its key elements. In certain respects this model is outmoded today; it also needs to be complemented on a few points. Resistance, for example, needs to be analysed with the help of sociology. Nonetheless, at a general level, Schumpeter's model provides a solid foundation on which to build today. The material in this box summarises the general, updated version of Schumpeter's full model.

Source: Joseph Schumpeter (1911 [2002]), 'New translation: *Theorie der wirtschaftlichen Entwicklung*', *American Journal of Economic and Sociology*, **61** (2), 405–37; (1934), *The Theory of Economic Development*, Cambridge, MA: Harvard University Press; (1928 [2003]), 'Entrepreneur', *Austrian Economic and Entrepreneurial Studies*, **6**, 235–65; (1939), *Business Cycles*, New York: McGraw-Hill; (1942 [1977]), *Capitalism, Socialism and Democracy*, New York: Harper & Row.

6.4   STEP 3: SCHUMPETER'S FULL MODEL OF NON-ECONOMIC ENTREPRENEURSHIP

In the first edition of *The Theory of Economic Development* (1911) Schumpeter devotes about ten pages to the topic of entrepreneurship in non-economic areas of society (Schumpeter, 1911 [2003]: 105–13). Non-economic entrepreneurship, he specifies, is 'closely analogous' to economic entrepreneurship, and it is to be found in areas such as 'politics, art, science, social life, moral considerations, etc' (Schumpeter, 1911 [2003]: 105, 110). While there are indications that Schumpeter continued to believe in the application of his theory of entrepreneurship to non-economic topics also after the 1910s, he would never again discuss this topic at any length (for example, Schumpeter, 1928 [2003]: 247–8; 1934: xi, 58–9, 82).

While one may differentiate between what Schumpeter literally says about non-economic entrepreneurship, on the one hand, and a more general version of his theory of non-economic entrepreneurship, on the other, I do not do so in this chapter. The reason for this is practical: Schumpeter wrote so little on this topic that it seems artificial to devote separate sections to each of these topics.

Schumpeter does not define non-economic entrepreneurship but we may extrapolate from his theory of economic entrepreneurship. This gives the following definition: non-economic entrepreneurship can be defined as the pushing through or successful introduction of a new combination of already existing material and forces in all areas of social life, except for the economy.

As to the motivation for non-economic entrepreneurship, Schumpeter states in *The Theory of Economic Development* that of his three motivations, only one is directly related to the requirement of private property, that is, to the economy (Schumpeter, 1934: 94). From this statement we can perhaps draw the conclusion that the remaining two – 'the will to conquer' and 'the joy of creating' – are relevant also for non-economic entrepreneurs (and for economic entrepreneurs in non-capitalist economies). To this may be added that if the motivation for the capitalist entrepreneurs is complex, the motivation for political entrepreneurs, scientific entrepreneurs, artistic entrepreneurs and so on is probably even more complex.

Schumpeter speaks of the themes in the non-economic areas of social life ('politics, art, science, social life, moral considerations, etc') as each occupying an 'area' or 'field'. The actors in each field are either leaders or followers. Followers are the passive products of the forces that determine the field, while leaders determine some space of their own through their independent actions – what Schumpeter calls the space of 'relative autonomy' (for example, Schumpeter, 1911 [2003]: 107). The actors in each respective field are usually named after the field; the actors in the field of art are artists, in politics, politicians, and so on. The same person can be active in several fields, but typically follows the rules in the field he or she is in at the moment. A businessman who is also a painter in his spare time, will for example not paint according to his economic convictions but adapt to the way of behaving in the field of art ('no picture is painted according to the law of marginal utility' – Schumpeter, 1911 [2003]: 106).

Schumpeter does not define what he means by a non-economic innovation. Following the general logic of his model of economic entrepreneurship, however, a non-economic innovation may be viewed as a new combination of the elements that make up the process of production in each field. This means that innovations can be conceptualised as going through the seven phases of production in Schumpeter's general model: (1) the conception of the item (in art, science etc.); (2) financing the venture; (3) its legal forms; (4) its organisation; (5) acquiring resources for its production; (6) method of production; and (7) marketing of the item.

Since Schumpeter wrote so little on non-economic innovations, I provide two brief examples, and in this way try to illuminate the logic of what I see as Schumpeter's argument. First, it should be stressed that it is once more innovations and not inventions that count. A scientific discovery, a brilliant painting or a brand new political institution would, in other words, not qualify as innovations.

What then constitutes a non-economic innovation? This is not so clear, but one possibility would be to stick to the idea that we are looking for a 'close analogy' to the production of a good that gets sold at a profit on the market because it incorporates a novelty. Let me therefore turn to my two examples: the Bolshevik party of Lenin (a political innovation) and the New York City Ballet of George Balanchine and Lincoln Kerstin (an artistic innovation).

The secret party of professional revolutionaries existed long before Lenin, but he picked up the idea, perfected it, and used it with such success in the Russian Revolution that it was soon imitated in many countries. Kerstin and Balanchine founded the New York Ballet in 1935, drawing on Kerstin's organisational talents and Balanchine's skills as a dancer and choreographer. The result was a ballet company that has deeply shaped US ballet culture through its systematic training of dancers and production of new ballets.

Resistance to non-economic innovations is, again, best handled by a sociological type of analysis – of habits, customs, norms and so on. We would also expect there to be special versions of these habits and so on in each specific area or field – artistic habits and so on in the area of art; scientific customs and so on in the area of science; and so on. Interest will strengthen the resistance; and in this case interest would be what Weber terms 'ideal interests' (as opposed to 'material interests' – Weber, 1946: 280).

To be successful, non-economic innovations have to be profitable, analogously to economic innovations. Exactly how to define profit in this context can be debated. Following the idea in Bourdieu that we may speak of different types of capital, one could conceivably also speak of different types of profit (political profit, scientific profit, artistic profit; for example, Bourdieu, 1986). Schumpeter himself seems to have taken a somewhat different route and instead focused on the successful and widespread institutional anchorage of some new practice, as indicated by his one and only concrete reference in this context to 'new developments, new "schools", new parties' (Schumpeter, 1911 [2003]: 110–11).[9]

One can construct a link to macro-level change also in the case of non-economic entrepreneurship. Schumpeter mentions, for example, that 'the art of a time' may change as a result of new combinations, and this change is presumably to be understood as the result of a process set in motion by swarms of artistic entrepreneurs (Schumpeter, 1911 [2003]: 112). Schumpeter also says that all non-economic areas or fields of society make up '*the social culture* of a nation' (ibid.; emphasis added), and presumably this culture would change or evolve under the impact of non-economic innovations.

The idea of creative destruction in the areas of politics, science, art and so on is intriguing and worth pursuing. Schumpeter makes us predict that successful innovations will not only lead to new developments, new 'schools' and new parties, but also to the destruction of existing ones. Again, in brief, there is good reason why we may want to follow Schumpeter's suggestion that one can see entrepreneurship in non-economic areas in analogy to what happens in the area of the economy (see Box 6.3).

BOX 6.3   SCHUMPETER'S FULL MODEL OF NON-ECONOMIC ENTREPRENEURSHIP

The Main Thesis

Non-economic entrepreneurship is 'closely analogous' to economic entrepreneurship (1911: 110). It can be defined as the pushing through or successful introduction of a new combination of already existing material and forces in '*all areas of social life*', except for the economy (1911: 105).

The Five Key Elements

1. Motivation
Non-economic entrepreneurs are driven by '*the will to conquer*' and '*the joy of creating*'; their motivation is complex (1934: 94).

2. Innovation
Innovations consist of new combinations in '*areas*' or '*fields*' such as '*politics, art, science, social life, moral considerations*' (1911: 105, 108, 110). Any part of the process or combination can be changed through innovation: (1) the conception of the item (in art, science etc.); (2) financing the venture; (3) its legal forms; (4) its organisation; (5) acquiring resources for its production; (6) method of production; and (7) marketing of the item. One way to visualise the seven elements that make up the whole process/combination is as follows:

1	2	3	4	5	6	7

⟶

3. Resistance
Obstacles include habits, customs, tradition, norms, routines, orders that may or may not be anchored in interests linked to some special field or area. Some of the obstacles to non-economic entrepreneurship differ from the obstacles to economic innovations.

4. Profit
Non-economic combinations lead to the creation of '*new developments, new "schools", new parties*' (1911: 110–11).

5. Link to macro-level change
A swarm of artistic entrepreneurs may, for example, affect a change in 'the art of a time' (1911: 110). Non-economic innovations cause creative destruction in the areas of politics, art, science and so on, and in this way affect '*the social culture* of a nation' (1911: 110–11).

Comment: Schumpeter wrote very little on non-economic entrepreneurship. Whatever we know comes basically from a brief discussion in the last chapter of the first edition of *The Theory of Economic Development* (1911). Non-economic entrepreneurship, Schumpeter states, is '*closely analogous*' to economic entrepreneurship (1911: 110).

Source: The references to 'Schumpeter (1911)' are to the translation of chapter 7 in *Theorie der wirtschaftlichen Entwicklung:* Joseph Schumpeter (1911 [2003]), 'The theory of economic development', in J. Backhaus (ed.), *Joseph Alois Schumpeter*, Boston, MA: Kluwer. See also Schumpeter (1928 [2003]), 'Entrepreneur', *Austrian Economics and Entrepreneurial Studies*, **6**, 247–8; (1934), *The Theory of Economic Development*, Cambridge, MA: Harvard University Press, pp. 93–4, 110; emphasis added.

6.5 FINAL STEP 4: SCHUMPETER'S FULL MODEL APPLIED TO SOCIAL ENTREPRENEURSHIP

It was noted at the outset of this chapter that while a huge literature on social entrepreneurship has started to emerge, there is no generally accepted theory that explains how it works. The term itself seems to have emerged spontaneously a few decades ago, even if one can find assertions in the literature to the effect that it was invented by so and so in some specific year. There is no consensus about the meaning of the term, although several sources argue that social entrepreneurship roughly refers to individuals who are driven by a sense of social mission to work for social change (for example, Bornstein, 2004; Dees, 2001; Martin and Osberg, 2007).

It is often noted that the social change has to be of a certain kind and that it does not, for example, include conservative or right-wing social change. To be more precise than this is hard, both since it raises difficult philosophical questions about what we mean by progressive values and since the literature is vague on this point. It would also seem that the novelty with social entrepreneurship has more to do with some individual accomplishing social change than with the values involved. The latter are usually of a standard type, such as reduction of poverty, improvement of the educational system and the like.

Schumpeter himself never touched on something that can be construed as social entrepreneurship. For one thing, he died many years before the idea as well as the term itself came into existence. He was also a conservative throughout his life; and his own ideal was 'intact capitalism' or what we today would call laissez-faire or neo-liberal capitalism (Schumpeter, 1946 [1951]: 187–90). Had he lived today, he would probably have disapproved of social entrepreneurship.

This does not mean that Schumpeter's model of entrepreneurship cannot be extended to the topic of social entrepreneurship. But does it make sense to do so? Here, the proof of the pudding is in the eating; and in this case the eating consists of successfully assisting with the following two tasks: conceptualising social entrepreneurship and explaining how it operates.

At one point in *The Theory of Economic Development*, Schumpeter summarises his theory of entrepreneurship as a *'mechanism of [economic] change'*, and this opens up the door to conceptualise social entrepreneurship as a *'mechanism of social change'* (Schumpeter, 1934: 61; emphasis added). Other ideas in Schumpeter's work allow us to give a more precise definition: social entrepreneurship is the pushing through or the successful introduction of social change, through a new combination of elements that make up some way of doing things. Certain values are implied in the notion of 'social change', such as everybody's right to economic progress, proper health care and the like.

As to motivation, our earlier discussion of non-economic entrepreneurship suggests that this type of entrepreneurs has complex motivations, and this would also seem to fit social entrepreneurs. There is, however, especially one motive or, better, one motivational force that would seem to characterise the social entrepreneur. This is a sense of *social mission*.

Schumpeter's fascination with the lone entrepreneur single-handedly accomplishing great things is usually severely criticised. Social entrepreneurs, however, would seem to be precisely this type of person. They tend to operate outside the existing power structure and on their own, rather than join traditional collective enterprises such as trade unions and co-operatives. What makes the social entrepreneur so attractive to many people is also that they show what a single individual can accomplish – if he or she has the right kind of idea and the will-power to push it through.

Still, even if the individual is central to social entrepreneurship it deserves to be emphasised that he or she – just as the economic entrepreneur – typically works with other individuals; and that the social dimension is strongly present in most everything that is done (for example, Light, 2006). Similarly, it is clear that social entrepreneurs typically do not invent some new type of behaviour. Instead they turn it into their mission to push some new type of behaviour through, and this means that the common way of acting in a population has to change. Again, we may view this process from idea to realisation as consisting of a number of elements, one of which needs to be changed in some novel way for the project to be successful.

According to Schumpeter's model, social entrepreneurship goes through seven steps: (1) the conception of some way of doing things; (2) financing the venture; (3) its legal forms; (4) its organisation; (5) acquiring resources for its production; (6) method of production; and (7) to turn it into the accepted way of doing things.

The social entrepreneur picks up a good idea and mobilises resources to promote it, typically through some organisation. He or she then attempts to make people change their behaviour, and the more this is done, the easier it becomes to turn the new behaviour into a solid form, such as an institution, behaviour that is endorsed by the state and the like.

While economic entrepreneurship is centred around a good that needs to be produced and sold, social entrepreneurship has to do with ways of doing things. The current way of doing things typically needs to be changed in such a way that it becomes easier to realise certain values, and this can only happen through sustained social change.

That resistance to change in social behaviour is typically a form of social behaviour itself that indicates that sociologists have an important role to play in analysing this particular type of entrepreneurship. In this, social entrepreneurship is similar to non-economic entrepreneurship. The product as well as the resistance to social entrepreneurship are primarily non-economic and social in nature. Economic factors nonetheless enter into the process at different stages, including the stage of resistance, for example, in the form of economic interests that are linked to the social behaviour in question.

What constitutes 'profit' in the case of social entrepreneurship, and is it necessary in the first place? By definition it is necessary, or at least something that is analogous to it, if we assume that social entrepreneurship is defined as behaviour that results in social change. To this can be added that so-called 'social businesses' according to this argument will have two different types of 'profits', since they operate both in the capitalist market and have a social mission. Their goal in the market is to stay in business, though they do not aim at a high market profit. They do, however, aim for a 'high' social profit.

Explaining the links between the individual actions of the single social entrepreneur and macro-level change adds to the understanding of social entrepreneurship. A successful social entrepreneur – say Muhammad Yunus – gets followers (imitators, in Schumpeter's terminology), who help to spread the innovation to other countries. There is also an element of social destruction involved in social entrepreneurship; the old type of behaviour gets pushed to the side (in the case of Yunus, borrowers' relationship to usurious private moneylenders). While this latter behaviour by definition is not progressive, it is also clear that unintended consequences may result from social entrepreneurship. Also in this way, social entrepreneurship helps to shape society's general evolution.

Let me return in more detail to Muhammad Yunus and micro finance to show what can be accomplished by looking at social entrepreneurship with the help of Schumpeter (for example, Bornstein, 1997; Yunus and Jolis, 1991). It was not Yunus who created the idea of giving loans to the poor, and in this way help them to get out of their poverty. This idea was instead invented by Akhtar Hameed Khan. Yunus, however, was driven by a strong sense of mission to push this idea through. His innovation, as I see it, consisted of something else, namely, in the way that he used social group pressure as collateral for loans to single individuals. While Khan had tried to make a village co-operative responsible for the loan, Yunus looked to the small private group (of five people) to guarantee the loan of the individual.

This group pressure could be used in various ways, and Yunus has tried out different versions. The basic principle nonetheless remains the same: use group pressure to ensure that the individual group member repays her loan. I say 'her loan' because Yunus chose to prioritise loans to women, since he found that he could accomplish more social change in this way.

Yunus's 'good' consisted of a small loan to an individual, guaranteed in some way by the group. He produced it with the help of money and people that he mobilised. The success of his approach helped to spread the innovation, which was finally legitimised not only through its own successful diffusion but also through the stamp of approval that institutions such as the World Bank and the Nobel Peace Prize Committee in Oslo provided.

6.6 CONCLUDING REMARKS: SKILL AND WILL; THE ENTREPRENEUR AS A RECOMBINATEUR

This chapter contains three novelties: an attempt to make a case for not only using single elements in Schumpeter's theory of entrepreneurship, but his *full theory*; an effort to show that Schumpeter views innovations in *two very different ways*; and an attempt to show that this full model can be used to provide an understanding and explanation of social entrepreneurship (see Box 6.4). While Schumpeter is often mentioned in the context of social entrepreneurship, it is usually casual mention or a reference to some single aspect of his model (for example, Martin and Osberg, 2007).

BOX 6.4   SCHUMPETER'S FULL MODEL APPLIED TO SOCIAL ENTREPRENEURSHIP

The Main Thesis

Social entrepreneurship can be defined as the pushing through or the successful introduction of social change through a new combination of elements that make up some way of doing things. Certain

---

values are implied in the notion of 'social change', such as every-body's right to economic progress and a humane health care.

The Five Key Elements

1. Motivation
Social entrepreneurs have complex motivations, centred around a sense of *mission* to create social change.

2. Innovation
Innovations are new combinations that produce social change. These combinations consist of the following elements, each of which can be the object of an innovation: (1) the conception of the way of doing things; (2) financing the venture; (3) its legal forms; (4) its organisation; (5) acquiring resources for its produc-tion; (6) method of production; and (7) to turn it into the accepted way of doing things. One way to visualise the seven elements that make up the whole process/combination of social change is as follows:

1	2	3	4	5	6	7

⟶

3. Resistance
Resistance to social change includes habits, customs, tradition, norms, routines and orders that may or may not be anchored in interests (economic, ideal and other).

4. Profit
Social change on the local, national and international level that typically entails the creation of new organisations, institutions and/or laws that help to realise some value.

5. Link to macro-level change
Social innovations lead to creative destruction and contribute to society's evolution.

Comment: Social change held little attraction to Schumpeter, who defined himself as a conservative and who did not believe in intervening in society's evolution. While Schumpeter did not discuss social entrepreneurship, it can be conceptualised accord-ing to his model.

I hope to have emphasised three elements in particular in Schumpeter's theory of entrepreneurship that are usually not singled out and looked at with theoretical interest: *innovation as a combination, resistance,* and *the link of entrepreneurship to the macro level.* While there is a general agreement in the literature that innovations are crucial, it contains no discussion or theoretisation of the fact that these can be conceptualised not only as single elements but also as *new combinations* (cf. Knudsen and Swedberg, 2007; Swedberg, 2006). While it is similarly well recognised that it is not easy to be an entrepreneur, and that he or she has to face and solve many practical problems, the more general category of resistance has not received any attention (cf. Knudsen and Swedberg, 2007; Swedberg, 2006). And while it is commonplace to criticise Schumpeter for his focus on the single entrepreneur, his attempt to link entrepreneurs (in plural!) to larger movements in economy and society has not been much explored.

In this chapter I have referred to Schumpeter's full theory as a 'model', and one might argue that a model should not be verbal but expressed in formal language. This is a valid point. Another valid point is that a verbal model is better than no model. I do think, however, that the elements of the model, verbal or formal, should be closely and logically linked, and that some work in this direction remains to be done in the case of the Schumpeterian model. This goes both for Schumpeter's model of economic entrepreneurship and when it has been adjusted to fit social entrepreneurship.

That this deficiency can be remedied also seems clear to me, and I briefly try to show how one might go about this. The motivation of the entrepreneur in the general version of Schumpeter's theory is complex and essentially serves to get the individual going in a certain direction. To this one might add that a better way to integrate this part of the model with the rest of the model, would be to emphasise the element of *skill* in the individual. The skill would be a skill to make combinations (which links it to innovation), a skill to overcome obstacles (which links it to resistance) and a skill to push through the whole thing to the profit (which links it to the will).

Innovation is directly linked to profit, and I have just linked it to motivation by noting that the entrepreneur has to be a bit of a *recombinateur.* Novelty (in a combination) is also linked to resistance in the sense that you can only do something new if you overcome what already exists.

It is a bit more difficult to tie the macro link closer to the other key elements in Schumpeter's model. This is also a point where one would like empirical research to suggest some likely links. One argument that could be made is that some macro events tend to facilitate future entrepreneurship, while others make it harder. Some macro changes also tend to cause suspicion of entrepreneurs and increase resistance to them, while others work in the opposite direction.

Can one also tighten up the theory of social entrepreneurship that was presented earlier in this chapter? The answer would seem to me to be 'yes', and that one could proceed more or less along similar lines. Instead of seeking to unlock the secrets of the entrepreneur's heart and motivation, a focus on skill seems more realistic. Again, the skill would be a skill to make new combinations, to overcome resistance and to push the whole thing through to the end. Once more, in short: skill and will; the entrepreneur as a *recombinateur*.

The elements that can be found in the model of social entrepreneurship are also closely linked in the sense that they all consist of social action. Resistance can be defined as the existing way of doing things, and innovation as a new way of doing things. Social change (or 'profit') would then be a way of 'locking in' new ways of doing things, with the help of laws and regulations or by turning them into social institutions.

Also the link to the macro level in social entrepreneurship can be understood in a similar manner to the equivalent link in economic entrepreneurship. Macro-level change represents what we may call societal change, rather than social change, and it concerns all of society, be it local, national or international. A revolution, from this perspective, may indeed represent an opportunity for societal change – but not more than that, since revolutions are difficult to steer.

The last point I would like to make in this chapter is that the spirit in which Schumpeter conceived the entrepreneur and entrepreneurship invites us to play around with his ideas, to seize them, hold them and recombine them. Also the theoretical entrepreneur, in short, has to be a bit of a *recombinateur*.

NOTES

1. Schumpeter uses the term 'development' in his very own sense. It is usually synonymous with 'entrepreneurship' – except for the cases where it indicates economic change from factors outside the economic sphere or incremental and very slow change.
2. One difficulty with outlining Schumpeter's full model of entrepreneurship has to do with the question of which elements to include. An obvious answer would be to include all the elements that Schumpeter does. This would mean that we would not only include the elements I have selected but also, say, his theory of interest. If it is true – contrary to what I argue – that one can accomplish more by also including the rest of Schumpeter's ideas, one part of my argument nonetheless stands firm, namely, that we need to take Schumpeter's full theory of entrepreneurship into account.
3. Some interpreters of Schumpeter equate his concept of innovations exclusively with *technological* innovations. This goes counter to Schumpeter's own view.

4. From a Schumpeterian perspective, a new organisational form represents a new organisational norm. Why this is the case will soon become clear.
5. A financial innovation can be described as a new way of financing the operations of an enterprise that result in a new high profit. If the goal of the enterprise was to sell financial products, one could in contrast speak of innovations in terms of new financial products.
6. I thank Laura Ford of Cornell University for this suggestion.
7. In getting arguments for including legal forms on Schumpeter's list for innovations, one may want to draw on what today constitutes the most underexploited source for Schumpeter's theory of innovation, namely, *Business Cycles*. Schumpeter notes, for example, at one point in this work that 'legal and financial devises had to be invented in quite the same sense as the steam engine had to be invented' (Schumpeter, 1939: 247). For an exemplary use of *Business Cycles* as a source for Schumpeter's theory of innovation, see Thomas McCraw (2007).
8. There is also the interesting possibility of having a new combination but no entrepreneur. This would be the case when a new combination is the result of an accident, along the lines of mutations to DNA.
9. See, for example, Schumpeter's statement about a general who 'earned corresponding "profit" in terms of social prestige' (Schumpeter, 1942 [1977]: 133).

REFERENCES

Baumol, W. (2002), *The Free-Market Innovation Machine: Analyzing the Growth Miracle of Capitalism*, Princeton, NJ: Princeton University Press.

Bornstein, D. (1997), *The Price of a Dream. The Story of the Grameen Bank*, Chicago, IL: University of Chicago Press.

Bornstein, D. (2004), *How to Change the World. Social Entrepreneurs and the Power of New Ideas*, Oxford: Oxford University Press.

Bourdieu, P. (1986), 'Forms of capital', in J. Richardson (ed.), *Handbook of Theory and Research for Sociology of Education*, Westport, CT: Greenwood, pp. 241–58.

Dees, J.G. (2001), 'The meaning of "social entrepreneurship"', working paper, Center for the Advancement of Social Entrepreneurship, Duke University.

Delude, C. (2005), 'Brain researchers explain why old habits die hard', *MIT News*, 19 October, see http://web.mit.edu/newsoffice/2005/habit.html, accessed 19 October 2007.

Heatherley, D., D. Leung and D. MacKenzie (forthcoming), 'The finitist accountant: classifications, rules and the construction of profits', in T. Pinch and R. Swedberg (eds), *Living in a Material World: Economic Sociology meets Science and Technology Studies*, Cambridge, MA: The MIT Press.

Knudsen, T. and R. Swedberg (2007), 'Capitalist entrepreneurship: making profit through the unmaking of economic orders', paper presented at conference on Capitalism and Entrepreneurship, Center for the Study of Economy and Society, Cornell University, 28–29 September.

Light, P. (2006), 'Reshaping social entrepreneurship', *Stanford Social Innovation Review*, Fall: 47–51.

Martin, R. and S. Osberg (2007), 'Social entrepreneurship: the case for definition', *Stanford Social Innovation Review*, Spring: 29–39.

McCraw, T. (2007), *Prophet of Innovation: Joseph Schumpeter and Creative Destruction*, Cambridge, MA: The Belknap Press of Harvard University Press.

Nelson, R. and S. Winter (1982), *An Evolutionary Theory of Economic Change*, Cambridge, MA: Harvard University Press.

Peirce, C.S. (1957), *Essays in the Philosophy of Science*, New York: Bobbs-Merrill.

Schumpeter, J.A. (1911), *Theorie der wirtschaftlichen Entwicklung*, Leipzig: Duncker & Humblot.

Schumpeter, J.A. (1911 [2002]), 'New translations: *Theorie der wirtschaftlichen Entwicklung*', *American Journal of Economics and Sociology*, **61** (2): 405–37.

Schumpeter, J.A. (1911 [2003]), 'The theory of economic development', in J. Backhaus (ed.), *Joseph Alois Schumpeter*, Boston, MA: Kluwer.

Schumpeter, J.A. (1928 [2003]), 'Entrepreneur', *Austrian Economics and Entrepreneurial Studies*, **6**, 235–65.

Schumpeter, J.A. (1934), *The Theory of Economic Development*, Cambridge, MA: Harvard University Press.

Schumpeter, J.A. (1939), *Business Cycles: A Theoretical, Historical and Statistical Analysis of the Capitalist Process*, 2 vols, New York: McGraw-Hill.

Schumpeter, J.A. (1940 [2000]), 'Letter to Simon Kusnetz dated March 18', pp. 321–2 in *Briefe/Letters*, Tübingen: J.C.B. Mohr.

Schumpeter, J.A. (1942 [1977]), *Capitalism, Socialism and Democracy*, New York: Harper & Row.

Schumpeter, J.A. (1946[1951]), 'Capitalism', pp. 184–205 in *Essays*, New Brunswick, NJ: Transaction Publishers.

Schumpeter, J.A. (1949 [1951]), 'Economic theory and entrepreneurial history', pp. 248–66 in *Essays*, Cambridge: Addison-Wesley.

Schumpeter, J. (1954), *History of Economic Analysis*, London: Allen & Unwin.

Swedberg, R. (1991), *Schumpeter – A Biography*, Princeton, NJ: Princeton University Press.

Swedberg, R. (2006), 'Social entrepreneurship: the view of the young Schumpeter', in D. Hjorth and C. Steyaert (eds), *Entrepreneurship and Social Change*, Cheltenham UK and Northampton, MA, USA: Edward Elgar, pp. 21–34.

Weber, M. (1946), *From Max Weber*, eds by H. Gerth and C.W. Mills, New York: Oxford University Press.

Weber, M. (1978), *Economy and Society: An Outline of Interpretive Sociology*, Berkeley, CA: University of California Press.

White, W. (1955), *Money and Motivation: An Analysis of Incentives in Industry*, New York: Harper & Row.

Yunus, M. and A. Jolis (1991), *Banker to the Poor: The Autobiography of Muhammad Yunus*, London: Aurum Press.

7. The culture of management: self-interest, empathy and emotional control

Eva Illouz

What an enormous price man had to pay for reason, seriousness, control over his emotions – those grand human prerogatives and cultural showpieces! How much blood and horror lies behind all 'good things'! (F.W. Nietzsche, quoted in Smith, 1971: 31)

7.1 INTRODUCTION

The impact of capitalism on social relations has been *the* central puzzle of classical sociology, with most of the founders of the discipline agreeing that capitalism posed a serious threat to our capacity to create meaning and maintain social relationships. This chapter shows that under the aegis of psychologists who started to massively intervene in the American corporation from the 1930s onward, the deployment of rationality inside economic organisations counter-intuitively went hand in hand with an intensification of emotional life. Second, the chapter argues that psychologists, acting simultaneously as professionals and as producers of culture, have not only codified emotional conduct inside the workplace but, more crucially, made 'self-interest', 'efficiency' and 'instrumentality' into valid cultural repertoires. Finally, the chapter argues that in becoming cultural repertoires of action, 'self-interest' and 'efficiency' actually generated and organised new models of sociability, most noticeably the model of communication. Psychological cultural frames drew from and merged with the cultural matrix of the market and thus came to orient the self, provide it with strategies of action and, perhaps more crucially, shape new forms of sociability.

For the study of social entrepreneurship, this cultural development is of interest for at least three reasons. First, it centrally involves the concept of 'empathy' that plays such a central role in the discourse of social entrepreneurship (Bornstein, 2004; Drayton, 2006,). If you want to be a 'good' social entrepreneur, should you study management (literature)? Second, the chapter argues that this notion of 'empathy' (and of emotional control) has historically evolved with the rise of the capitalist corporation and the needs of managing a corporation (and working for it). If following Schumpeter's influential work, typically entrepreneurship and management are juxtaposed as two competing modes, we are faced with the puzzle that social entrepreneurship appears to have taken on board a crucial development of management. Third, the chapter argues that this development is not least due to the import of a cultural lexicon that imports 'feminine' concerns typically attributed to 'family life' into the workplace of corporations. It thus illuminates one link between work and family life, a relation that is so far generally bracketed in social entrepreneurship discussions. As a result, this chapter points to a number of further questions: Is the 'empathy' of social entrepreneurs a descendant of the 'empathy' demanded in the capitalist corporation? Why has capitalism largely moved away from the 'heroic' lexicon of earlier capitalist entrepreneurs and the associated value set (Schumpeter, 1934)? Does social entrepreneurship imply a 'feminisation' of entrepreneurship?

Throughout the twentieth century, under the aegis of the therapeutic discourse, emotional life became imbued with the metaphors and rationality of economics; conversely, economic behaviour was consistently shaped by the sphere of emotions and sentiments. The rationalisation of emotions created its own converse, which could be characterised as the 'emotionalisation of economic conduct'. This reciprocal process points to a broader cultural process that I dub *emotional capitalism* (Illouz, 2006). In emotional capitalism emotional and economic discourses mutually shape one another so that affect is made an essential aspect of economic behaviour, and emotional life, especially that of the middle classes, follows the logic of economic relations and exchange. Market-based cultural repertoires shape and inform interpersonal and emotional relationships. Knowing how to forge and maintain interpersonal relationships becomes central to how economic relationships are thought of and imagined. What I call emotional capitalism is a cultural process through which new scripts of economic relationships are formulated and intertwined with interactional-emotional scripts, as illustrated by the prevalent cultural frames of 'cooperation' and 'teamwork'. These scripts, born of the professional language of psychologists and of the corporate language of efficiency, have reshaped the ways actors conceptualise horizontal and vertical hierarchies, power, and even, to a limited but definite extent, gender relations. Nowhere has this reciprocal influence of psychological and economic discourses been more apparent than in the key cultural motif of 'emotional control'.

7.2 EMOTIONAL CONTROL IN THE SOCIOLOGY OF ORGANISATIONS

While emotions have often been absent from economic sociology, they do appear in the sociology of organisations, though in a negative form, under the heading of 'emotional control'. Studies of the corporation have consistently found that the twentieth-century American workplace demanded a much stricter control of emotions than its predecessors, the nineteenth-century shop floor or factory. C. Wright Mills's *White Collar: The American Middle Classes* from 1951 and William Whyte's *The Organization Man* from 1956 were among the first works to draw sociologists' attention to the new emotional requirements of economic organisations (Mills, 1951; Whyte, 1956). Inspired by the disquieting Weberian vision of the domination of faceless bureaucratic structures, these (and other subsequent) studies suggested that in the course of the twentieth century large corporations exerted a new kind of pressure on their employees to 'manage' their inner life and emotions. Sociologist Arlie Hochschild's seminal 1983 study of airline flight attendants, *The Managed Heart*, extended this line of thought by suggesting that a considerable amount of emotional control ('emotional work') goes into attendants' interactions with passengers as they are encouraged to adopt the company's ideology regarding how they should feel in a variety of situations (Hochschild, 1983). Hochschild suggested that women working in the service industries were the most likely to become 'emotional laborers', workers who had to repress their emotions in order to sell the image of their company. In a similar vein, Gideon Kunda's study of the culture of a 'high-tech' corporation argued that modern corporations exert 'normative control', attempting to control the 'minds and hearts' of their employees (Kunda, 1992).

In these accounts, emotional control is a variant of social and economic control. They suggest that emotional control has a strong cultural affinity with the sphere of capitalist economic activity, not only in the Weberian sense that it is a precondition for the rational and dispassionate pursuit of gain but also in the sense that it reflects contemporary modes of social control inside the capitalist workplace. Most sociological accounts presume a somewhat direct relationship between the social and economic power to issue commands on the one hand and individuals' exercise of emotional control on the other. In this view, individuals are (somewhat incoherently) both passive recipients of orders and sophisticated actors who can wear masks and lie to others and to themselves about their 'true' selves. Moreover, implicitly contained in these studies is the idea that emotional self-control represses the truly 'human element' of interactions because it inscribes economic rationality at the very centre of relations inside the organisation. This view has been complemented by feminist perspectives on organisations, which have argued that the ideal of rational self-control consecrates attributes of male identity and excludes women by rejecting care-oriented and emotionally expressive female styles of management.

My approach here significantly differs from all of the above. First, I argue that we cannot understand the emergence of the emotional norm of self-control inside the American workplace without understanding the broader models of social competence with which self-control has frequently been associated. Indeed, one element consistently overlooked by the sociology of organisations is that emotional control figured in our moral vocabulary long before the emergence of capitalism and that it has come to stand as an extended metaphor for self-mastery, self-possession, and moral autonomy, all marks of a properly groomed selfhood (Hemphill, 1998; Stearns and Stearns, 1986). Being able to control one's bouts of anger, lust or depression is not simply the effect of the 'commodification of emotion' (as Hochschild and others argue); it is an essential element of social competence writ large. As the sociologist Erving Goffman astutely observed:

> During any conversation, standards are established as to how much the individual is to allow himself to be carried away by the talk, how thoroughly he is to permit himself to be caught up in it. He will be obliged to prevent himself from becoming so swollen with feelings and a readiness to act that he threatens the bounds regarding affect that have been established for him in the interaction . . . When the individual does become over-involved in the topic of conversation, and gives others the impression that he does not have a necessary measure of *self-control over his feelings and actions* . . . then the others are likely to be drawn from involvement in the talk to an involvement in the talker. *What is one's man [sic] over-eagerness will become another man's alienation.* (Emphasis added)[1]

One might argue that Goffman takes for granted and naturalises what are in fact highly gendered emotional attributes of masculinity. But such a view itself reproduces the pernicious and erroneous stereotype according to which women have little or no control over their emotionality. Goffman refers here to a (relatively) gender-blind form of social competence shared and endorsed by men and women, even if its modalities vary from one gender to the other.

The exercise of such competence cannot be easily distinguished from the repressive self-control that sociologists of organisations have analysed.[2] Following Norbert Elias's thesis in his monumental *Civilizing Process,* we may view emotional control as the result of the modern (that is, since the seventeenth century) differentiation of functions and of networks of interdependency that thus orient the self toward a greater number of social interactions. As these interactions increase in frequency and variety, the individual is compelled to adjust his or her conduct to an increasing number of others, thus making the self more self-regulated and predictable (Elias, 1939). According to this view, emotional control has become a dominant way of shaping one's emotion, not only because it is a form of corporate control and because it naturalises male identity, but also because it mobilises forms of social competence made more necessary by the multiplication and lengthening of chains of social interactions.

Finally, unlike the sociologists (Elias included) who treat emotional control as a monolithic category, I argue that there are many different forms of emotional control, for the simple reason that emotional control draws primarily on culturally shaped conceptions of the self. The flight attendant's self-control is a far cry from, say, the Stoic's ataraxia. As I show in the following analysis, the therapeutic self-control advocated in economic organisations is characterised by its inclusion, rather than exclusion, of women's point of view, by its mix of rationality and emotionality, and by its very capacity to make emotions central to the self.

7.3 THE POWER OF CONTROL AND THE CONTROL OF POWER

The period from the 1880s to the 1920s has been dubbed the golden age of capitalism, during which 'the factory system was established, capital was centralised, production standardised, organisations bureaucratised, and labour incorporated in large firms' (Shenhav, 1998: 20). Most conspicuous was the rise of the large-scale corporation, employing thousands and even tens of thousands of workers, thus making corporations bureaucratically complex and hierarchically much more integrated.[3]

In his seminal study on the rise of the corporation, sociologist Reinhard Bendix has suggested that during the nineteenth century managers' rhetoric was a mix of self-help (inspired by religious Puritanism) and (Spencerian) theory of the 'survival of the fittest'. Managers were managers by virtue of their merits, and these merits could not be questioned. Similarly, those who were in subaltern positions lacked, by definition, physical, moral, and intellectual qualities.[4]

As the volume and pace of industrial production began to swell, the sheer mass of work and workers that were to be supervised grew (Chandler, 1977). As they grew, the organisation became faced with what it saw as the increasing complexity of managing people who had to produce efficiently and quickly. From the increasing number of workers and the need to discipline them emerged a managerial class who were neither owners nor workers and who viewed themselves as vested with the social mission of increasing production by managing workers, who were viewed as basically stupid, immoral, dependent and the main source of society's ills. Against the backdrop of labour unrest and in an atmosphere of antagonism between workers and capitalists, the American mechanical engineer and leader of the efficiency movement, Frederick Taylor, proposed a theory of scientific management that promised to secure material wealth and social harmony. Taylor's aim was to remove the 'cause for antagonism' and, to that end, as he famously claimed, a 'revolution in mental attitude' was demanded.[5] He asserted that 'the man at the head of the business under scientific management [must be] governed by rules and laws which have been developed through hundreds of experiments just as much as the workman, and the standards which have been developed [must be] equitable'.[6] Taylor has been frequently pilloried for inventing an inhuman system of management ultimately serving capitalists' interests. But from a cultural standpoint the reverse is true, for his use of science served to undermine the traditional basis of legitimacy of leadership and to establish the foundation and perceived need for psychologists' intervention, which would in turn attempt to codify and formalise the 'human' element in the corporation. Instead of regarding success as self-explanatory (success being the proof that a man was deserving in the first place), Taylor's theories suggested that the duties of managers needed to be (re-)examined.

This had the effect of subtly changing the definition of what constituted a good manager. As long as they had regarded success as a sign of merit, no further justification of industrial leadership was necessary. But Taylorist views of management suggested that failures were not an unavoidable outcome of inherent and inborn incompetence. Instead, the causes of failures had to be investigated and prevented through the development of appropriate managerial policies. As Bendix has suggested, there was a subtle but significant change in the image of the worker: from a person who had to be taught virtue and proper manners, he had become an object of scientific scrutiny and interrogation whose aptitudes and attitudes had to be tested (Bendix, 1956: 298). In that process, the definition of success and leadership also changed: while in the nineteenth century success had been a self-evident sign of one's social superiority, which was then self-justified, leadership gradually became a more elusive category, a quality to be proven rather than a quality inevitably and tautologically bestowed. This in turn implied a new degree of uncertainty regarding what constituted a good manager. Compared to its predecessors, the religious or Darwinian legitimation of leadership, management theory seems to have created a process of collective scrutiny and questioning, thereby creating new social forms of uncertainty and anxieties, which in turn would generate new forms of organisational control. The new cultural anxiety about the nature of the good worker and the idea that the deployment of adequate knowledge could help find solutions to improve workers' performance constituted the backdrop for the growing intervention of psychologists inside the corporation.

7.4 PSYCHOLOGISTS ENTER THE MARKET

By the 1920s, 86 per cent of all wage earners were employed in manufacturing (Bendix, 1956). Even more conspicuous was the fact that the American firm had the largest proportion of administrative workers worldwide (18 administrative workers for each 100 production workers; Shenhav, 1998). The expansion of firms went hand in hand with the consolidation of management theories that aimed to systematise and rationalise the production process. Indeed, the management system shifted the locus of control from traditional capitalists to technocrats. Using the rhetoric of science, rationality and general welfare to establish their authority, technocrats claimed that the interests of both the employers and the employees would presumably be met. The critical theorist and sociologist Yehouda Shenhav views this transformation as the seizure of a new form of power by engineers who acted as a class of professionals. A new ideology of management was imposed that conceived of the workplace as a 'system' in which the individual would be eradicated and general rules and laws would be formalised and applied to the worker and to the work process. In contrast to capitalists, who had frequently been portrayed as greedy and selfish, managers in the new ideology of management emerged as rational, responsible, and predictable and as the bearers of new rules of standardisation and rationalisation (Shenhav, 1998: 197).

Yet if until the 1920s the engineers' rhetoric of the workplace as system prevailed,[7] soon afterward psychologists initiated another discourse that paid a great deal of attention to individuals and to their emotions.[8] At the same time that corporations were trying to figure out how to maximise the production process and make it more efficient, psychologists were struggling to establish themselves as a professional group that offered a competing lexicon for making sense of problems of productivity.

Psychologists produced a battery of tests to find out whether intelligence was correlated with productivity. The results consistently suggested that the relationship was so trivial as to be insignificant. However, psychologists did find that character traits such as honesty, loyalty and dependability were significantly related to productivity.

The psychologist and organisation theorist Elton Mayo was one of the first in a long list of 'management theorists' to provide guidelines for shaping the identity that managers sought. Mayo must be given a place of honour in any account of management theory because 'there can be few disciplines or fields of research in which a single set of studies or single researcher and writer has exercised so great an influence as was exercised for quarter of the century by Mayo and the Hawthorne studies' (Carey, 1967: 403).

Mayo essentially suggested that *personality* was paramount to success in the corporation. If the skills in human relations were skills in handling persons *as persons*, then successful management depended substantially on managers' ability to understand others and to handle human relations in general. Managers would now be evaluated not only according to their skill and technical competence but also according to diffuse and imprecise criteria such as 'having the right personality', 'knowing how to handle human situations' and 'knowing how to resolve conflict'. However, where experimental psychologists had viewed moral qualities such as 'loyalty' or 'reliability' as important attributes of the efficient personality, Mayo's famous Hawthorne experiments (conducted from 1924 to 1927) paid historically unprecedented attention to emotional transactions per se, for their main finding was that productivity increased if work relationships were characterised by care and attention to workers' feelings. In place of the Victorian language of 'character', Mayo used the amoral and scientific language of psychology to conceive of human relations as technical problems to be alleviated by proper knowledge and understanding.[9] In other words, because American corporations were struggling to increase their productivity and because they delegated the solution to this question to people who had been trained in the emerging science of psychology, a new cultural category emerged: that of the 'human relationship'.

In Mayo's first experiments at General Electric the subjects were all women. Unbeknown to himself, Mayo's initial findings were highly gendered. An analysis of the cases addressed by Mayo is instructive both of the ways in which his approach to work conflicts was influenced by a psychological worldview and of the ways in which the problems he unravelled among women workers were gendered. For example, 'one woman worker . . . discovered during an interview that her dislike of a certain supervisor was based upon a fancied resemblance to a detested stepfather. Small wonder that the same supervisor had warned the interviewer that she was "difficult to handle"' (Mayo, 1949: 69). Two other women workers were offered a transfer to another and better section. But, as Mayo observes,

> to accept would mean leaving their group and taking a job in another department: they refused. Then representatives of the Union put some pressure on them, claiming that, if they continued to refuse, the Union organisers 'might just as well give up' their efforts. With reluctance, the girls reversed their decision

and accepted the upgrading. Both girls at once needed the attention of an interviewer: they had liked the former group in which they had earned informal membership. Both felt adjustment to a new group and a novel situation as involving efforts and private discontent. From both much was learned of the intimate organisation and common practices of their groups, and their adjustments to their new groups were eased, thereby effectively helping to reconstitute the teamwork in those groups. (Mayo, 1949: 71)

As a further example:

The interviewer was able to establish that a woman's performance was suffering because her mother had pressured her to ask for a raise. She talked her situation out with an interviewer, and it became clear that to her a raise would mean departure from her daily companions and associates. Although not immediately relevant, it is interesting to note that after explaining the situation to the interviewer she was able to present her case dispassionately to her mother . . . The mother immediately understood and abandoned pressure for advancement, and the girl returned to work. This last instance illustrates one way in which the interview clears lines of communication of emotional blockage – within as without the plant. (Mayo, 1949: 72)

Notice how these analyses put interpersonal relationships and emotions at the centre of the cultural imagination of the workplace. But they also point to the ways in which *women* experienced the workplace. Because their social role was primarily defined as that of breadwinner, it is doubtful that many men would have felt torn between a raise and their friends or that they would have preferred to give up the former over the latter. If the question of how to form and maintain social bonds inside the corporation became a key motif for Mayo and subsequent theorists, it is because his initial findings were (unknowingly) gendered, reflecting women's emotional culture, in which nurturance, care, display of affection, outward expressions of support, and linguistic communication were central to their social identity. Mayo's subsequent experiments with men only further confirmed his views that gentle supervision and an atmosphere of trust were conducive to higher productivity.

Few have noticed that Mayo's interview method had *all* the characteristics of a therapeutic interview except the name. This is how Mayo defines his method of interviewing:

Workers wished to talk, and to talk freely under the seal of professional confidence (which was never abused) to someone who seemed representative of the company or who seemed, by his very attitude, to carry authority. The experience itself was unusual; there are few people in this world who have had the experience of finding someone intelligent, attentive, and eager to listen without interruption to all that he or she has to say. But to arrive at this point, it became necessary to train interviewers how to listen, how to avoid interruption or the giving of advice, how generally to avoid anything that might put an end to free expression in an individual instance. Some approximate rules to guide the interviewer in his work were therefore set down. These were, more or less, as follows: 1. Give your whole attention to the person interviewed, and make it evident that you are doing so. 2. Listen – don't talk. 3. Never argue; never give advice. 4. Listen to: (a) what he wants to say, (b) what he does not want to say, (c) what he cannot say without help. 5. As you listen, plot out tentatively and for subsequent correction the pattern (personal) that is being set before you. To test this, from time to time summarise what has been said and present for comment (e.g., 'is this what you are telling me?'). Always do this with the greatest caution ... 6. Remember that everything said must be considered a personal confidence and not divulged to anyone. (Mayo, 1949: 65)

I do not know a better definition of a therapeutic interview. Because Mayo was using the conceptual tools of psychology, he could elicit a form of speech that was essentially private and emotional. Moreover, because the subjects of his milestone experiments were women, he inadvertently initiated a process in which the emotional attributes of women were incorporated into the workplace, which was then still largely dominated by the male workforce.

If, as many feminists have claimed, masculinity is implicitly inscribed in the instruments of classification and evaluation inside the workplace, surely Mayo's findings are an example of the reverse, namely, the inscription of femininity in seemingly 'universal' claims. Mayo used a 'female method' – based on speech and on the communication of emotions – to unravel women's problems, that is, problems that had a fundamentally interpersonal and emotional nature, and applied them to highly gendered male organisations. In so doing, Mayo had initiated a process of redefinition of masculinity inside the workplace.

7.5   A NEW EMOTIONAL STYLE FOR WORKERS AND MANAGERS

Mayo's findings were applied to defining an adequate work environment not only for workers but also for management. Who would be a successful manager? According to Mayo, the 'new' leader was someone who acted as an investigator of social sentiments and who could further collaboration between managers and workers to achieve organisational goals (Wren, 1979: 318). Moreover, by suggesting that conflicts were not a matter of competition over scarce resources but rather resulted from tangled emotions, personality factors and unresolved psychological problems, Mayo constructed a discursive *continuity between the family and the workplace*. Because the psychologists hired to increase productivity worked with a terminology derived from studies of the family, the language of and solutions to conflicts in the workplace typically emerged from that realm.[10]

According to Mayo, conflict was the result of emotional transactions, and harmony could be reached by the acknowledgment of such emotions and mutual understanding. Mayo's theory of management helps reconcile the conflicting interests of capitalists and workers. His theory acted (or at least seemed to act) as a conduit for workers' critiques of their work conditions (Boltanski and Chiapello, 1999). But it also offered techniques to quell those critiques. For example, when workers voiced grievances, Mayo and his team noticed that the simple fact that a manager would listen to someone who was angry and let the person express that anger would assuage the angry person. In the same vein, conflicts at work were reconceptualised as stemming from personality problems and a troubled childhood, not from the defective structural organisation of capitalism. For the first time, each single individual and his or her emotions were scrutinised, and the language of productivity became slowly intertwined with that of the psyche. Being a good manager meant being able to display the attributes of a psychologist: it required that one grasp and deal with the complex emotional nature of social transactions in the workplace.

Mayo's object of study and his objectives were in many ways radically different from those of clinical psychology. Yet by insisting on the human factor in the workplace, on such intangibles as emotions and human relations, and on an invisible thread linking the family and the workplace, Mayo's theory made actors working in corporations far more receptive to the new definitions of leadership propagated by the discourse of popular psychology. In the context of new uncertainties that were created by the insecure economic environment of the 1930s, success in the corporation was made to depend on having the right personality and therefore on one's correct management of emotions. Consequently, by making the notion of 'personality' central to economic behaviour, psychologists could not only form new connections between the language of the psyche and that of economic efficiency but also ascertain and legitimate their authority in the corporation and in society at large.

When in the 1950s the Mayoist consensus about human relations was challenged by the 'new' view that conflicts of interest between labour and management were natural and inevitable, the language of emotions and human relations persisted, for it had become part of the conventions that psychologists and management theories had successfully established. The texts of the 1940s and 1950s still typically postulated that the 'feelings' of people were more important than the 'logic' of organisation intangibles, such as charts, rules and directives (Stagner, 1948: 131; emphasis added) As the historian Daniel Wren put it, 'in general, the texts of the early 1950s emphasised feelings, sentiments, and collaboration' (Wren, 1979: 475). In the 1960s, under the influence of the immensely popular psychology of Abraham Maslow, this tendency only deepened with new approaches, including 'industrial humanism' or 'organisational humanism', that sought to offset the authoritarian tendencies of organisations and to integrate individual and organisation goals. The extraordinary cultural power of psychology thus seems to have resided in its capacity to inscribe the individual – his or her needs, claims and critiques – within the very structure and culture of economic organisations.

The point of this rather cavalier overview is obviously not to retrace the complex and contradictory history of management.[11] Rather, it is simply to suggest that amid the variety and complexity of management theories, one central cultural repertoire emerged: traditional work relationships based on authority and even force were criticised and rejected, and were recast as emotional and psychological entities, thus enabling a (seeming) harmony between the organisation and the individual.

7.6 EMOTIONAL CONTROL

One of Mayo's teachings, endlessly recycled by popular psychologists, was that anger needed to be banished from the workplace and that emotional control was a precondition for being a good (middle-ranking) manager. The norm of anger control, inspired by a Puritan view of the family, had always prevailed in the American family (Stearns and Stearns, 1986). During the nineteenth century, such standards of anger control remained the bulwark of the family but do not seem to have been observed in the workplace, or at least not as strictly as they were in the family. The new injunction of emotional control captured the corporate imagination because it recast the old Puritan norm of anger control in the double psychological language of emotionality and of economic efficiency. New cultural scripts promoting emotional control could gain quick legitimacy because the link between rationality and emotional self-control had had a long and venerable history and because it reflected one of the most important organisational myths, that of rationality. As Frank Dobbin suggests in his analysis of the emergence of new forms of economic behaviour, 'new practices must conform to the wider understanding of what is rational' (Dobbin, 2004: 11).

In his 1933 *The Human Problems of an Industrial Civilization*, Mayo suggested that angry reactions were like nervous breakdowns in that they necessitated appropriate measures and that one of the chief problems of proper management would be to control or prevent them (Mayo, 1933). The human relations movement increasingly suggested that the *control* of anger was an attribute of leadership because it was a prerequisite for higher productivity and efficiency. In their history of anger, Stearns and Stearns documented how, from the 1930s onward, corporations developed an organisational apparatus to train their personnel in the art of this new emotional ethos, not only for the sake of higher efficiency and productivity, but also because handling workers' emotions would presumably help reduce the level of workers' anger and therefore the incidence of discontent and strikes as well (Stearns and Stearns, 1986). A frequently used strategy to cope with anger was to claim that complaints and anger had nothing to do with the workplace but were simply re-enactments of early family conflicts (Stearns 1994, 123).

The injunction to emotional control was directed not only at workers but perhaps first and foremost at managers. Foremen were commanded to listen to workers' grievances and to hold their temper in close check. 'The foreman's checklist: do I correct the mistakes of my workers considerately, and in a manner to indicate that I am more interested in helping them to avoid future mistakes than I am in the opportunity merely to "bawl them out"?' (Stearns, 1994: 124). In the 1950s, T-groups (sensitivity training programmes) bombarded foremen with examples of the bad old days of 'foremen who shouted, put down worker grievances' (quotes in Stearns and Stearns, 1986: 132). In these groups, foremen learned that they should be 'friendly but impersonal' and that remaining 'cool' was an important attribute of competence (Stearns, 1994: 124).

Studies of the contemporary corporation amply confirm that the ethos of self-restraint has become pervasive (Hochschild, 1983; Jackall, 1988; Kunda, 1992). For example, in his study of managers, sociologist Robert Jackall argues that the most important managerial quality is self-control and that in the contemporary corporation self-control is a crucial asset for those in the lower ranks who wish to signal their candidacy for leadership or professionalism. Or to give another example from popular advice literature: 'Expressing anger spontaneously . . . usually means losing control. That reflects badly on you – no matter how justified your outburst may be. There's something about seeing a colleague out of control that shakes up everyone. You're breaking office rules, breaching professional decorum' (Curran, 1985: 115).

These new cultural repertoires are most salient in the popular advice literature on management and leadership. Addressing an 'ideal-type' manager (or would-be manager), popular psychologists left the intricacies of management theory per se and assumed instead the broader cultural role of articulating the type of selfhood that could deliver the key to corporate success. Although the texts of popular psychology cannot straightforwardly inform us of the practical uses of therapeutic language, they do point to the publicly available languages that shape self-understandings and help interpret the behaviour of others.

7.7 EMPATHY

The self-control advocated by psychologists does not entail the overall suppression of emotions. The contrary is true: empathy is as strongly advocated as self-control and is viewed as an essential addition to self-control. For example, in 1936, in the immensely popular book *How to Win Friends and Influence People,* Dale Carnegie asserts:

> If as a result of reading this book, you get only one thing – an increased tendency to think always in terms of the other person's point of view, and see things from his angle as well as your own – if you get only that one thing from this book, it may easily prove to be one of the milestones of your career. (Carnegie, 1937 [1981]: 218)

In 1956, Leonard Jarrard, then teaching at the Carnegie Institute of Technology, wrote in the journal *Personnel Psychology* that 'empathy appears to be a necessary requisite for supervisory success' (Jarrard, 1956: 157).

Anyone familiar with the corporation knows that the emotional self-control advocated by organisational consultants and psychologists is a far cry from the stern repression of emotions usually associated with its Victorian predecessor. In its therapeutic version, self-control must be manifested in an upbeat, smiling, agreeable attitude. From the 1930s onward, almost *all* guidebooks on successful management emphasised the value of positive talk, empathy, enthusiasm, friendliness and energy, with the more recent guidebooks advocating a blend of spirituality with a therapeutic call to dispel performance anxieties, to nurture oneself, and to entertain positive thoughts about oneself and others. Indeed, positive energy, as marked by appearing to be problem-free and enthusiastic, is another important attribute of the manager, whose self-control must always be personable and friendly. The mix of self-control and empathy advocated by organisational psychologists aims at creating the conditions for what organisational researchers call 'ingratiation' strategies (Rosenfeld et al., 1995: 28–47), strategies aiming at making one likable by projecting friendliness, a positive attitude toward others, and the capacity to acknowledge them. What is at stake in the construction of such emotional personas is the capacity to establish trust and trustworthiness.

Thus the argument positing that psychology has strengthened managers' grip on minds and hearts or that the economy debases a genuine realm of emotions is simplistic. The capitalist workplace, far from being devoid of emotions, has been saturated with a kind of effect committed to and commanded by the imperative of cooperation. Because capitalism demands and creates networks of interdependence and has positioned effect in the heart of its transactions, it has also brought about a dismantling of the very gender identities it helped establish in the first place. In commanding that we exert our mental and emotional skills to identify with others' point of view, the 'psychological ethos' orients the manager's self to the model of traditional female selfhood. It *blurs gender divisions* by inviting men and women to control their negative emotions, be friendly, view themselves through others' eyes, and empathise with others (Roos and Ashmore, 1993). For example, one 1990s manual entitled *Social Skills at Work* states that

> in professional relationships men don't have to be identified always with 'hard' masculine qualities and women with 'soft' feminine ones. Men can and should be just as capable as women of sensitivity and compassion . . . and of the arts of cooperation and persuasion, while women should be just as capable as men of self-assertion and leadership and of the arts of competition and direction. (Fontana, 1990: 8)

Emotional capitalism has realigned emotional cultures, harnessing the emotional self more closely to instrumental action.

Of course, I do not claim that the injunctions and instructions of advice literature have straightforwardly shaped corporate life or that they have miraculously erased the harsh and often brutal reality of the corporate world and of male domination of women. What I am saying, however, is that new models of emotionality, formulated by psychologists and consultants in management and human relations, have subtly but surely altered modes and models of sociability inside the middle-class workplace and have redrawn the cognitive and practical emotional boundaries regulating gender differences.

As the self-appointed experts on relationships inside organisations, psychologists have introduced emotions into the discourse on management and productivity. By linking professional competence with emotions, they have constructed managerial identity around the idea that 'personality attributes' and emotional style are a legitimate basis for managerial authority, with the ultimate economic justification that they are conducive to cooperation and productivity. Psychologists have redefined the 'moral fitness' of the leader as emotional competence, in which one signals and signifies the mastery of one's inner self simultaneously through distance from others (through self-control) and through an empathy and friendliness aimed at demonstrating one's capacity to cooperate with others. This redefinition has transformed the traditional male modes and models of domination inside the corporation.

7.8   EMOTIONAL CONTROL AND POWER

For these business psychologists, power is established by keeping one's emotions in check. According to one 1950s book of business psychology, for example,

> it goes without saying that in order to help other people relieve emotional tension and to direct emotional stirrings into the desired pattern, the individual in charge of the situation must be able to keep himself under control. Displays of emotion tend to engender similar responses in other people. This means that if the person is to control the situation he must not allow himself to be stimulated by the emotionality of the other person. (Beach and Clarck, 1959: 97)

Here two agents, one in power and one receiving orders, can have their own will realised *by not reacting*: the employer establishes her authority by controlling her negative emotions, but the employee can also realise his strength by, say, not reacting to a bullying boss. Further, by avoiding an expression of anger or protest, an employee can be made to be the subtle victor of an interaction with a bullying boss. Not reacting becomes the mark of self-control, which in turn signals a hidden and subtle psychological power that can in fact bypass hierarchical status and power.

In the psychological literature, overt reactions to others' offences are repeatedly and forcefully discouraged. In a famous 1991 manual for managers, *Getting Past No*, the Harvard Business School professor William Ury admonishes, 'when you react, you are hooked' (Ury, 1991: 15). The public defence of one's honour, understood as the social value bestowed on the self by others, is always systematically discouraged. This is because, according to the therapeutic ethos, the fully mature adult prefers to react strategically and defend his interests rather than his honour. People who are likely to prefer their honour over their interest are deemed emotionally 'incompetent' and therefore lacking in 'true' power.

We arrive at the following astonishing paradox: 'real' psychological strength consists in being able to secure one's interests without defending oneself by reacting or counterattacking. In this way, securing self-interest and power in an interaction is established by showing self-confidence, which is in turn equated with a lack of defensiveness or overt aggressiveness. Power thus becomes divorced from the outward display of hostility and from the defence of one's honour, responses that have traditionally been central to definitions of masculinity. Self-control means that one is governed by calculated reason and that one is predictable and consistent in one's interactions.

To conclude, as corporations grew bigger and created more layers of management between employees and upper management and as American society became oriented toward a service economy (on its way to the so-called post-industrial society), a scientific discourse dealing primarily with persons, interactions and emotions was the natural candidate to shape the language of selfhood in the workplace. The psychological discourse became prevalent in American culture for a number of reasons. One was that psychologists offered a language – of persons, emotions, motivations – that seemed to correspond to and make sense of the large-scale transformations in the American workplace. Moreover, psychology claimed to provide new tools to orient oneself in the increasingly complex maze of American organisations and the American economy. As Karl Manheim put it in his classic 1929 study *Ideology and Utopia*, 'it is not men in general who think, or even isolated individuals who do the thinking, but men in certain groups who have developed a particular *style of thought in an endless series of responses to certain typical situations characterising their common position*' (Mannheim, 1929 [1936]: 3; emphasis added). Because corporate hierarchy demanded an orientation to persons as well as to commodities, and because work in the corporation demanded coordination and cooperation, the management of the self in the workplace increasingly became a 'problem'. It was only natural that the response to this 'problem' would be addressed by psychologists. Psychologists acted as 'knowledge specialists' who developed ideas and methods to improve human relations and who thereby transformed the 'structure of knowledge or consciousness that shapes the thinking of laypersons' (Arditi and Swidler, 1994: 306).

With the recession of the late 1920s and the steep rise in unemployment rates that accompanied the recession, work was becoming more uncertain (Kimmel, 1996). In this context, the discourse of psychology offered symbolic guidance and seemed to secure both labour's and management's interests. On the management's side, psychologists seemed to promise that they would increase profits, fight labour unrest, organise manager–worker relationships in a non-confrontational way, and neutralise class struggles by casting them in the benign language of emotions and personality. On the workers' side, the language of psychology seemed far more democratic than previous theories of leadership because it now made good leadership depend on personality and on the capacity to understand others rather than on social position. After all, in the previous system of control over the workers, 'workers had to submit to the authority of foremen in issues such as hiring, firing, pay, promotion, and workload. Most foremen used a "drive system," a method involving strict supervision and verbal abuse' (Shenhav, 1998: 21). In addition, psychologists paid attention to workers' critiques of the workplace and seemed to be concerned with the satisfaction of their needs in an unprecedented way. While most sociologists have viewed the early uses of psychology inside the corporation as a form of subtle and hence powerful control, I suggest instead that it held a significant appeal for workers because, at least at face value, it seemed to give audience to workers' critiques and to democratise what had been relations of dominance and subordination between workers and managers (this is why Mayo's intervention at General Electric was so effective). Such seeming democratisation was associated with the new belief that one's personality, deemed to be independent of social status, was the key to managerial success and that managers needed to attend to the human dimension of work relationships.[12]

Finally, the psychological discourse shaped and framed the cultural repertoires through which both labour and management understood, communicated and acted upon not only their emotions but also, and perhaps most crucially, their interests. Interests, like other motives for action, are culture bound. The idea that self-interest should guide action was not self-evident, for psychologists had to muster a battery of arguments and rhetoric to convince workers, managers and would-be managers that they should act for its sake. Far from being pre- or a-cultural, interests are made meaningful through public vocabularies and indeed were instilled as a principle of action by the many experts and professionals who entered the corporate field (psychologists, organisational consultants, and so on). These findings accord with Weber's famous claim that 'ideas have, like switchmen, determined the tracks along which action has been pushed by the dynamic of interest' (Weber, 1922 [1993]: 280). But they go even further and suggest that the very notion of 'interest', far from being an invariant property of social action, was in fact intensively culturally elaborated by psychologists. In other words, psychologists not only made emotions central to the workplace but relentlessly codified the notion of self-interest itself, arguing that mature individuals are defined by their ability to secure their self-interest, in turn expressed by self-control and by the capacity to forgo expressions of power.

7.9 THE COMMUNICATIVE ETHIC AS THE SPIRIT OF THE CORPORATION

Knowledge systems, no less than morality plays, stories or myths, offer cultural prescriptions and models of behaviour. In fact, one of the reasons why knowledge is such an intrinsic part of culture is that many knowledge systems offer an image of the good or worthy person as well as a set of the rules through which one is to become such a person. The different theories that were elaborated by popular psychologists writing guidebooks on management converged around the 1970s in one cultural model that has become widely pervasive and authoritative, namely, the model of 'communication'. Psychologists increasingly refined the rules of emotional conduct by principally reformulating the cognitive and linguistic rules of interaction and by offering a model of sociability based on 'communication'. This model explains conflict and problems as the result of imperfect emotional and linguistic communication; conversely, it views adequate linguistic and emotional communication as the key to achieving desirable relationships.

The model of 'communication' aims at providing linguistic and emotional techniques to reconcile diverging imperatives: namely, to assert and express the self, yet cooperate with others; to understand others' motives, yet manipulate oneself and others to reach desired goals; and to be self-controlled, yet personable and accessible. Communication is thus an 'ethical substance' in which it is impossible to separate self-interest from attention to others.

The main aspect of the self concerned with moral conduct is how one appears to others through language and emotional expression. According to the ethos of communication put forth by popular psychology, a prerequisite of good relationships with others demands that one evaluates oneself 'objectively', which implies that one ought to understand how one appears to others. Numerous guidebooks on successful leadership prescribe that one evaluate and compare one's self-image with the image others have of oneself. As an advice book puts it: 'Without the management training course [a communication workshop] Mike's career might well have remained stagnant, not because he lacks ability but because he *didn't understand that he was giving other people the wrong impression of himself*' (Fontana, 1990: 23; emphasis added).The advice literature on successful management incessantly requires that one examine oneself as if through someone else's eyes. This self-knowledge enables one to manipulate and control oneself and others more skilfully without, however, inviting a cold or cynical approach to others. In fact, self-awareness is contiguous with the injunction to identify with others and to listen to them. As a book for leaders puts it: 'This book is designed to help managers and staff members better understand why people do the things they do and feel the way they feel. The goal is to develop the skill of stepping outside the situation to ask, "what is really going on, and why?"' (Mann, 1993: 4).

The concept and practice of communication, initially presented as a technique and as an ideal definition of personality and selfhood, are now applied to characterise the ideal corporation. For example, the giant corporation Hewlett Packard advertises itself in this way: 'HP is a firm where one can breathe a spirit of communication, a strong spirit of inter-relations, where people communicate, where you go towards others. It is an affective relationship' (Aubert and de Gaulejac, 1991: 148). In fact, communication has come to define the model of corporate selfhood in general:

> In a recent survey of recruiters from companies with more than 50,000 employees, communication skills were cited as the single most important decisive factor in choosing managers. The survey, conducted by the University of Pittsburgh's Katz Business School, points out that communication skills, including written and oral presentations, as well as an ability to work with others, are the main factor contributing to job success.[13]

This peculiar mix of self-interest and sympathy, of attention to oneself and manipulation of others, articulates a historically new type of selfhood that I dub r*eflexive selfhood* (Giddens, 1991). A reflexive self has internalised strong mechanisms of self-control to maintain its self-interest, not through the blatant display of selfish competitiveness, but through the art of mastering social relations. A reflexive self occupies the space that makes up the modern idea of the 'individual' but is a far cry from the Robinson Crusoe prototype because it incorporates the other's point of view by imagining and identifying with it both sympathetically and strategically.

Reflexivity is woven into the very fabric of work in the contemporary corporation, which demands at once a dexterity with symbols and a fluency in transactions with others.[14] Managers operate in a complex hierarchy of signs and persons; they are managed by others and in turn manage others; they compete with equals but are constrained to build coalitions with them and to decipher the hidden cues of competitors or superiors. This dense hierarchical structure was codified by the therapeutic persuasion as requiring a reflexive self centred on the control of emotions, on the semiotic skills to decipher interactions, and on the capacity to signal (or hide) one's own moves through 'communication skills'. Psychologists have thus constructed personality as a form of symbolic currency, defined by its ability to *master, manage, and manipulate social bonds themselves.* Projecting a communicative selfhood signals at once self-mastery and the capacity to master others through a complex mix of linguistic clarity and the emotional capacity to blend opposites, such as assertiveness and recognition.

By a peculiar detour of cultural history, psychologists have articulated a language of selfhood that resuscitates Adam Smith's complex view of the self. In his *Theory of Moral Sentiments*, Smith posited that the self was split between what he called an 'impartial spectator' and a self that could sympathetically identify with the plight of another (Smith, 1759).

Two sociologists suggest that '[Smith's] idea that aggressive impulses are tempered by the internalised expectations of others creates the contemporary equation of honour and reason that help[s] pacify economic conduct' (Baxter and Margavio, 2000: 4). In his *Wealth of Nations*, Adam Smith conceived of a model of society in which each person's pursuit of his own economic self-interest would be a source of social harmony, for in a society where labour is carefully and minutely divided, individuals would all need each other and would therefore enter a civil relationship with others on the basis of their own self-interest (Smith, 1776). The ethos of communication taps directly into this model of social interaction by suggesting that it is in all people's best interest to control their emotions, to listen to each other, to communicate with each other and to exercise empathetic feelings. The deployment of rational management of people in the contemporary corporation contributes to the constitution of a complex personality structure that both masters and expresses emotions, that is both rational and sympathetic, that both masters one's self-image and is able to decipher others' motives. Thus, by an ironic twist of cultural history, the self-interested *Homo economicus* of Adam Smith has been recast by psychologists as a *Homo communicans* who reflexively monitors his words and emotions, controls his self-image, and pays tribute to the other's point of view.

The reasons why communication has become so central in the definition of competent corporate selfhood are many and have to do with the transformations of capitalism. With the changing normative structure entailed in the democratisation of social relationships, procedural rules had to be set up to reconcile the increasingly hierarchical structure of corporate organisations with the increasing democratisation of social relations. Moreover, the increasing complexity of the economic environment, the ever-growing pace of new technologies, and the consequent rapid obsolescence of skills made criteria for success changing and contradictory, and had the effect of overburdening the self with tensions and uncertainties and of making it solely responsible for managing them. Communication has thus become an emotional skill for navigating an environment fraught with uncertainties and conflicting imperatives and collaborating with others. Finally, the flexibility demanded by the therapeutic persuasion has an affinity with the flexibility required in the so-called post-Fordist era. Indeed, in the 1970s and 1980s, capitalism moved toward customised production, decentralisation of production, and the creation of a core workforce that had multiple skills (Kumar, 2005), all of which placed much greater burdens on the self in an unstable economic environment.

It is also in the late 1970s, early 1980s that the concept of social entrepreneurship was coined and popularised via the work of Ashoka. Its founder, William Drayton, identifies three skills that people must have in such an economic environment: 'applied empathy, teamwork, and leadership . . . applied empathy [requires that] that we contemplate each action, we must comprehend how it will impact everyone at several removes around us and long into the future – and then guide our behaviour accordingly' (Drayton, 2006: 10). Drayton argues that this skill is necessary in a complex environment where rules 'are increasingly in conflict, changing, or have yet to be developed' (ibid.). This observation raises the question if and how the culture of management and its 'feminine' model of empathy and emotional control have been and are transferred to the world of entrepreneurship that had traditionally been associated with masculine virtues of conquering and fighting.[15]

7.10   CONCLUSION

The above discussion points to an important paradox. The French sociologist Pierre Bourdieu has suggested that one of the concepts most contrary to *interest* is not so much disinterestedness as *indifference.* Bourdieu's characterisation of indifference corresponds quite closely to the kind of emotional life advocated by the therapeutic ideal of self-control. 'To be indifferent is to be unmoved by the game: like Buridan's donkey . . . Indifference is an ethical state of non-preference as well as a state of knowledge in which I am not capable of differentiating the stakes proposed . . . *Illusio* is the very opposite of ataraxy: it is to be invested, taken in and by the game' (Bourdieu and Wacquant, 1992: 116). The therapeutic ethic of self-control presents itself as a vast cultural attempt to instil in actors a way of playing the game without seeming to be moved by it. Its aim is to instil an indifferent attitude, an attitude of not being taken in by the game, with the goal of securing one's best interests. While the therapeutic person dwells excessively on his or her emotions, he or she is simultaneously required not to be moved by them.

   Thus the therapeutic ethos offers the following sociological puzzle: it fosters a form of sociability based on communication; it encourages a strong individualism based on enlightened self-interest, but always with the aim of maintaining the self within a network of social relations. The therapeutic ethos fosters a procedural approach to one's emotional life as opposed to a thick or substantive one. Shame, anger, guilt, offended honour, admiration are all emotions defined by moral content and by a substantive view of relationships, and these emotions have been progressively made into signs of emotional immaturity or dysfunction.

   What is commanded instead is the capacity to control emotions and to master the rules of *communicating* with a wide variety of others: to be 'emotional', as this therapeutic adjective suggests, is to disturb the expected smoothness of social interactions. In sociological terms, however, being 'emotional' simply means foregrounding one's relationship with another: anger, contempt, admiration and affection are the names we give to feelings about social relationships when these relations are threatened or at stake. This means that the precondition for 'communication' or 'cooperation' is, paradoxically, the *suspension of one's emotional entanglements in a social relationship*. To the extent that emotions point to the entanglement of the self in a social relation, they also point to one's dependence on others. Emotional control thus points to a model of sociability in which one must display the ability to remove oneself from the reach of others in order to better cooperate with them. The emotional control of the type propounded by the therapeutic persuasion is at once the mark of a *disengaged self* (busy with self-mastery and control) and of a *sociable self* – bracketing emotions for the sake of entering into relations with others.

NOTES

1. Goffman, quoted in MacIntyre (1984: 115).
2. The injunction to self-control is a motif that has accompanied the development of what is conventionally called Western civilisation. Temperance (or emotional control) appears to be one of the cardinal categories which, from Plato onward, has been consistently viewed as the precondition of the exercise of discernment as well as the precondition for cooperation. With a few noticeable exceptions in the history of Western thought, almost no thinker, whether inspired by Augustinian faith or straightforward rationalism, has seriously objected to the necessity to control one's emotions. 'There is hardly any variety of moral theory – whether developed in terms of law and duty or in terms of happiness and virtue, whether appealing to *a priori* principles or to criteria of utility empirically applied – which does not recommend the discipline of desire by reason and which does not condemn sensuality, self-indulgence, unchecked appetites, or passions run wild' (Adler, 1952: 684). Indeed, whether what is advocated is religious modesty, rational control, Aristotelian moderation or Macchiavelian strategic thinking, emotional control has been deemed central to social existence, spiritual progress, virtue and social success.
3. Firm owners increasingly pushed away contractors, which until then controlled the production process, and gained control of the workers, of the firing and hiring.
4. An opinion of the time makes this clear: 'Many a man is entirely incapable of assuming responsibility. He is success as the led, but not as the leader' quoted in Bendix (1956: 259).
5. Quoted in Bendix (1956: 278).
6. Quoted in Bendix (1956: 278).
7. Because Shenhav focused almost exclusively on engineers, he was led to over-generalize from their own rhetoric to the corporation in general. Indeed engineers tended to think of men as machines to be carefully monitored, and of the corporation as an impersonal system to operate.
8. Frederick Taylor himself was not impervious to the emotional atmosphere of the shop floor as 'talked about his shock at the choleric surliness of many factory workers'. The mental revolution propounded by Frederick Taylor targeted the workers' moods and emotions no less than their work performance (Stearns, 1994: 122).

9. Warren Susman has documented the passage from a 'character' oriented society to a personality-oriented culture (Susman, 1984). He confirms that the emphasis on 'personality' had corporate origins and that the psychologists' intervention in the cultural arena made 'personality' something to 'play' with, 'work on' and manipulate.
10. See in particular Trahair's biography of Elton Mayo (Trahair, 1984).
11. For works that accomplish this task very well, see, for example, Guillen (1994), Shenhav (1995) and Wren (1979).
12. Elton Mayo himself was no democrat, but his ideas could be easily interpreted as such (O'Connor, 1999).
13. www.mindtools.com/CommSkll/CommunicationIntro.htm, last accessed 28 July 2008.
14. As an advice book on corporate success puts it, 'whereas the skills needed to make a success at Level 1 are relatively straightforward [relationships with subordinates], those from Level 2 [with equals] onwards become increasingly complex' (see Fontana, 1990: 12).
15. With respect to the motivations of the entrepreneur, Schumpeter writes of 'the dream and the will to found a private kingdom, usually, though not necessarily, also a dynasty . . . the will to conquer: the impulse to fight, to prove oneself superior to others, to succeed for the sake, not of the fruits, but of success itself . . . the joy of creating, of getting things done, or simply of exercising one's energy and ingenuity' (Schumpeter, 1934: 93). See also the chapter by Swedberg in this volume.

REFERENCES

Adler, M.J. (ed.) (1952), *The Great Ideas: A Synopticon of Great Books of the Western World*, Chicago: Encyclopaedia Britannica.

Arditi, J. and A. Swidler (1994), 'The new sociology of knowledge', *Annual Review of Sociology*, **20**, 305–29.

Aubert, N. and V. de Gaulejac (1991), *Le Cout de l'Excellence*, Paris: Seuil.

Baxter, V. and A. Margavio (2000), 'Honor, status, and aggression into economic exchange', *Sociological Theory*, **13** (3), 1–18.

Beach, L.R. and E.L. Clarck (1959), *Psychology in Business*, New York: McGraw-Hill.

Bendix, R. (1956), *Work and Authority in Industry: Ideologies of Management in the Course of Industrialization*, New York: J. Wiley & Sons.

Boltanski, L. and E. Chiapello (1999), *Le Nouvel Esprit du Capitalisme*, Paris: Gallimard.

Bornstein, D. (2004), *How to Change the World: Social Entrepreneurs and the Power of New Ideas*, Oxford and New York: Oxford University Press.

Bourdieu, P. and L. Wacquant (1992), *An Invitation to Reflexive Sociology*, Chicago, IL: University of Chicago Press.

Carey, A. (1967), 'The Hawthorne studies: a radical criticism', *American Sociological Review*, **32** (3), 403–16.

Carnegie, D. (1937 [1981]), *How to Win Friends and Influence People*, New York: Simon & Schuster.

Chandler, A.D. (1977), *The Visible Hand: The Managerial Revolution in American Business*, Cambridge, MA: Harvard Belknap.

Curran, A. (1985), 'Is it OK to sob on the job?', *Redbook*, March, 115.

Dobbin, F. (2004), 'The sociological view of the economy', in F. Dobbin (ed.), *The Economic Sociology: A Reader*, Princeton, VJ: Princeton University Press, pp. 1–46.

Drayton, B. (2006), 'Everyone a changemaker: social entrepreneurship's ultimate Goal', *Innovations – Technology, Governance, Globalization*, Winter, 1–32.

Elias, N. (1939 [1968]), *The Civilizing Process: The History of Manners and State Formation and Civilization. trans. Edmund Jephcott*, Oxford: Blackwell.

Fontana, D. (1990), *Social Skills at Work*, Leicester and New York: British Psychological Society, Routledge.

Giddens, A. (1991), *Modernity and Self-identity: Self and Society in the Late Modern Age*, Cambridge: Polity Press.

Guillen, M. (1994), *Models of Management: Work, Authority, and Organization in a Comparative Perspective*, Chicago, IL: University of Chicago Press.

Hemphill, C.D. (1998), 'Class, gender, and the regulation of emotional expression in revolutionary era conduct literature', in P.N. Stearns and J. Lewis (eds), *An Emotional History of the United States*, New York: New York University Press, pp. 33–51.

Hochschild, A. (1983), *The Managed Heart: The Commercialization of Human Feeling*, Berkeley and Los Angeles, CA: University of California Press.

Illouz, E. (2006), *Cold Intimacies: The Making of Emotional Capitalism*, Oxford: Polity Press.

Jackall, R. (1988), *Moral Mazes: The World of Corporate Managers*, New York: Oxford University Press.

Jarrard, L. (1956), 'Empathy: the concept and industrial applications', *Personnel Psychology*, **9** (2), 157–67.

Kimmel, M. (1996), *Manhood in America: A Cultural History*, New York: Free Press.

Kumar, K. (2005), *From Post-Industrial to Post-Modern Society: New Theories of the Contemporary World*, Malden, MA; Oxford: Blackwell.

Kunda, G. (1992), *Engineering Culture: Control and Commitment in a High-Tech Corporation*, Philadelphia, PA: Temple University Press.

MacIntyre, A. (1984), *After Virtue: A Study in Moral Theory*, Notre Dame, IN: University of Notre Dame Press.

Mann, R.B. (1993), *Behavior Mismatch: How to Manage 'Problem' Employees Whose Actions Don't Match Your Expectations*, New York: Amacom Books.

Mannheim, K. (1929 [1936]), *Ideology and Utopia: An Introduction to the Sociology of Knowledge*, New York: Harcourt Brace Jovanovich.

Mayo, E. (1933), *The Human Problems of an Industrial Civilization*, New York: Macmillan.

Mayo, E. (1949), *The Social Problems of an Industrial Civilization*, London: Routledge & Kegan Paul.

Mills, C.W. (1951), *White Collar: The American Middle Classes*, New York: Oxford University Press.

O'Connor, E.S. (1999), 'The politics of management thought: a case study of the Harvard Business School and the Human Relations School', *Academy of Management Review*, **24** (1), 117–31.

Roos, V. and R.D. Ashmore (1993), 'The multifaceted self: androgyny reassessed by open-ended self-descriptions', *Social Psychology Quarterly*, **56** (4), 278–87.

Rosenfeld, P., R. Giacalone and C. Riordan (1995), *Impression Management in Organizations*, New York: Routledge.

Schumpeter, J.A. (1934), *The Theory of Economic Development. Translation of the 2nd edition by Redvers Opie*, Cambridge, MA: Harvard University Press.

Shenhav, Y. (1995), 'From chaos to systems: the engineering foundations of organization theory', *Administrative Science Quarterly*, **40**, 557–85.

Shenhav, Y. (1998), *Manufacturing Rationality*, Oxford: Oxford University Press.

Smith, A. (1759 [2004]), *The Theory of Moral Sentiments*, Cambridge: Cambridge University Press.

Smith, A. (1776 [1910]), *The Wealth Of Nations*, London: J.M. Dent.

Smith, Roger Winston (ed.) (1971), *Guilt: Man and Society*, New York: Anchor Books.

Stagner, R. (1948), 'Psychological aspects of industrial conflict: I. Perception', *Personnel Psychology*, **1**, 131–44.

Stearns, P. (1994), *American Cool: Constructing the 20th Century Emotional Style*, New York: New York University Press.

Stearns, C.Z. and P.N. Stearns (1986), *Anger: The Struggle for Emotional Control in America's History*, Chicago, IL: University of Chicago Press.

Susman, W.I. (1984), *Culture as History: The Transformation of American Society in the Twentieth Century*, New York: Pantheon Books.

Trahair, R. (1984), *The Humanist Temper: The Life and Work of Elton Mayo*, New Brunswick, NJ: Transaction Books.

Ury, W. (1991), *Getting Past No: Negotiating with Difficult People*, New York: Bantam Books.

Weber, M. (1922 [1993]), *The Sociology of Religion*, Boston, MA: Beacon Press.

Whyte, W.H. (1956), *The Organization Man*, New York: Doubleday.

Wren, D.A. (1979), *The Evolution of Management Thought*, New York: Wiley.

8. Forgotten antecedents: entrepreneurship, ideology and history

Rob Boddice

'Well! I've often seen a cat without a grin', thought Alice; 'but a grin without a cat! It's the most curious thing I ever saw in all my life!' (Carroll, 1865 [2007]: 94)

8.1 INTRODUCTION: SOCIAL ENTREPRENEURSHIP – A GRIN WITHOUT A CAT

Judging by the historical perspective of contemporary scholars in the field, social entrepreneurship is an entirely new and unprecedented activity. Researchers struggle to define the concept and its associated activities, often trying to determine the novel, contemporary circumstances that gave rise to this unfamiliar phenomenon; sponsors of social entrepreneurs, meanwhile, herald the heretofore unseen sweeping of the field by heroic personalities who succeed as entrepreneurs and as social developers/reformers where governments and charities have previously failed.[1] Not only that, but social entrepreneurs are credited with a unique vision, seeing the roots of problems beyond their symptoms, and forming ingenious strategies to overcome difficulties and implement change that is valuable, sustainable and profitable. These people are, as Ashoka points out, of exceptional ethical fibre. Social entrepreneurs, it would seem, are at the forefront of human evolution, and their existence was scarcely possible until now.[2]

It will be my contention that such a view really just presents the symptoms without the causes. The apparent newness of social-entrepreneurial activity belies the traditions upon which it rests, and panegyrics in its favour (often put forward by sponsoring groups) tend to draw a veil over the substance and variety of motives and ideologies carried by social entrepreneurs themselves. It is this current tendency to herald the originality of social entrepreneurship that leads me, inspired by Ronan MacDonald's thoughts on the Geist of capitalism in Weberian theory, to identify such rhetoric as the 'grin without a cat' (MacDonald, 1971). Social entrepreneurship does come from somewhere, but as yet there has been little research as to its origins, the traditions it draws on and the kinds of ideology employed, sometimes unconsciously, in the execution of it.

A brief survey is revealing of the neglect in this regard. Social entrepreneurship's grandest protagonist, Bill Drayton, chair and Chief Executive Officer (CEO) of Ashoka, claimed that in about 1700 'the West broke out from 1,200 years of stagnation', and that 'for the last 300 years this profound innovation [entrepreneurial/competitive business] in how humans organise themselves has been the defining, decisive historical force at work'. But he follows what is already far too broad a brushstroke really to mean anything with a wildly inaccurate and historically nonsensical statement: 'However, until 1980, this transformation bypassed the social half of the world's operations.' Save for Florence Nightingale and the 'anti-slavery leagues', mere islands, he tells us, the social sector languished without change, suffering from 'poor self-esteem and élan' (Drayton, 2006a: 5–6). Of course, anyone with any knowledge at all of social history in the West from 1700 to 1980 would know that this is untrue, and historians might baulk at the way in which a tendentious historical 'analysis' is put forward with the specific intention of promoting a particular socio-political vision.[3] Even where there *is* acknowledgement of the precedents set by nineteenth-century entrepreneurs, the analysis is curiously naive: 'What distinguished them and the sector they were creating was the object of this entrepreneurial fervor: not the accumulation of wealth or the production of goods, but the betterment of their fellow men.'[4] The question, 'according to what standard?' is left out of the equation, and we are left with a motley crew of imperialists, evangelical Christians of various denominations, priests and Methodist ministers, aristocrats and industry magnates whose ideological and self-interested motives are left out of the picture.

Drayton's 'islands' serve as a case in point. Florence Nightingale, for example, is described by David Bornstein as an example of an 'ethically driven social entrepreneur' in a chapter on her life in his book *How to Change the World* (Bornstein, 2007: 47). Interestingly, the chapter immediately precedes the one on Drayton himself and begins by connecting the two: when Drayton 'calls someone a leading entrepreneur, he is describing a specific and rare personality type . . . He means someone like Florence Nightingale' (Bornstein, 2007: 42). It is extraordinary that the term 'ethical' can supplant the term 'religious', and that Nightingale's determination to make change can be seen as an end in itself, not as a representation of the need to serve God. Florence Nightingale received her 'calling' to God's service, according to her own private notes, on 7 February 1837

(Woodham-Smith, 1950: 17) and even spent considerable time writing *Suggestions for Thought to the Searchers after Truth among the Artizans of England* (1860), a work of her own radical theology which found (some) favour and attention with the likes of J.S. Mill and Benjamin Jowett (Woodham-Smith, 1950: 349–51). The social benefits that Nightingale's work brought about are not in question here, but it is to misrepresent the past to extract it from its context. To call Nightingale an 'ethically driven social entrepreneur' is simply an anachronism.

Such fantasies would be frivolous if they were not dangerous. What appears to be profoundly new, or value neutral, may well just be the 'grin without a cat', and if we are adequately to assess what social entrepreneurship is, and what it is good (or bad) for, then it is imperative that we know about the body of the cat – the historical forces and ideologies behind entrepreneurial activity – even if at first glance it does not appear to be there. Any 'movement' that refuses to confess or acknowledge its ideological foundations – and let us be clear from the start, social entrepreneurship does have ideological foundations, however implicit – or to pay heed to historical example, or to learn from the mistakes and misadventures of the past, is not sufficiently accountable.[5] I do not mean the term 'ideology' to be employed as a pejorative (although it could be), but simply to draw attention to the fact that no ideology can claim universal, unequivocal support. Even the claim that social entrepreneurs act in such a way as to avoid partisan politics and provide basic services begs a question, first, of the kind of political outlook implied by being non-partisan in different political climates; and second, of the ethnographical and historical assumptions brought to bear on such a concept as 'basic services'. No social action is value neutral, and acting independently does not ensure that you act accountably. Who oversees social entrepreneurs? On what basis are decisions made if not by example? Can any activity make a claim for social virtue if it is not cognisant of the historical forces that have shaped a given 'problem'? Moreover, if social entrepreneurs and their sponsoring organisations make no attempt to see which forces have produced and shaped themselves, if they refuse to concede that those forces have been driven by particular ideologies, then the tendentiousness of their activities will remain veiled and open to cynical and suspicious attack.

Up until the late 1950s there existed an active field of research in the history of entrepreneurship, later absorbed in 'business studies' and consequentially stripped of an historical awareness.[6] There is some hope that the subject is seriously back on the agenda, with the opening in 2003 of the Rock Center at Harvard Business School.[7] Yet it is striking that the cutting-edge of research in the field of entrepreneurship was, in the 1950s, becoming aware precisely of the social implications of the activities of entrepreneurs in the past, present and future. There was a distinct feeling that entrepreneurs were about to cast their net wider in the post-war world, and it came with some warnings. Joseph Schumpeter pointed to the inevitable social instrumentality of entrepreneurial activity, where such activity was possible:

> Naturally . . . the mere emergence of a quantitatively significant number of entrepreneurs presupposes, and its existence contributes to, a certain type of civilization and a certain state of the public mind. Entrepreneurs will be few and without great importance in situations where this activity is despised and frowned upon, and entrepreneurial success in turn will tend to change such a situation . . . [T]o some extent entrepreneurial activity impresses the stamp of its mentality upon the social organism. (Schumpeter, 1949: 81–2).

This statement came together with a warning, one which he felt was so obvious it barely needed stating, that the range of views on the importance of the entrepreneurial leader in producing economic and social change (extending from insignificance to 'nothing short of everything') all bore 'the stamp of ideological preconception' (Schumpeter, 1949: 72). The activities of entrepreneurs, their public image, and their reception in the environment in which they work, all hinged on some ideological formulation (often unstated) about the value of the entrepreneurial individual or outfit and the environment in which he, she or it worked.

In 1949 there seemed to be a widespread recognition of this fact, which was represented in the various projects that the Harvard University Research Center in Entrepreneurial History suggested should be carried out. The first of these, which so far as I can tell was *not* carried out, got right to the heart of the matter.[8] Entitled 'Entrepreneurship and economic development: a comparative study', its outline was explicit: 'Entrepreneurship is itself an historical product, not a mere response of an unchanging human nature to changing economic conditions.' The key variables in establishing the nature of entrepreneurs, it proposed, are 'those social pressures with which anthropologists deal in terms of "culture" and related notions'. It went on to note that 'very little has been done, however, to establish precisely what kinds of social pressures are important at particular times or places, or the way in which they specifically operate through personality to affect entrepreneurial performance and dynamic changes in economy and society'. The ultimate end of this project would be to guide future entrepreneurs in their policy of development in 'backward areas' by examining a range of entrepreneurial cultures dating back to the late nineteenth century, both in Europe and in Africa, as well as in India, China, and North and South America. Its two key questions were: what has been the effect, in terms of development, of entrepreneurs? What factors affect the 'characteristics of entrepreneurship'? (Research Center in Entrepreneurial History, 1949: 179–80). Social entrepreneurs and the organisations that nurture and sponsor them should, as a starting point, be fully aware that entrepreneurship is a mutable category, with a role in shaping, but also being shaped by, the social environment in which it operates. The kind of inquiry envisaged by the Harvard University Research Center in Entrepreneurial History was designed precisely to equip future entrepreneurial activities with the knowledge of the ways in which particular historical circumstances affect outcomes, with as much to learn from success as failures (see Vasi in this volume), and with a tacit recognition that a good idea is only 'good' insofar as it is congruous with the specific circumstances of time and place. The intention was not to 'use' or distort history so as to promote new ventures, but merely to better understand those cultural and political environments into which entrepreneurs might enter in the future, so as to increase the chance of success. This chapter, in drawing attention precisely to the specific historical contexts that have affected the characteristics of entrepreneurship, and to their developmental effect in those contexts, aims to show that a value neutral approach to the 'social' is impossible.[9] It should also show that, the label aside, 'social entrepreneurship' is far from a new phenomenon.

The chapter's focus on some of the apparently forgotten historical antecedents of social entrepreneurship is meant to lead to conjecture about some of the likely implications of facing up to (or not facing up to) these productive forces. Casting a wide net, temporally and geographically, I aim to show that social entrepreneurship has its roots in a variety of movements stretching back to the beginning of the industrial revolution. In chronological order, not to show their connectedness, but their ideological disparateness, these are early forms of socialism in Britain, Catholic social reform in France, early twentieth-century tycoon philanthropy in the USA, and 1960s computer construction, also in the USA. I make no claim here to have uncovered anything heretofore unknown; nor am I suggesting any direct lines of provenance – the historical intertwining of the motive to be socially developmental and to be entrepreneurial is far too complex for such a simplistic reduction. These examples are therefore merely sketches, designed to beg a question. The big question for social entrepreneurs and their sponsoring groups will be how to support a claim for being ideologically neutral when confronted with the profoundly ideologically partisan qualities exhibited by their antecedents. Historical inquiry has brought these actors to account, which is not to say that they have been judged; it is merely that their motives, aims and ambitions have been exposed and contextualised in sources other than their own rhetoric. I will suggest that social entrepreneurs should be subject to the same kind of analysis. Ultimately, the term 'social entrepreneurship' itself is challenged as being too broad an umbrella, since it masks ideological intent and hinders dissent.

8.2   INDUSTRIALISATION IN BRITAIN: ENTREPRENEURS, EDUCATORS AND SOCIALISTS

It is not a profound remark to say that the industrial revolution's most troubling 'problem' was what to 'do' with society. The indications that city populations would explode, without sufficient social infrastructure to sustain any kind of life befitting the 'civilised' world, were all too plain to see. At the same time, the countryside was being depleted of its workforce and was plunged into greater poverty than was usual. These social problems, caused precisely by the rapidity of economic change, were the chief concerns of reforming minds who valued the money-making opportunities that the industrial revolution wrought, but who could not abide the human cost. Various sketches of situations urban and rural from the late eighteenth century and throughout the nineteenth century drew stark attention to the fact that *something must be done* (Booth, 1902; Cobbett, 1830 [1967]; Disraeli, 1845 [1981]; Engels, 1844 [1999]; Malthus, 1807–24 [1986]; Mayhew, 1851–62).

The fact that such studies continued to be carried out, even gaining in depth and complexity, suggests that if anything the situation only worsened in the period. But several significant entrepreneurs developed models of social betterment that would still allow an uninterrupted flow of industrial output. These few 'organisers of change' were regarded, according to Charles Wilson, 'with the respect and even awe properly attributable to those who had been instrumental in delivering society from the fate predicted for it by Malthus' (Wilson, 1955: 129). Wilson's assessment of the situation and its solution ought to sound familiar to modern-day social entrepreneurs. Quoting Ashton's *Industrial Revolution*, Wilson agrees that:

> the central problem of the age was how to feed and clothe and employ generations of children outnumbering by far those of any other time . . . She was delivered . . . not by her rulers, but by those who, seeking no doubt their own narrow ends, had the wit and resource to devise new instruments of production and new methods of administering industry. (Wilson, 1955: 130)

These new methods of administering industry entailed new methods of alleviating or ameliorating social problems. Economic development required social innovation. Early pioneers in this regard included Matthew Boulton and Josiah Wedgwood, known for their high-quality production in conjunction with an awareness that the well-paid, well-looked-after, well-educated worker ensured the quality of that production.[10] Wilson again:

> Boulton and Wedgwood were not only cultivated men but just employers who regarded a humane code of labor relations as an efficient system of production and gave a lead to others in such matters as the provision of schemes of social welfare and education. They were imitated by scores of others even unto the second and third generations; so that even in the 1850s when elementary education was a recognized public charge, Price's Patent Candleworks were still running an elaborate and expensive set of schools for their boy and girl workers at Battersea. (Wilson, 1955: 140–41)

It has to be remembered, however, that such apparent benevolence was value and ideology laden. Wedgwood and his like had a clear notion of the ways in which the lives of workers should be *managed*, to maximise output, even if they also thought this would benefit the workforce. The working week was to be rigorously organised, strictly conforming to the rigours of the clock, to the point where the perception of time changed for the industrial classes. The working week, Monday to Saturday, so many hours a day, with leisure in allotted segments that would not impinge on production – all these factors fundamentally reoriented the way in which life was lived for the industrial masses (see Reid, 1976; 1996; Thompson, 1967). To work for one of these social benefactors no doubt led to an improvement of one's lot, but at the price of sharing their social vision (or at least not resisting it).

This vision was reinforced through the administering, but also control, of education. The notion that the provision of education should be part and parcel of industrial leadership was taken up by Robert Owen and later adopted by Owenites in the USA (see Bestor, 1948, 1950; Cole, 1925; Harrison, 1967; Podmore, 1906). Owen, a wealthy cotton spinner and captain of industry, incorporated the communal happiness of the population into the ideal of the industrial future. He was driven by his ambition 'not to be "merely a manager of cotton mills" but "to change the condition of the people"' (Taylor, 1983: xii). The bases for his experiment were the communities of New Lanark in Scotland (from about 1817) and New Harmony, Indiana (from about 1825). The communitarian project was to provide permanent employment and living conditions conducive to the happiness of the population. It was also designed to usher in the 'New Moral World', and Owen's inhabitants were to go to schools for the building of character. As one Owen scholar has pointed out, the 'regime at New Lanark was very strongly paternalist, with all the initiative and control in the hands of Owen', who was undemocratic and unsympathetic to dissent (Harrison, 1967: 86). Owen's own corpus stands as a testament to his ideological position, ending ultimately in a millenarian anticipation of the era of "'universal love" and the condemnation of "the false religions of the nations of the earth"' (Harrison, 1967: 87).[11] According to one contemporary scholar, the term 'social entrepreneur' was coined in reference to Robert Owen (Nicholls, 2006: 7[12]), but even at the time it was not clear to contemporaries of Owen that his work and ideas were 'good'. According to Taylor, Owenites 'were, and knew themselves to be, an iconoclastic vanguard whose views tended to be well in advance of even the most progressive-minded of their contemporaries' (Taylor, 1983: xiii). Moreover, 'Owenite commitment to collectivised family life and female equality set them apart from not only their conservative opponents but also from most other radical movements of the period (including Chartism)'. Given the ways in which Owen's drive to foster 'good' and sustainable social change rested on such controversial ideological foundations, does it not make sense that people who profess to be, currently, social entrepreneurs, reveal their own ideological roots? Otherwise, what guarantees do we have that social entrepreneurs and their backers will make changes that are desired by those whose society is to be changed, as opposed to changes construed from a point of view extrinsic to that society? What impact will such changes have on the broader economic and political structures of a given place? How does one distinguish between a 'good' project of sustainable change, and a 'bad' project liable to cause instability to a desirable status quo, unless the ideological backgrounds of the different points of view are fully unpacked? If our understanding of why certain social entrepreneurial activity succeeds is dependent on an appreciation of the 'contentious interactions between various social actors',[13] then this in turn requires an understanding of why there might be a difference of opinion in the first place. Presumably, one group objects to the other on the basis of a threat to its interests. The rightness or wrongness of these interests is determined by an ideological position. There is no intrinsic reason to assume that social entrepreneurs can lay claim to 'rightness' simply by dint of being social entrepreneurs.

Owen was also distinctly aware of his own profile and went to great lengths and expense to cultivate it.[14] Social reformers who followed have attracted similar observations, if not criticisms:

> The leading entrepreneurs may well turn out to have a just claim to rank high amongst those who not only swept and garnished their own houses but initiated a national process of social amelioration in an age facing insuperable problems of social adjustment. Some of the most vigorous social reformers, like Robert

Peel, Samuel Whitbread, and Harriet Martineau, came from this class and the tradition lasted down to the enlightened capitalists of the late 19th and early 20th century like the Levers and the Cadburys with their new housing schemes. It was not merely their own success but their palpable contribution to material national well-being and their consciousness of social responsibility which drew to them popular esteem and social prestige. (Wilson, 1955: 141)[15]

In short, from its beginnings, the combination of entrepreneurial activity with a social mission has been characterised by a combination of altruism and self-interest; the amelioration of local, regional or national social ills coupled with the economic drive to personal enrichment (monetary or prestige). We should not, on the one hand, *assume* that social entrepreneurs are driven by a personal or political 'philosophy' which their projects seek to concretise or generalise. But, on the other hand, we should be wise to ask if they are, and they ought to be self-aware enough to be able to tell us without reference to glib slogans (such as 'everyone a changemaker'). Those organisations who support individual social entrepreneurs ought also to hold their 'heroes' to account, as well as being upfront about their own motivations, beyond simply 'making change'.

8.3   LÉON HARMEL AND *FIN-DE-SIÈCLE* FRANCE

Across the English Channel, the striking differences in social and cultural context led to different solutions to the social ills of industrialisation. The key difference in the following case was the combination of industrialism and social conscience with staunch Catholicism.[16] Yet its beginnings have much in common with the work of those reformers who had come earlier in Britain. There was, of course, a strong and growing culture of socialism, but social Catholics tended to define themselves precisely against this 'godless' movement (Misner, 1991: 4). In language which again sounds strikingly familiar to Drayton-esque descriptions of today's social-entrepreneur set, Joan Coffey describes the social situation in *fin-de-siècle* France and the motivation of one of the key social Catholics of the era, Léon Harmel:

> *La belle époque* was made to order for the privileged set, while the lower classes, victimised by the industrial revolution, waited impatiently for the government to gradually ameliorate their living and working conditions. Not willing to stand by until the government enacted labor reform, Harmel began earlier and operated amid the political, economic, and social vortex of the times. (Coffey, 2002: 2)[17]

Harmel was, like Owen, a mill owner with a passionate care for the condition of his employees. But unlike Owen, Harmel's social mission was driven by his devout Catholicism and his personal ties to Rome. In the Val-des-Bois, the location of Harmel's mill, he established a Christian corporation with a 'family wage and factory' council. There were also Catholic worker circles and factory-worker 'pilgrimages' to Rome. Harmel instituted Christian democratic congresses, a 'factory chaplain project' and a programme of Social Weeks for young clergy, as well as a 'fraternal union' for commercial and industrial workers. He also played a key role in the Christian trade unions (Coffey, 2002: 5). Harmel's vision consisted in the triumvirate of family unity, worker happiness and the Lord's work. While Coffey points out that 'his deep religious faith was the inspiration for social reform', she might also have pointed out that inclusion in Harmel's social project entailed acquiescence (at least publicly) in his values (Coffey, 2002: 6). His method of alleviating social problems actually served to deepen the division of *les deux Frances*: 'clerical versus anticlerical, churched versus unchurched'. Harmel's project therefore served as a launching pad for attacks against the 'positivist bourgeoisie as well as sorties out into the great hostile portions of the working class' (Misner, 1991: 133). Nevertheless, Coffey makes the point implicitly, as Harmel's religious and social missions were always fully intertwined. He:

> deemed essential the study of religious doctrine and contemporary social problems if truth were to successfully combat error and if successful proselytizing were to occur; this became the impetus for Harmel's involvement with workers' study groups in *L'Oeuvre des Cercles Catholiques d'Ouvriers* and *Les Cercles Chrétiens d'Études Sociales*. (Coffey, 2002: 43)

The very definition of the social problem was, for Harmel, attributable to a lack of religious observance that ought to have been key to ensuring the smooth process of industrial development. If material existence was to be difficult, moral rectitude could at least provide a way of dealing with it, and perhaps ultimately an answer to it. The way out of poverty was the sanctity of the family under conditions of fair employment. The family was sanctified through God; the employer was benevolent according to his own piety. Harmel therefore put together the cause and solution to the problem under the common head of religion. 'Pauperism', he thought, 'was a product of "industrialization without religion and without faith. It united material misery with moral abasement and was the incurable malady of modern society"' (Coffey 2002, 26). Through religious education, a stable home life, and a secure and accountable working life, society's ills could be ironed out. Much like Owen concluded, the answer was in education, but it would be education in the mode of Harmel and with the stamp of Rome. Its results were noteworthy:

With increased literacy and political enfranchisement, with increased wages and benefits, with greater worker representation and avenues to discuss grievances with management, the lines between the *grands* and the *petits* became less distinct for society in general and Harmel in particular with the passage of time. (Coffey, 2002: 44)

Where today's social entrepreneurs are working in religious idioms (still true even where they are not), Cho's concern about the particular vision of society that a reformer holds is especially valid: 'if "society" is more fragmented and conflictual than the notion of a discursively achievable consensus suggests, [social entrepreneurship] might also include initiatives that divide rather than integrate' (Cho, 2006: 43). Harmel's cause may have been worthy, but it was not inclusive. His social 'goods', his motivations, energy, and successes were all couched in terms of his ideology. The ultimate vindication of the project of social Catholics was the issue, by Pope Leo XIII, of the social encyclical, *Rerum novarum*, upon which Harmel instituted study groups (Coffey, 2002: 5; Misner, 1991: 4 and ch. 11). For those suffering from social problems who did not share their faith, vision and allegiances, we can only assume that the 'problem' was in part exacerbated by social Catholics themselves. To guard against this takes a remarkable degree of self-reflection on the part of the social entrepreneur. The extent to which social entrepreneurial endeavour necessarily entails some form of ideological imposition, as well as the degree to which social development has a 'waste product' of social alienation, ought always to be at the forefront of the social entrepreneur's mind.

8.4   HENRY FORD, TYCOON PHILANTHROPIST[18]

If the historical antecedents so far mentioned push the boundaries of what social entrepreneurship might be and from where it came, the idea of including one of America's foremost business tycoons would perhaps raise the accusation of having gone too far. But why is someone like Henry Ford not considerable as a social entrepreneur? After all, he completely revolutionised the way in which the whole of society *moved*. His product was cheap, desirable and undoubtedly made things 'better' according to his own vision. It mobilised the workforce, especially in Detroit and permanently changed the face of transportation. Was he an entrepreneur? Yes. Did he have a vision of society working in a different, improved, way? Yes. Did he realise this in part through tremendous personal charisma and force? Yes. He may well be suitably classified as an old-fashioned Victorian moralist who believed in hard work and laissez-faire economics, but this temporal and ideological position surely no more disqualifies him than it would disqualify anyone else. He fits the Weberian mould perfectly[19] and is also undeniably a social entrepreneur by modern standards, if not for the changes he wrought in the world of transport, then through the social services and 'benefits' he provided through economically innovative and sustainable means.

Ford's chief social achievement (other than making affordable cars) was the introduction of the $5 day in 1914, doubling wages for his employees.[20] He led the field in changing industrial standards of pay and conditions. His social improvements, however, were mitigated by the conditions his employees had to meet in order to benefit from them. Much as in Harmel's and Owen's cases, there was a price to pay to be included in a better social future, and this, generally speaking, was moral conformity to the standards of the entrepreneur.

Watts has succinctly enumerated the many sociological conditions, based largely on Ford's own backward-looking Victorian morality, to be met in order to qualify for the $5 day: 'the employee needed to demonstrate that he did not drink alcohol or physically mistreat his family or have boarders in his home, and that he regularly deposited money in a savings account, maintained a clean home, and had a good moral character' (Watts, 2005: 200–201). To ensure these criteria were met, Ford's team of investigators visited employees' homes and judged them, advised them, and made decisions instrumental to their future lives, serving Ford's 'inclination to manufacture men as well as cars' (Watts, 2005: 203–5). The benefits of the scheme to Ford's employees were no doubt enough to make conformity to it worthwhile, but today's social entrepreneurs might well be obligated to count the costs of such a scheme. One man's vision of a social 'problem' and his corresponding set of solutions according to no other standard than his own (or those of his own culture or class) would be insufficient, today, to justify acting. It is irrelevant, in this case, that Ford was motivated by profit, and naive to say that he was *only* motivated by profit. Ford's social development ideals were as important as his drive to manufacture. This, by itself, makes the case relevant for current social entrepreneurs. The case becomes even more relevant if we are to critically assess the accountability structures (or lack thereof) in the 'hybrid value-added chain' work promoted by Ashoka and the like, which encourages the for-profit finance sector to collaborate with the 'citizen sector' (Drayton, 2006a: 17–24).

8.5   WILLIAM NORRIS, CIVIL RIGHTS AND COMPUTER EDUCATION[21]

My final example, though the most recent, is probably the least known. Nevertheless, I make no claim to have discovered the plight of this social entrepreneur. I use the term in the case of William Norris with no fear of anachronism, since his methods and business model look typically social entrepreneurial. Norris was a successful high-tech computer entrepreneur, stirred by the racial hatred in the USA and the social difficulties this wrought. His solution was to take his business to the poor (and black) community and operate it from there, fostering trust, jobs and social inclusion.

The first of these endeavours came in the north side of Minneapolis in 1967, precisely to aid the integration of the black community. Norris was clear that charity did not work. He 'regarded most non-profit organisations as ineffectual because they palliated the symptoms of social ills rather than addressing the causes' (O'Toole, 1998: 285). In stark contrast to the general movement away from the cities of growing businesses, which advantaged those who could afford to move their domestic lives accordingly, Norris shied away from the usual suburban and inaccessible location of manufacturing plants and instead opened shop directly within the community whose problems he sought to alleviate. He reformed the application process so as to stress the applicant's future rather than the past, and made the plant integral to the business so as to demonstrate its long-term importance and to stress its permanence (O'Toole, 1998: 282–5). By 1969, 70 per cent of the 412 employees at this plant were on the official US Department of Labor's list as 'certifiably disadvantaged' (O'Toole, 1998: 286). This initial success prompted more development, and further expansion deliberately targeted the poorest neighbourhoods. At the same time, Norris was pioneering education by computer software, so as to try to improve the general educational lot of American youth (O'Toole, 1998: 291–4).

Norris's business ambitions eventually added up to nought. The pressures of international competition and a general business-world lack of support emanating from Wall Street made the going particularly tough. 'Addressing social needs takes time' Norris said, but it also takes a favourable climate (O'Toole, 1998: 297). The business world was not interested in Norris's social mission, only profit. Yet the obscurity into which Norris fell still left a legacy of employee assistance programmes, mothers' hours, day care and telecommuting for the handicapped (O'Toole, 1998: 299). This social entrepreneurial programme failed but it pointed the way to the future.

The irony, however, is in Norris' motive. Norris, too, was interested in profit. He was in business to make money. His attempts to integrate black communities into the (white) 'American Way', his implicit entry into civil rights politics and his unflinching approach to the raw nerve of modern American life, all this he did because for him the bottom line was clear: he thought business was impossible in a society which was 'burning', some-times literally. Profit was the underlying motive, because a society that worked (in both senses) would ultimately make business better. Profit is not value neutral. A profit motive is ideological. The 'fixing' of social prob-lems is therefore not free of the risk of creating new ones. Even for social entrepreneurs like Norris there are searching, self-reflective questions to be asked concerning what 'problem' is being solved, and what problems, in turn, that might *create*. This is no less true for social entrepreneurs who have no obvious profit motive, in the financial sense. It is, in fact, a broader point about the formulation 'society will be better if . . .'. Whose vision of society is this? Who is included/excluded by it? Against what and whose standards is the term 'better' placed? Posing these questions to Norris's case reveals the ethnocentrism, however well intentioned, of his definition of 'better'. Do social entrepreneurs and their promoters ask these questions enough? Who holds them to account?

8.6   CONCLUSION: FINDING A CAT FOR THE GRIN

The motive of social entrepreneurs, and in particular of those organisa-tions which exist to promote them, remains unclear. This curious mix of altruism and solipsism which desires to foster sustained social change while at the same time, presumably, making a living for the agent, still begs a question of 'Why?' Even if the social entrepreneur's motive is to 'make change' (for which I read, 'do good'), this motive's status as an end in itself is questionable. From where does the desire to 'make change' or to 'do good' come? Furthermore, why execute this desire as an entrepreneur (as opposed to a social worker, charitable volunteer, or any one of countless other 'do-gooding' idioms)?

Ronan MacDonald offers one possibility in his work outlining the con-nections between the social theories of Max Weber and J.A. Schumpeter. *The Protestant Ethic and the Spirit of Capitalism* argued that the religious 'calling' remained as the Geist of capitalism after religious fervour had been swept away: this was the 'grin without the cat' with which I began this chapter (MacDonald, 1971: 79; Weber, 1930 [1992]). In Weber's words, MacDonald reminds us, it was feasible that a 'man exists for the sake of his business instead of the reverse' (MacDonald, 1971: 78–9). Nevertheless, for both Weber and Schumpeter, the man of innovation was of 'unusually strong character', had 'clarity of vision and ability to act', had a 'capac-ity for making decisions' and the 'vision to evaluate forcefully' (the first two are Weber's, the latter two Schumpeter's): all strong qualities of the entrepreneur (MacDonald, 1971: 78).

Why should social entrepreneurship not acknowledge the possibility that it is the latest part of this process in which the motivations in business enterprises become increasingly opaque: the ever-widening grin of a decreasingly visible cat? Why is it not just another atavism? Even if it protests that it is not related, the case should be proven and not just dismissed. The pieces do slot together satisfactorily, and I would suggest that social entrepreneurship is a plausible epilogue to the 'spirit of capitalism'. The process is not hard to imagine. People leading meaningless but financially enriching lives reach a crossroads at which value needs to be added to the meaning of their activities, rather than to the bottom line, for the sake of their own sense of self-worth (through doing 'good works'). A process that began in religious 'good works' therefore ends in secular 'good works', the latter with no knowledge of its connections to the former. Entrepreneurial business did not, according to Weber's thesis, have to justify itself. It just *was*. And until Weber pointed out *why* that was the case, no one engaged in it seemed to have minded that it just *was*. It seems fairly likely that today's breed of social entrepreneurs have not read Max Weber (or Schumpeter, for that matter), and feel no need to account for the ideological background to their plans and their actions. But their provenance is likely the same as the secular form of capitalism described by Weber, only a generation or two further on.

In an otherwise unproven theory of personality types and economic stagnation in traditional societies, Everett Hagen wrote one passage that stands out as a remarkably prophetic description of the social entrepreneur as an engine of social change, making sense of this notion that the social entrepreneur adds (moral) value back on to the business 'calling':

> there gradually emerges a group of individuals, creative, alienated from traditional values, driven by a gnawing burning drive to prove themselves (to themselves, as well as to their fellows), seeking for an area in which to do so, preferably an area in which they can gain power, and preferably also one in which in some symbolic way they can vent their rage at the elites who have caused their troubles. (Hagen, 1971: 136)

This serves as a useful reminder that the buzz surrounding social entrepreneurship has as much to do with the person and personality of the entrepreneur him or herself as it has to do with making change in society, a point fully acknowledged and encouraged by groups such as Ashoka. The need to prove oneself, the drive, commitment – all these things may result in positive change, but they arise from, and in fact depend on, a personal calling, and perhaps a sense of personal anger or injustice, or a sense of vicarious anger and injustice for the problems of others. The meaninglessness of capitalist endeavour reaches a tipping point at which meaning becomes the primary goal of these capitalists. This self-oriented element of social entrepreneurship is in fact an old element of entrepreneurship and socio-economic invention (Hagen mentions Henry Ford), philanthropy and charitable work, and it suggests the *because* (however tenuous) behind a Weberian calling. The kind of broad-ranging social change envisaged by social-entrepreneurial groups for their social entrepreneurs ultimately lies, therefore, on this post-Weberian individuation. It is an irony of social entrepreneurship that global visions of sustainable change and development depend on an individual focus. I have begun to unpack this phenomenon, but it requires more work. Historians are able to ascribe motives to past actors, to place 'changemakers' within a context that can explain the nature of their actions. It is not for the sake of accountability or judgement so much as it is about understanding the effects of an intersection of historical forces that produce social climates at odds with personality types, who in turn are fitted to try to reconcile the world to their vision. Through a preliminary examination of some of the antecedents of contemporary social entrepreneurship, dwelling on the ideological motivations of those actors, I hope to have provided a means whereby current actors can adequately begin to question their own motives. Social entrepreneurs at present seem not to engage in this kind of internal reflection, and, after all, not everyone is entirely comfortable with the 'defining quality of leading social entrepreneurs': 'they cannot come to rest until they have changed the pattern in their field *all* across society' (Drayton, 2006b: 45; original emphasis).[22] Acting in a certain way because it is thought, by the actor, to be the right (or necessary) thing to do, is not a good enough justification for acting. It pays no heed to the tendentious nature of right and wrong, of cultural chauvinism and of historical mutability (compounded by differences in geography).[23] 'Why am I doing this?' ought to be the question social entrepreneurs ask themselves frequently, and the answer needs to place emphasis on the 'I' and the 'this'. To do something *for* someone else still does not explain why it is that *you* are the one to do it, nor how that thing in particular came to be perceived as a 'problem' in the first place.

NOTES

1. For definitions see Nicholls (2006: 10–13), Cho (2006: 35–7) and Dees (1998).
2. Even those who have tried to establish a genealogy or tradition of social entrepreneurship have done so without due attention to scholarly rigour. Martin Morse Wooster's small collection *By their Bootstraps: The Lives of Twelve Gilded-Age Social Entrepreneurs* (New York, n.d.) certainly tries to cast an historical light on the subject, but the work is published by the Manhattan Institute's Social Entrepreneurship initiative and is cast in the kind of rhetoric utilised by involved sponsors of social entrepreneurship. Nevertheless, the list of names therein, including founder of the boy scouts, Robert

Baden Powell and founder of the Salvation Army, William Booth, ought to be enough to make social entrepreneurs take note of the latent ideologies behind 'good works'.

3. Drayton's is a vision of society in which the welfare state and governmental financial institutions have failed and should be replaced, which is by no means either historically accurate, nor an unquestionable policy for the future (Drayton, 2006a: 15–17). Elsewhere, and equally unconvincingly, Drayton claims that since about 1980 'the operating half of the world that deals with social issues has gone through an historical transformation of unprecedented speed and scale. It has gone from pre-modern to entrepreneurial.' It is the state which is overlooked in such a construction, but this is an oversight that the weight of evidence will not bear (2006b: 45).

4. Henry Olsen, 'Introduction' to Wooster (n.d.: i).

5. Here I follow Schumpeter's assertion, developing Marxian theory and adding a dose of Weber, when he says: 'Obviously we cannot say: everywhere else is ideology; we alone stand on the rock of absolute truth.' His particular caution is precisely against the notion of a 'modern radical intellectual who stands indeed upon the rock of truth, the unbiased judge of all things human'. It is this mantle that social entrepreneurs have unwittingly adopted. As Schumpeter points out, 'if anything can be called obvious in this field, it is the fact that this intellectual is just a bundle of prejudices that are in most cases held with all the force of sincere conviction' (Schumpeter, 1954 [1994]: 34–7). Even where there is a call for historical research, or an awareness that social entrepreneurs are subject to 'time, place, form, actor, and practice' it seems implicit that the scope of such research would be limited to the kind of temporal frame established by Drayton. A long-view historical approach, though it is not explicitly discarded, is not seriously considered (see Austin, 2006: 23–8, esp. 24).

6. The Harvard University Research Center in Entrepreneurial History, founded in 1948, was closed just ten years later due to a shift in research focus and lack of funds. See the working paper, published online, by Jones and Wadhwani (2006: 6–7).

7. Which has produced such articles as Jones and Khanna (2006).

8. Jones and Wadhwani (2006: 8–24) eloquently summarise the work on entrepreneurial history that was done. Its extensiveness only makes the lack of reference to these works all the more conspicuous in the rhetoric produced by social-entrepreneurial organisations.

9. There is, of course, no entirely value neutral historical inquiry either, but historiography is subject to accountability by virtue of the historical record, necessarily limiting what can be claimed to be 'true'. It is not my intention to claim that social entrepreneurs should 'use' history – I am uncertain that it can ever be so directly applied – but simply that they should be historically aware; to ask questions that currently go unasked; to see how 'good ideas' transpired to be not so good from other points of view; to see how the passage of time has revealed those agents in the past who claimed to be doing good – providing basic services and social development – to be tendentiously and ideologically motivated, exclusionary, self-interested and ethnocentric. If history has any 'use' here, it is in heightening the contextual self-awareness of social actors.

10. For Boulton (and Watt) see Jones (1999); for Wedgwood see McKendrick (1961).

11. Owen's key works are as follows: *A New View of Society: or essays on the principle of the formation of human character* (1816); *Report to the County of Lanark, of a plan for relieving public distress and removing discontent by giving permanent productive employment to the poor and working classes* (1817); *Book of the New Moral World* (1836–44).

12. Nicholls cites the originator of this idea, J.A. Banks (Banks, 1972).

13. See Vasi in this Volume, Chapter 9.

14. Harrison points out that 'in the summer of 1817 [Owen] embarked on an intensive propaganda [campaign], deluging the newspapers with texts of his addresses which they printed in full. He spent £4000 in two months and made himself a nationally known figure' (Harrison, 1967: 78). To put this in perspective, the equivalent spend on self-promotion in 2006 would be in the order of £3 million. For the rationale behind this calculation, see www.measuringworth.com, last accessed 18 November 2007.

15.	For Peel see Newbould (1983); for Whitbread see Rapp (1987); for Martineau see Roberts (2002); for Lever see Lewis (2008).
16.	For general treatments of social Catholicism, see Misner (1991) and Vidler (1964).
17.	For more on the work and context of Léon Harmel, see Caldwell (1966) and Nord (1984).
18.	The following précis of Ford's social contribution is inspired by Watts (2005). For an additional account of Ford's mixed motives, see Raff and Summers (1987: esp. 57–72).
19.	Ford was a fierce Protestant who also happened to believe in reincarnation. See Watts (2005: 319–21).
20.	Peter Drucker places the responsibility for this innovation on Ford's partner, James Couzens, but the structures built up around the scheme had Ford's moral stamp (Drucker, 1985: 204–5).
21.	The life and career of William Norris is detailed in O'Toole (1998). My précis of Norris's work is based on this text, though the analysis of his ideological motives and the implications for social entrepreneurs are mine.
22.	Nor is everyone comfortable with the cultivation of the 'Invisible Hand' in the field of 'normative' values, as put forward by Geoff Mulgan (Mulgan, 2006: 74–95, esp. 75). There seems to be a deep caesura between the deeply individualistic action of the social entrepreneur and the environment in which he or she works which depends on 'consent, and mutual commitment'. Society surely cannot be changed consensually by one person or by one group. Society's acquiescence, if it comes, surely comes after the process of changing it has begun, which is a morally questionable circumstance for the 'changemaker'.
23.	Rowena Young is one of the few who have called for social entrepreneurs to be 'highly reflective about the significance of their interventions' (Young, 2006: 72).

REFERENCES

Austin, J.E. (2006), 'Three avenues for social entrepreneurship research', in J. Mair, J. Robinson and K. Hockerts (eds), *Social Entrepreneurship*, London: Palgrave Macmillan, pp. 22–33.

Banks, J.A. (1972), *The Sociology of Social Movements*, London: Macmillan.

Bestor, A.E. (1948), *Education and Reform at New Harmony: Correspondence of William Maclure and Marie Duclos Fretageot, 1820–1833*, Indianapolis, IN: Indiana Historical Society.

Bestor, A.E. (1950), *Backwoods Utopias: The Sectarian and Owenite Phases of Communitarian Socialism in America, 1663–1829*, Philadelphia, PA: Pennsylvania University Press.

Booth, C. (1902), *Life and Labour of the People in London*, London: Macmillan.

Bornstein, D. (2007), *How to Change the World: Social Entrepreneurs and the Power of New Ideas*, Oxford and New York: Oxford University Press.

Caldwell, T.B. (1966), 'The Syndicat des employés du commerce et de l'industrie (1888–1919)', *International Review of Social History*, **11**, 228–66.

Carroll, L. (1865 [2007]), *Alice's Adventures in Wonderland and Through the Looking Glass*, Scituate, MA: Digital Scanning.

Cho, A.H. (2006), 'Politics, values and social entrepreneurship', in J. Mair, J. Robinson and K. Hockerts (eds), *Social Entrepreneurship*, London: Palgrave Macmillan, pp. 34–56.

Cobbett, W. (1830 [1967]), *Rural Rides*, ed. G. Woodcock Harmondsworth: Penguin.

Coffey, J.L. (2002), *Entrepreneur as Catholic Social Reformer*, Notre Dame, IN: University of Notre Dame Press.

Cole, G.D.H. (1925), *Robert Owen*, London: E. Benn.

Dees, J.G. (1998), 'The meaning of "Social Entrepreneurship"', www.fuqua.duke. edu/centers/case/documents/dees_SE.pdf, original draft 31 October 1998, reformatted and revised 30 May 2001, accessed 15 August 2007.

Disraeli, B. (1845 [1981]), *Sybil, or the Two Nations. Edited by S. M. Smith*, Oxford: Oxford University Press.

Drayton, B. (2006a), 'Everyone a changemaker: social entrepreneurship's ultimate goal', *Innovations – Technology, Governance, Globalization*, Winter, 1–32.

Drayton, B. (2006b), 'The citizen sector transformed', in A. Nicholls (ed.), *Social Entrepreneurship*, Oxford: Oxford University Press, pp. 45–55.

Drucker, P. (1985), *Innovation and Entrepreneurship: Practice and Principles*, New York: Harper & Row.

Engels, F. (1844 [1999]), *The Condition of the Working Class in England*, Oxford: Oxford University Press.

Hagen, E.E. (1971), 'How Economic Growth Begins: A Theory of Social Change', in P. Kilby (ed.), *Entrepreneurship and Economic Development*, New York: Free Press, pp. 123–37.

Harrison, J.F.C. (1967), '"The steam engine of the new moral world": Owenism and education, 1817–1829', *Journal of British Studies*, **6** (2), 76–98.

Jones, G. and T. Khanna (2006), 'Bringing history (back) into international business', *Journal of International Business Studies*, **37** (4), 453–68.

Jones, G. and R.D. Wadhwani (2006), 'Entrepreneurship and business history: renewing the research agenda', www.hbs.edu/research/pdf/07-007.pdf, accessed 17 July 2008.

Jones, P.M. (1999), 'Living the Enlightenment and the French Revolution: James Watt, Matthew Boulton, and their sons', *Historical Journal*, **42** (1), 157–82.

Lewis, B. (2008), *So Clean: Lord Leverhulme, Soap and Civilisation*, Manchester: Manchester University Press.

MacDonald, R. (1971), 'Schumpeter and Max Weber: central visions and social theories', in P. Kilby (ed.), *Entrepreneurship and Economic Development*, New York: Free Press, pp. 71–94.

Mair, J., J. Robinson and K. Hockerts (eds) (2006), *Social Entrepreneurship*, London: Palgrave Macmillan.

Malthus, T.R. (1807–24 [1986]), *Essays on Population. Edited by E. A. Wrigley and D. Souden*, London: W. Pickering.

Mayhew, H. (1851–62), *London Labour and the London Poor*, London: Griffin, Bohn.

McKendrick, N. (1961), 'Josiah Wedgwood and factory discipline', *Historical Journal*, **4** (1), 30–55.

Misner, P. (1991), *Social Catholicism in Europe: From the Onset of Industrialization to the First World War*, New York: Crossroad.

Mulgan, G. (2006), 'Cultivating the other invisible hand of social entrepreneurship: comparative advantage, public policy, and future research priorities', in A. Nicholls (ed.), *Social Entrepreneurship*, Oxford: Oxford University Press, pp. 74–95.

Newbould, I. (1983), 'Sir Robert Peel and the Conservative Party, 1832–1841: a study in failure', *English Historical Review*, **98**, 529–57.

Nicholls, A. (ed.) (2006), *Social Entrepreneurship*, Oxford: Oxford University Press.

Nightingale, F. (1860), *Suggestions for Thought to the Searchers after Truth among the Artizans of England,* privately printed.

Nord, P.G. (1984), 'Three views of Christian democracy in fin de siècle France', *Journal of Contemporary History*, **19** (4), 713–27.

O'Toole, P. (1998), *Money and Morals in America: A History*, New York: Clarkson Potter.

Podmore, F. (1906), *Robert Owen: A Biography*, London: Hutchinson.

Raff, D.M.G. and L.H. Summers (1987), 'Did Henry Ford pay efficiency wages?', *Journal of Labor Economics*, **5** (4), S57–S86.

Rapp, D. (1987), *Samuel Whitbread (1764–1815): A Social and Political Study*, New York: Garland.

Reid, D. (1976), 'The decline of Saint Monday, 1766–1876', *Past and Present*, **71** (1), 76–101.

Reid, D. (1996), 'Weddings, weekdays, work and leisure in urban England, 1791–1911: the decline of Saint Monday revisited', *Past and Present*, **153** (1), 135–63.

Research Center in Entrepreneurial History, Harvard University (ed.) (1949), *Change and the Entrepreneur: Postulates and Patters for Entrepreneurial History*, Cambridge, MA: Harvard University Press.

Roberts, C. (2002), *The Woman and the Hour: Harriet Martineau and Victorian Ideologies*, Toronto and Buffalo, NY: University of Toronto Press.

Schumpeter, J.A. (1949), 'Economic theory and entrepreneurial history', in Research Center in Entrepreneurial History, Harvard University (ed.), *Change and the Entrepreneur: Postulates and Patters for Entrepreneurial History*, Cambridge, MA: Harvard University Press, pp. 63–84.

Schumpeter, J.A. (1954 [1994]), *History of Economic Analysis*, Oxford and New York: Oxford University Press.

Taylor, B. (1983), *Eve and the New Jerusalem: Socialism and Feminism in the Nineteenth Century*, New York: Pantheon.

Thompson, E.P. (1967), 'Time, work-discipline and industrial capitalism', *Past and Present*, **38**, 56–97.

Vidler, A.R. (1964), *A Century of Social Catholicism: 1820–1920*, London: SPCK.

Watts, S. (2005), *The People's Tycoon: Henry Ford and the American Century*, New York: Vintage.

Weber, M. (1930 [1992]), *The Protestant Ethic and the Spirit of Capitalism*, London and New York: Routledge.

Wilson, C. (1955), 'The entrepreneur in the Industrial Revolution in Britain', *Explorations in Entrepreneurial History*, **7** (3), 129–45.

Woodham-Smith, C. (1950), *Florence Nightingale, 1820–1910*, London: Constable.

Wooster, M. Morse (n.d.), *By their Bootstraps: The Lives of Twelve Gilded-Age Social Entrepreneurs*, New York: Manhattan Institute.

Young, R. (2006), 'For what it is worth: social value and the future of social entrepreneurship', in A. Nicholls (ed.), *Social Entrepreneurship*, Oxford: Oxford University Press, pp. 56–73.

PART III

Contexts

9. New heroes, old theories? Toward a sociological perspective on social entrepreneurship

Ion Bogdan Vasi

9.1 INTRODUCTION

The concept of social entrepreneurship has received growing attention in the mass media over the recent years. At the beginning of the 1990s hardly any articles in US newspapers mentioned social entrepreneurship; by 2000 almost 40 articles mentioned this concept, and by 2007 more than 150 articles did so. Similarly, the number of articles dedicated to social entrepreneurship in major, world newspapers has increased exponentially. In 1995 fewer than 20 articles discussed social entrepreneurship in English-language world newspapers; by 2000 that number increased to over 70, and by 2007 to over 300.[1] Television has also recently become interested in social entrepreneurship: for example, in 2005 the Public Broadcasting Service has aired a four-hour series on social entrepreneurs, hosted by Robert Redford and having the title 'The New Heroes'.

Social entrepreneurship has become an increasingly popular topic in some academic environments as well. More and more business schools have established research centres and now offer courses on social entrepreneurship.[2] Columbia University, for example, was one of the first to create a Research Initiative on Social Entrepreneurship in early 2002 with the declared mission 'to study and disseminate knowledge about the markets, metrics and management of for-profit and non-profit social enterprise and social venturing'.[3] A recent survey of business schools in the United States has found that the percentage of schools that require students to take a course on business and society issues has increased from 34 per cent in 2001 to 63 per cent in 2007.[4] And in 2005, the first International Social Entrepreneurship Research Conference was organised in Barcelona.

Despite its recently found popularity in the mass media and in business schools, the concept of social entrepreneurship remains relatively poorly understood and undertheorised. Very few academic articles and only a handful of books have been published so far on social entrepreneurship

(Mair et al., 2006; Nicholls, 2006). As the authors of a recently edited volume have recognised, we are now in the 'emerging excitement' phase of the social entrepreneurship concept's life cycle (Mair et al., 2006). Moreover, very few sociological studies of social entrepreneurship have been published to date – see Nicholls and Cho (2006) and Grenier (2006) for attempts to develop theoretical perspectives rooted in sociology.[5] That the sociological literature has almost nothing to say about social entrepreneurship is surprising, given the importance of social entrepreneurship as a process through which significant social change occurs in contemporary societies.

My goal in this chapter is to specify how a sociological framework can contribute to our understanding of social entrepreneurship. I begin by reviewing some of the definitions of social entrepreneurship. I argue that the most common interpretations, which focus on social entrepreneurs' 'heroic' personality, are inadequate for a sociological analysis. Next, I review two bodies of sociological literature that can bring a significant contribution to the social entrepreneurship debate: various theories of social movements and the sociological theories of organisational innovation and entrepreneurship. Building on these theories, I highlight a few perspectives that will help us understand not only social entrepreneurship's origins but also its different outcomes. More specifically, I argue that it is important to focus on social entrepreneurs' perception of political and discursive opportunities, on their mobilisation of organisational resources and on their interpretive work.

I conclude that a sociological perspective informed by 'old theories' can help us move beyond a simplistic understanding of social entrepreneurs as 'new heroes' and tackle three main issues. First, it can move beyond futile attempts to identify social entrepreneurs by their 'entrepreneurial personality' and build models that explain variation in social entrepreneurial outcomes. Second, it can overcome the implicit bias in studies that consider social entrepreneurship to be simply business entrepreneurship 'with a conscience'. Finally, it can avoid the common mistake of selecting only successful social enterprises.

9.2   LIMITATIONS OF EXISTING DEFINITIONS AND MODELS OF SOCIAL ENTREPRENEURSHIP

Most attempts to introduce the topic of social entrepreneurship in the academic environment are rooted in economic theory. Many definitions of social entrepreneurs, for example, merely expand definitions of entrepreneurs originating in the work of economists such as Jean-Baptiste Say, who was writing at the beginning of the nineteenth century. Arguably the most influential idea about entrepreneurship is that of the Austrian economist Joseph Schumpeter, who defined the entrepreneur as the person who identifies a commercial opportunity and organises a venture to implement 'a new combination of means of production' (Schumpeter, 2000: 58).[6] What distinguishes entrepreneurs from heads of firms, managers or capitalists, in Schumpeter's conception, is the fact that entrepreneurs are agents of change that propagate innovations to the point of 'creative destruction', a state at which the new venture renders existing products or business models obsolete (Schumpeter, 1975; see also Richard Swedberg's chapter in this volume).

A great deal of research on entrepreneurship has focused on describing the motivations, goals and personal characteristics of the entrepreneur. This is partly because Schumpeter has portrayed entrepreneurs in heroic terms, and partly because many researchers wanted to be able to 'pick winners' and identify techniques that would identify those most likely to start and grow successful businesses (Birley, 1998). Some researchers have focused on identifying the general behavioural patterns that are specific to the 'entrepreneurial personality' (de Vries, 1998), while others have focused on specific factors considered essential for entrepreneurship, such as risk taking propensity (Brockhaus, 1998; Liles, 1998).[7] Yet, as researchers have gradually recognised, it is virtually impossible to 'pick winners' and the association between psychological attributes and corporate performance is very weak (Begley and Boyd, 1998).

Recent definitions of social entrepreneurship emphasise that social entrepreneurs are simply a special case of entrepreneurs. As J. Gregory Dees notes, 'social entrepreneurs are one species of the genus entrepreneur' – in other words, social entrepreneurs are 'entrepreneurs with a social mission'. Consequently, many attempts to define social entrepreneurship have emphasised the personal characteristics of entrepreneurs (Dees, 2001: 2). According to Dees, social entrepreneurs play the role of resolute change agents in the social sector by:

> adopting a mission to create and sustain social value; recognising and relentlessly pursuing new opportunities to serve that mission; engaging in a process of continuous innovation, adaptation, and learning; acting boldly without being limited by resources currently in hand, and exhibiting heightened accountability to the constituencies served and for the outcomes created. (Dees, 2001: 4)

Similarly, Roger Martin and Sally Osberg argue that social entrepreneurship has three components:

1) identifying a stable but inherently unjust equilibrium that causes the exclusion, marginalisation, or suffering of a segment of humanity that lacks the financial means or political clout to achieve any transformative benefit on its own; 2) identifying an opportunity in this unjust equilibrium, developing a social value proposition, and bringing to bear inspiration, creativity, direct action, courage, and fortitude, thereby challenging the stable state's hegemony; and 3) forging a new, stable equilibrium that releases trapped potential or alleviates the suffering of the targeted group, and through imitation and the creation of a stable ecosystem around the new equilibrium ensuring a better future for the targeted group and even society at large. (Martin and Osberg, 2007: 35)

Some researchers have attempted to move beyond definitions and typologies by sketching theoretical models of social entrepreneurship. Johanna Mair and Ernesto Noboa have developed a model of social entrepreneurial intention formation (Mair and Noboa, 2006). Their model is centred on two sets of factors that determine social entrepreneurial behaviours. On the one hand, it emphasises that these behavioural intentions are influenced by perceived desirability, which is in turn shaped by the individuals' ability to develop empathy and moral judgement. On the other hand, it highlights that these behavioural intentions are influenced by perceived feasibility, which is in turn shaped by the individuals' perception of self-efficacy and social support.

Most of the existing definitions and models of social entrepreneurship are not very useful for a sociological analysis, for three main reasons. First, while some of these definitions allow for clear distinctions between social entrepreneurs and related concepts, they present a narrow perspective on social entrepreneurship. Martin and Osberg, for example, argue that social entrepreneurs are different from social activists because the latter are engaged in indirect action, that is, they attempt to improve 'an unfortunate and unstable equilibrium' by influencing governments, NGOs, consumers and other groups to take action (Martin and Osberg, 2007: 37). They argue that social entrepreneurs are also significantly different from social service providers because the latter are not creating and maintaining a new superior equilibrium – in other words, social service providers have a limited impact such that their service area is restricted to a local population. Yet, as Martin and Osberg themselves recognise, 'in the real world there are probably more hybrid models than pure forms' (Marting and Osberg, 2007: 38). Indeed, it is common for social activists to also be social entrepreneurs, and vice versa. Therefore, a sociological model of social entrepreneurship should examine all processes through which social entrepreneurs create change, and these processes may include both direct and indirect action.

Second, these definitions and models emphasise agency at the expense of structure. According to Martin and Osberg, social entrepreneurs see an opportunity to create something new in a suboptimal equilibrium, rather than an inconvenience to be tolerated, because of their unique personal characteristics – inspiration, creativity, courage, and so on (Martin and Osberg, 2007). Similarly, David Bornstein identifies six qualities of successful entrepreneurs: willingness to self-correct, to share credit, to break free of established structures, to cross disciplinary boundaries, to work quietly and a strong ethical impetus (Bornstein, 2004). Nonetheless, social entrepreneurs' personality characteristics are a necessary but insufficient condition for successful entrepreneurship. There are, obviously, numerous social entrepreneurs who have the same personal characteristics as those identified above but fail in their social enterprise. To understand why some succeed and some fail, it is important to examine closely the social context in which they operate, since macro-social factors often determine the availability of resources for social entrepreneurship.

Third, these theoretical frameworks do not pay sufficient attention to social conflict. Most of these perspectives are rooted in economic analyses which assume that individuals are rational actors who imitate successful entrepreneurs and, thus, create a stable ecosystem around a new 'optimum equilibrium'. Social entrepreneurs, however, are rarely creating an equilibrium that is taken-for-granted as optimal. To put it differently, one group's optimal equilibrium may be another group's suboptimal equilibrium. Indeed, many social entrepreneurs may fail in their enterprises not simply because they cannot overcome resistance to social change or because they are not sufficiently skilled at marketing their ideas, as Bornstein seems to suggest (Bornstein, 2004). Rather, they may fail because they face considerable opposition from powerful elites, or because they lack organisational resources and support from influential allies. Understanding why only some social entrepreneurs succeed requires a careful examination of the potentially contentious interactions between various social actors.

9.3 A SOCIOLOGICAL DEFINITION OF SOCIAL ENTREPRENEURSHIP

Although the concept of social entrepreneurship is relatively new, people have obviously solved social problems in the past by releasing their 'entrepreneurial spirit'. Indeed, as scholars have noted, 'the practice of social entrepreneurship may be well ahead of the theory' (Alvord et al., 2002: 3; see also the chapter by Robert Boddice in this volume). Rather than adapting a definition that restricts social entrepreneurship to commercial enterprises with social impacts, this study employs a definition that emphasises the catalytic effect of social entrepreneurship on social transformation *beyond* solutions to social problems that are immediate causes of concern. I adapt the definition proposed by Sarah Alvord, David Brown and Christine Letts: 'social entrepreneurship is an individual or collective action that attempts to create innovative solutions to immediate social problems as well as to mobilise ideas, capacities, resources, and social arrangements required for long-term, sustainable social transformation' (Alvord et al., 2002: 3).

Depending on the type of innovation it promotes, social entrepreneurship can take at least three somewhat distinct forms. First, some social entrepreneurship initiatives focus on *disseminating a package of innovations* needed to solve common problems. This form of social entrepreneurship attempts to serve widespread needs because it assumes that 'information and technical resources can be reconfigured into user-friendly forms that will make them available to marginalised groups' (Alvord, 2002: 10). Once such a package is constructed by various experts – a difficult task, because it requires substantial creativity to adapt materials and resources for low-cost usage – it can be disseminated by individuals and agencies with relatively few resources. For example, once Muhammad Yunus came up with the idea to provide group-based loans without collateral for poor and marginalised Bangladeshi people in the late 1970s, the micro-credit innovation disseminated so quickly that, by 2008, over 4 million families in 27 countries were directly benefiting from it.

Second, some forms of social entrepreneurship involve *building local capacities* or working with marginalised populations to identify capacities needed for self-help. This approach is grounded in two main assumptions: that local groups possess the best knowledge about which issues are most important, and that local actors may solve many of their problems if they have access to more resources and better capacity to act. Therefore, social entrepreneurship directed at capacity building requires paying special attention to local constituents and resource providers. An example of this form of social entrepreneurship is the Amazon Conservation Team (ACT), an organisation created in 1996 to develop the capacity of the indigenous peoples of the Amazon to provide enduring protection of the rainforest. Working with 26 indigenous groups across different South American countries, the ACT has shown that indigenous people are reliable stewards of their own territory when given the opportunity and appropriate training.[8]

Third, some social entrepreneurship initiatives focus on *mobilising grassroots groups* to form alliances against abusive elites or institutions. As Alvord, Brown and Letts note, the assumption underlying this approach is that marginalised groups can solve their own problems if they have increased access to political institutions (Alvord et al., 2002). Yet, because social entrepreneurs often have to mobilise local groups in order to increase the political voice of marginalised individuals and solve their problems, this form of social entrepreneurship is highly politicised and may involve activities that challenge powerful antagonists. One example of such social entrepreneurship is the Self-Employed Women's Association, formed in the early 1970s in order to prevent the exploitation of poor, self-employed Indian women workers and to provide services otherwise unavailable to manual labourers and home-based producers.

The above definition and typology have the merit of emphasising that social entrepreneurship is similar to social movement activism in at least two ways. One similarity is that, because social activism and social entrepreneurship are inherently political phenomena, both charismatic movement leaders and creative social entrepreneurs have to overcome resistance to social change by mobilising resources, taking advantage of political opportunities, and engaging in framing processes. This is particularly the case for those forms of social entrepreneurship that require building local capacities or mobilising grassroots groups. Indeed, in these cases the decisions made by social entrepreneurs and social movement actors are influenced by the same contextual factors. Yet, even when they have to disseminate a package of innovations, social entrepreneurs frequently have to act as social movement activists. In other words, they have to organise resources, find influential allies, or engage in framing processes that resonate with important segments of the population.

Another similarity is that the outcomes of both social movements and social entrepreneurship are complex phenomena that are irreducible to organisational creation and growth. One outcome of social movement activism is the creation of new social movement organisations; similarly, one outcome of social entrepreneurship is the creation of social enterprises. But just as the success of social movements cannot be judged based on the number or the size of new social movement organisations, the success of social entrepreneurship cannot be reduced to the creation of viable businesses. A more adequate – and more difficult – way of measuring how social movements and enterprises matter is to examine the degree to which they have secured medium- and long-term collective benefits for their constituents as well as for the larger population (Amenta and Caren, 2004; Amenta and Young, 1999). Indeed, it would be short-sighted to consider that a movement has been successful simply because it created an organisation that lobbied for the adoption of a new policy, without examining how effectively it was implemented and whether it had the intended consequences. It would be equally short-sighted to consider that a social enterprise has been successful because it created an efficient organisation for distributing a package of innovations, without considering whether those innovations are actually used by the intended beneficiaries, and whether they have the intended consequences.

Although social entrepreneurship and social movement activism have numerous similarities, it is important to point out that the two concepts are not interchangeable. While social movement activism is limited to collective actions, social entrepreneurship may consist only of individual actions. Wealthy philanthropists, for example, have the necessary resources to create an innovative solution to a pressing social problem and to mobilise capacities for sustainable social change without having to rally large numbers of people. Another important difference is that social entrepreneurship may attempt to create social change without challenging an existing authority. Unlike social movements, social entrepreneurs may push for an innovative solution by working within the institutionalised channels and reproducing 'the rules of the game', without challenging the hegemony of governments or business models.

9.4 USING SOCIOLOGICAL THEORIES OF MOVEMENTS AND ENTREPRENEURSHIP TO UNDERSTAND SOCIAL ENTREPRENEURSHIP

How can we develop a sociological perspective on social entrepreneurship? I argue that the best strategy is to combine insights from social movement scholarship and the sociology of entrepreneurship. This is particularly important for studies that examine the factors that account for variation in social entrepreneurship's outcomes, rather than trying to explain who becomes an entrepreneur and why.[9]

While traditional research on social movements has assumed that states are the main source of power (Gamson, 1990; McAdam, 1982; Tilly, 1978), more recent research has shown that numerous movements challenge not only the state but also different areas of civil society such as education (Binder, 2004; Rojas, 2007), science (Moore, 1999), the workplace (Morrill et al., 2003; Raeburn, 2004), or religion (Katzenstein, 1999). An original study of protest events in the US between 1968 and 1975 has shown that all movements direct some protests at non-state institutions, and that some movements – women's, gay and lesbian, and civil rights – target non-state institutions more frequently than they target governments (van Dyke et al., 2004). Consequently, a growing number of scholars have issued calls for refocusing social movement research on various challenges to authority and for developing a multi-institutional approach to social movements (Armstrong and Bernstein, 2008; Snow, 2004).

These new developments in social movement research have important consequences for our understanding of social change processes such as social entrepreneurship. By recognising that social movement activity can be directed not only at states but also at non-state institutions, it is possible to analyse much of the social entrepreneurial activity using social movement theories. A sociological analysis of social entrepreneurship will have to start from the observation that social entrepreneurship activity, just like social movement activity, frequently targets multiple institutions: governments, education, the workplace, and so on. It will also have to take into account the fact that social entrepreneurs often act as social movement actors who engage in 'venue shopping' and 'forum shifting', shopping around for the most vulnerable targets and rapidly switching targets according to perceived chances of success (Armstrong and Bernstein, 2008: 87).

One promising line of inquiry is to examine the processes through which social entrepreneurs – not only individuals but also organisations – mobilise different types of resources in order to increase their chance of success. Social movement research conducted under the resource mobilisation framework has demonstrated that a significant amount of coordination and strategic effort is required to convert individually held resources into collective resources that can be used in collective actions (Jenkins and Eckert, 1986; McCarthy and Zald, 1977; Minkoff, 1995). Some scholars have shown that social movements' success depends on the totality of moral resources – legitimacy, sympathetic support, celebrity – bestowed upon them by external sources (Cress and Snow, 1996). Other researchers have shown that movements' outcomes are shaped by their ability to produce their own resources such as cultural products, social networks and organisations (Edwards and McCarthy, 2004). Still other scholars of social movements have emphasised that movements gain resources through mechanisms such as social appropriation, the 'political activation' of organisations and institutions that have previously been politically inactive, or brokerage, the connection of previously unconnected sites (McAdam et al., 2001).

The resource mobilisation framework from social movement studies is similar to sociological studies of entrepreneurship centred on social networks. In comparison to social movement research, studies of entrepreneurship have had a 'parochial status' in sociology (Ruef and Lounsbury, 2007: 13).[10] However, an important line of research has focused on the relationship between entrepreneurship and interpersonal networks, such as the social networks that form between extended families or ethnic groups. Mark Granovetter shows that extended kinship ties are essential for small-scale entrepreneurship because they provide two key ingredients for successful entrepreneurship: trust and solidarity (Granovetter, 1995).

Similarly, Ronald Burt demonstrates that the emergence of entrepreneurial opportunities is connected to the structure of personal networks and, in particular, to the presence of structural holes (Burt, 1993). More generally, research on immigrant entrepreneurship finds that the extensive social networks that exist at the community level between different ethnic groups, such as Cuban or Chinese immigrants in the US, determine the level of entrepreneurial activity (Pang and Rath, 2007; Portes and Shafer, 2007).

Research on social entrepreneurship outcomes can benefit by examining the processes through which social entrepreneurs increase their chances of success by mobilising moral and organisational resources. Consider the case of Victoria Hale, a social entrepreneur who created in 2000 the first non-profit pharmaceutical company whose mission is to develop safe and affordable new medicines for people with infectious diseases in the developing world (the Institute for OneWorld Health). According to Martin and Osberg, the preliminary success of this social venture is due to the fact that Hale identified an opportunity to remedy an unjust equilibrium in the pharmaceutical industry and applied 'inspiration, creativity, direct action, and courage in launching a new venture to provide options for a disadvantaged population' (Martin and Osberg, 2007: 36).

A sociological account of Hale's success, however, must focus on the processes through which the Institute for OneWorld Health overcame the initial distrust of many governmental agencies and pharmaceutical companies, which viewed a non-profit pharmaceutical company as unfeasible. By collaborating with established agencies such as the National Institute of Allergy and the World Health Organisation, this social enterprise appropriated other organisations' moral and financial resources. By connecting academic research at different universities – Yale University, University of Washington and University of California, Berkeley – with pharmaceutical companies that have chemical libraries, Hale's institute engaged in brokerage and created new resources for innovative medical research. And by building formal connections with the Bill and Melinda Gates Foundation, the Skoll Foundation and the Lehman Brothers Foundation, the Institute for OneWorld Health was able to fund research that produced new treatments and proved that its project was feasible.

Another promising direction is to examine how social entrepreneurs employ framing processes to increase their ventures' legitimacy and, consequently, their chance of success. Because many social enterprises are outside the business mainstream, social entrepreneurs have to frame their activities such that they are perceived as legitimate. Social movement research shows that social activists have to change people's perceptions such that 'the social arrangements that are ordinarily perceived as just and immutable must come to seem both unjust and mutable' (Piven and

Cloward, 1977). Activists and movement entrepreneurs frequently engage in framing processes; in other words, they 'assign meaning to and interpret relevant events and conditions in ways that are intended to mobilise potential adherents and constituents, to garner bystander support, and to demobilise antagonists' (Snow and Benford, 1988: 198). Moreover, studies show that variation in one or more dimensions of collective action frames has important consequences not only for social movement organisations' ability to mobilise their constituents (Gerhards and Rucht, 1992), but also for their outcomes (Cress and Snow, 2000).

The framing perspective from social movement studies connects with an ecological perspective from sociological studies of entrepreneurship, which focuses on the influence of both material and cultural environments on the institutional development of entrepreneurship. Studies conducted under this perspective show that the key to success for many institutional entrepreneurs lies in their ability to legitimise their ventures. For example, Carol Caronna shows that certain 'heavy-weight' institutional entrepreneurs, such as Kaiser Permanente, are able to negotiate the dynamic relationship between new organisational identities – what would come to be known as a health maintenance organisation – and existing institutions in order to sustain illegitimate identities and institutionalise innovative organisational forms (Caronna, 2007). Luca Solari shows that black or grey market entrepreneurs obtain legitimacy by negotiating difficult paths between endorsing audiences and opponents (Solari, 2007).

An approach that focuses on the framing processes employed by social entrepreneurs to legitimate their ventures can be particularly useful for explaining variation in entrepreneurial outcomes. Consider the case of Van Jones, a social entrepreneur who was elected to the Ashoka Fellowship in 2000 in recognition of developing programmes that aim to systemically change criminal justice policies. Although Van Jones launched the Bay Area Police Watch as a hotline for victims of police brutality in 1995, he changed the name of this organisation to the Ella Baker Center in 1996. By naming the organisation after an 'unsung champion' of the civil rights movement and proclaiming that 'this is not your parents' civil rights organisation', Van Jones transformed the initial frame of the issue of police brutality into a broader frame that resonated with both old and young civil rights activists.[11]

A second frame transformation occurred when Van Jones and the Ella Baker Center launched the Green-Collar Jobs Campaign, which has the goal to bring 'green collar' jobs to Oakland, California. The Ella Baker Center identified under-employment and over-pollution as the most pressing social problems in Oakland. By using statements such as 'we envision eco-industrial parks on land once blighted by brownfields and prisons' and 'we want to move urban America from jail cells to solar cells', the Ella Baker Center developed a prognostic frame that resonated with both civil rights and environmental activists. Because of Van Jones's innovative framing and creative strategies, the Ella Baker Center attracted new resources and became recognised as one of the most effective and innovative social enterprises in America.

Still another promising line of inquiry is to examine how social entrepreneurs' perception of various opportunities impacts on their ventures' outcomes. The concept of political opportunity structures has been used by social movement scholars to account for variation in movements' repertoires and outcomes. The crucial features of political opportunity structures are the multiplicity of independent centres of power, the openness to new actors, the instability of existing political alignments, the availability of influential allies and the extent to which the regime represses or facilitates collective claim making (Tilly and Tarrow, 2007: 57). While this concept has been applied mainly to national political contexts, some studies show that transnational or supranational opportunity structures also impact the way movements make claims (della Porta and Kriesi, 1999; Tarrow, 2001). Other studies show that opportunity structures are not restricted to the political regime; cultural and discursive opportunities can also determine which ideas become accessible and are perceived as legitimate by the public (Koopmans and Stratham, 1999). Additionally, research shows that mass media plays a key role in the availability of discursive opportunities through reporting of protest events, thereby selecting which movements' messages and ideas are transmitted to the public (Gamson and Meyer, 1996).

A brief example illustrates the importance of focusing future research on the way in which social entrepreneurs' perceptions of political, discursive, and business opportunities shape their strategies and contribute to their endeavours' success. Consider the case of Javed Abidi, a social entrepreneur who has tirelessly worked to improve the lives of millions of disabled Indians. According to Bornstein, Abidi's success is due to his extraordinary diligence and to the fact that 'he has been preparing all his life for the role he has assigned himself as the executive director of the National Center for the Promotion of Employment for Disabled People (NCPEDP) in Delhi' (Bornstein, 2004: 210).

A closer examination, however, reveals that NCPEDP's various degrees of success are associated with the changes in the structures of political, discursive and business opportunities. The availability of influential political allies such as Sonia Gandhi was crucial in getting the Persons with Disabilities Act adopted by the Indian Parliament in 1995. Abidi's experience working for one of the major national newspapers, *The Times of India*, and his connections with other journalists allowed him to seize a discursive opportunity and to organise rallies that, although relatively small by Indian standards, got significant positive media coverage.[12] And, due to Abidi's networking with the Confederation of Indian Industry and Indian-based high-tech firms such as IBM, Apple Computer, Oracle or Microsoft, the NCPEDP had influential business allies who pushed for an effective implementation of the Persons with Disabilities Act.

To summarise, social entrepreneurship is an inherently complex process that requires combining insight from social movement studies and socio-logical research on entrepreneurship. Unlike 'regular' entrepreneurship, social entrepreneurship is by nature a political phenomenon because 'the act of defining the domain of the social inevitably requires exclusionary and ultimately political choices about which concerns can claim to be in society's "true" interest' (Cho, 2006: 36). Moreover, while the test of a successful business enterprise is the creation of a viable and growing busi-ness, the test of social entrepreneurship is often the creation of change in the social systems that produced and maintained the problem. Thus, the organisation created to solve the problem may get smaller as it succeeds (Alvord et al., 2002). A sociological analysis of social entrepreneurship requires specifying how societies negotiate among different, potentially contentious choices about social benefits, as well as understanding how social change occurs beyond the creation of new organisations or ventures. Researchers should examine how social entrepreneurs' mobilisation of organisational resources, interpretive work, and perception of political and discursive opportunities influence their selection of targets and ability to create long-term, positive social change.

9.5 CONCLUSION

Social entrepreneurship improves the lives of millions of people around the world. While the concept of social entrepreneurship has received growing attention in the mass media and business schools, social scientists know very little about the processes that facilitate the emergence of innovations that solve immediate social problems and also result in long-term, sustain-able social transformation. In this concluding section I highlight the main promises and challenges of developing a sociological research agenda on this topic.

First, sociological research can move beyond futile attempts to iden-tify social entrepreneurs by general behavioural patterns specific to the 'entrepreneurial personality'. Just as the presence of collective grievances does not guarantee the emergence of sustained mobilisations, the existence of creative individuals with great ideas for improving suboptimal social equilibriums is no assurance of the emergence of social entrepreneurship. A sociological perspective recognises that social entrepreneurs face considerable resistance to social change and aims to identify the social conditions that are conducive to social entrepreneurship. A particular challenge in developing this perspective, however, is to avoid moving from an under-socialised to an over-socialised approach; in other words, from an exclusive focus on individuals' characteristics to an exclusive focus on social structures. To avoid this problem, for example, sociological research should focus not only on the existence of concrete political, discursive or business opportunity structures for social entrepreneurship, but also on the way in which social entrepreneurs attribute existing opportunities and construct new ones. Sociological research should also focus on social entrepreneurs' actions and examine how they mobilise moral and organisational resources, and how they frame their actions to increase their ventures' legitimacy and attract additional support.

Second, a sociological perspective can overcome the implicit bias in studies that consider social entrepreneurship to be simply a new form of business entrepreneurship 'with a conscience'. Unlike the test of a successful business enterprise, the test of a successful social enterprise cannot be reduced to the creation of a new and growing venture. Instead, similar to the way in which a social movement is successful when it secures medium- and long-term collective benefits for its constituents, social entrepreneurship is successful when it creates a long-term solution to an imminent social problem. Social entrepreneurs can find long-term solutions to social problems without creating new viable enterprises, by building local capacities or working with existing grassroots groups. This poses a special problem for social researchers because they have to find a measure of social entrepreneurial outcomes that is independent from enterprise creation and growth. One way of addressing this issue is to examine how social entrepreneurs 'shop around' for the most vulnerable targets and attempt to create long-term positive change not only by creating new ventures, but also by working with governments for the adoption of new policies or with existing businesses for the adoption of innovative practices. To put it differently, this requires acknowledging that social entrepreneurship and social activism are often 'two sides of the same coin' that may involve creating innovative social enterprises as well as pushing for administrative and organisational reforms.

Finally, a sociological perspective can recognise that social entrepreneurship sometimes fails and, thus, avoids the common mistake of selecting only successful social enterprises. A growing number of organisations – such as Ashoka, New Profit, the Skoll and Schwab Foundations – have supported social entrepreneurs who have already had significant accomplishments, attempting to 'pick winners' and to scale up their success. Existing case studies of social entrepreneurship are, therefore, based on highly mediatised success stories but ignore cases of entrepreneurs who are less successful, 'part-time' or are not in the media spotlight. It will be difficult to know what produces social entrepreneurship until comparative research is completed to systematically analyse social enterprises with varying degrees of success. While identifying less successful or media-unsavvy social entrepreneurs is likely to be challenging, it is also imperative in order to advance our understanding of the conditions under which social entrepreneurs can solve the vast social problems of our times.

NOTES

1.   The numbers are based on my Lexis-Nexis search of the total number of newspaper articles in the US and around the world that included the term 'social entrepreneur' in the period 1990–2007.
2.   Studies suggest growing student interest in corporate social responsibility and social entrepreneurship. For example, a 2007 survey of MBA students has found that 81 per cent of students surveyed believe companies should try to work toward the betterment of society, and 79 per cent say they will seek socially responsible employment at some point during their careers. 'New leaders, new perspectives: a net impact survey of MBA student opinions on the relationship between business and social/environmental issues', a report produced by NetImpact' accessed online in March 2008 at, www.netimpact.org/associations/4342/files/MBA%20Perspectives.pdf.
3.   Accessed online in March 2008 at: www.riseproject.org/.
4.   'Beyond grey pinstripes, 2007–2008', a report produced by the Aspen Institute: The Center for Business Education, accessed online in March 2008 at, www.beyondgreypinstripes.org/rankings/bgp_2007_2008.pdf.
5.   I have searched all 47 sociological journals that are accessible through JSTOR using 'social entrepreneur(s)' in the title or abstract – no items matched the search.
6.   As Swedberg (2000: 17) notes, in his later writings Schumpeter made it clear that the entrepreneur does not have to be a person but can also be either a political or economic organization.
7.   For a literature review see Birley (1998).
8.   Accessed online in March 2008 at, www.amazonteam.org/about.html.
9.   For recent sociological research that addresses the question who becomes an entrepreneur and why, see Aldrich and Kim (2007) and Sorensen (2007).
10.   While the majority of entrepreneurial research has been conducted from a 'supply-side' perspective, which considers that societies need an adequate supply of special types of individuals who create entrepreneurship in order to advance economically, new studies have criticised the causal logic and methodology used by this research. For example, a common research design flaw of the 'supply-side' perspectives has been sampling on the dependent variable, or on successful entrepreneurs and firms (Thornton, 1999). More generally, this perspective has been criticised for underestimating the role of external structural influences and for making entrepreneurial activity too much a function of individuals (Martinelli, 1994). For different reviews of sociological studies of entrepreneurship, see Thornton (1999), Swedberg (2000) and Ruef and Lounsbury (2007).
11.   Ella Baker Center: a brief history, accessed online in March 2008 at, www.ellabaker-center.org/page.php?pageid=19&contentid=152.

12. Abidi's organization also attracted mass media's attention by organising the Helen Keller awards to recognise individuals and companies that supported people with disabilities, by recruiting movie stars as 'disability ambassadors', and by producing documentaries that were distributed nationally (Bornstein, 2004: 225).

REFERENCES

Aldrich, H. and P. Kim (2007), 'A life-course perspective on occupational inheritance: self-employed parents and their children', in M. Ruef and M. Lounsbury (eds), *The Sociology of Entrepreneurship*, Research in the Sociology of Organizations, vol. 25, Amsterdam and Oxford: Elsevier, pp. 33–82.

Alvord, S., D. Brown and C. Letts (2002), '*Social entrepreneurship and social transformation: an exploratory study*', Working Paper No. 15, available from the Social Science Research Network Electronic Paper Collection, Hauser Center for Nonprofit Organizations.

Amenta, E. and N. Caren (2004), 'The legislative, organizational, and beneficiary consequences of state-oriented challengers', in D. Snow, S. Soule and H. Kriesi (eds), *The Blackwell Companion to Social Movements*, Oxford: Blackwell, pp. 461–88.

Amenta, E. and M. Young (1999), 'Making an impact: conceptual and methodological implications of the collective goods criterion', in M. Giugni, D. McAdam and C. Tilly (eds), *How Social Movements Matter*, Minneapolis, MN: University of Minnesota Press, pp. 22–41.

Armstrong, E. and M. Bernstein (2008), 'Culture, power, and institutions: a multi-institutional politics approach to social movements', *Sociological Theory*, **26** (1), 74–99.

Begley, T. and D. Boyd (1998), 'Psychological characteristics associated with performance in entrepreneurial firms and smaller businesses', in S. Birley (ed.), *Entrepreneurship*, Aldershot: Ashgate, pp. 155–70.

Binder, A. (2004), *Contentious Curricula: Afrocentrism and Creationism in American Public Schools*, Princeton, NJ: Princeton University Press.

Birley, S. (1998), *Entrepreneurship*, Aldershot: Ashgate.

Bornstein, D. (2004), *How to Change the World. Social Entrepreneurs and the Power of New Ideas*, Oxford: Oxford University Press.

Brockhaus, R. (1998), 'Risk taking propensity of entrepreneurs', in S. Birley (ed.), *Entrepreneurship*, Aldershot: Ashgate, pp. 137–48.

Burt, R. (1993), 'The network entrepreneur', in R. Swedberg (ed.), *Explorations in Economic Sociology*, New York: Russell Sage Foundation.

Caronna, C. (2007), 'Turning identity into form: the cause and consequences for Kaiser Permanente of becoming and HMO', in M. Ruef and M. Lounsbury (eds), *The Sociology of Entrepreneurship*, Research in the Sociology of Organizations, vol. 25, Amsterdam and Oxford: Elsevier, pp. 309–36.

Cho, A.H. (2006), 'Politics, value, and social entrepreneurship: a critical appraisal', in J. Mair, J. Robinson and K. Hockerts (eds), *Social Entrepreneurship*, London: Palgrave Macmillan, pp. 34–56.

Cress, D. and D. Snow (1996), 'Mobilization at the margins: resources, benefactors and the viability of homeless social movement organizations', *American Sociological Review*, **61** (6), 1089–109.

Cress, D. and D. Snow (2000), 'The outcomes of homeless mobilization: the influence of organization, disruption, political mediation, and framing', *American Journal of Sociology*, **105**, 1063–104.

Dees, G. (2001), 'The meaning of "social entrepreneurship"', paper available online at, www.fuqua.duke.edu/centers/case/documents/dees_SE.pdf, accessed 18 April 2008.

Dyke, N. van, S. Soule and V. Taylor (2004), 'The targets of social movements. Beyond a focus on the state', in D.J. Myers and D.M. Cress (eds), *Authority in Contention*, Research in Social Movements, Conflicts and Change, vol. 25, Amsterdam: Elsevier, pp. 27–54.

Edwards, B. and J. McCarthy (2004), 'Resources and social movement mobilization', in D. Snow, S. Soule and H. Kriesi (eds), *The Blackwell Companion to Social Movements*, Oxford: Blackwell, pp. 116–52.

Gamson, W. (1990), *The Strategy of Social Protest*, Belmont, CA: Wadsworth.

Gamson, W. and D. Meyer (1996), 'Framing political opportunity', in D. McAdam, J. McCarthy and M. Zald (eds), *Comparative Perspectives on Social Movements: Political Opportunities, Mobilizing Structures, and Cultural Framings*, Cambridge: Cambridge University Press, pp. 275–90.

Gerhards, J. and D. Rucht (1992), 'Mesomobilization: organizing and framing in two protest campaigns in West Germany', *American Journal of Sociology*, **98**, 555–95.

Granovetter, M. (1995), 'The economic sociology of firms and entrepreneurs', in A. Portes (ed.), *The Economic Sociology of Immigration*, New York: Russell Sage Foundation, pp. 128–65.

Grenier, P. (2006), 'Social entrepreneurship: agency in a globalizing world', in A. Nicholls (ed.), *Social Entrepreneurship. New Models of Sustainable Social Change*, Oxford: Oxford University Press, pp. 119–43.

Jenkins, C. and C. Eckert (1986), 'Channeling black insurgency: elite patronage and professional social movement organizations in the development of the black movement', *American Sociological Review*, **51**, 249–68.

Katzenstein, M. (1999), *Faithful and Fearless. Moving Feminist Protest inside the Church and Military*, Princeton, NJ: Princeton University Press.

Koopmans, R. and P. Stratham (1999), 'Ethnic and civic conceptions of nationhood and the differential success of the extreme right in Germany and Italy', in M. Giugni, D. McAdam and C. Tilly (eds), *How Social Movements Matter*, Minneapolis, MN: University of Minnesota Press, pp. 225–52.

Liles, P. (1998), 'Who are the entrepreneurs?', in S. Birley (ed.), *Entrepreneurship*, Aldershot: Ashgate, pp. 87–96.

Mair, J. and E. Noboa (2006), 'Social entrepreneurship: how intentions to create a social venture are formed', in J. Mair, J. Robinson and K. Hockerts (eds), *Social Entrepreneurship*, New York: Palgrave Macmillan, pp. 121–35.

Mair, J., J. Robinson and K. Hockerts (eds) (2006), *Social Entrepreneurship*, New York: Palgrave Macmillan.

Martin, R. and S. Osberg (2007), 'Social entrepreneurship: the case for definition', *Stanford Social Innovation Review*, Spring, 27–39.

Martinelli, A. (1994), 'Entrepreneurship and management', in N. Smelser and R. Swedberg (eds), *The Handbook of Economic Sociology*, Princeton, NJ: Princeton University Press, pp. 476–503.

McAdam, D. (1982), *Political Process and the Development of Black Insurgency, 1930–1970*, Chicago, IL: University of Chicago Press.

McAdam, D., S. Tarrow and C. Tilly (2001), *Dynamics of Contention*, Cambridge: Cambridge University Press.

McCarthy, J. and M. Zald (1977), 'Resource mobilization and social movements. A partial theory', *American Journal of Sociology*, **82**, 1212–41.

Minkoff, D. (1995), *Organizing for Equality. The Evolution of Women's and Racial-Ethnic Organizations in America, 1955–1985*, New Brunswick, NJ: Rutgers University Press.

Moore, K. (1999), 'Political protest and institutional change: the anti-Vietnam War movement and American science', in M. Giugni, D. McAdam and C. Tilly (eds), *How Social Movements Matter*, Minneapolis, MN: University of Minnesota Press, pp. 97–118.

Morrill, C., M. Zald and H. Rao (2003), 'Covert political conflict in organizations: challenges from below', *Annual Review of Sociology*, **29**, 391–415.

Nicholls, A. (2006), *Social Entrepreneurship: New Models of Sustainable Social Change*, Oxford: Oxford University Press.

Nicholls, A. and A.H. Cho (2006), 'Social entrepreneurship: the structuration of a field', in A. Nicholls (ed.), *Social Entrepreneurship. New Models of Sustainable Social Change*, Oxford: Oxford University Press, pp. 99–118.

Pang, C.L. and J. Rath (2007), 'The force of regulation in the land of the free: the persistence of Chinatown, Washington DC, as a symbolic ethnic enclave', in M. Ruef and M. Lounsbury (eds.), *The Sociology of Entrepreneurship*, Research in the Sociology of Organizations, vol. 25, Amsterdam and Oxford: Elsevier, pp. 191–218.

Piven, F.F. and R. Cloward (1977), *Poor People's Movements*, New York: Vintage.

Porta, D. della and H. Kriesi (1999), 'Social movements in a globalizing world: an introduction', in D. della Porta, H. Kriesi and D. Rucht (eds), *Social Movements in a Globalizing World*, London: Macmillan, pp. 2–22.

Portes, A. and S. Shafer (2007), 'Revisiting the enclave hypothesis: Miami twenty-five years later', in M. Ruef and M. Lounsbury (eds), *The Sociology of Entrepreneurship*, Research in the Sociology of Organizations, vol. 25, Amsterdam and Oxford: Elsevier, pp. 157–90.

Raeburn, N. (2004), *Changing Corporate America from Inside Out. Social Movements, Protest and Contention, Volume 20*, Minneapolis, MN: University of Minnesota Press.

Rojas, F. (2007), *From Black Power to Black Studies: How a Radical Social Movement Became an Academic Discipline*, Baltimore, MD: Johns Hopkins University Press.

Ruef, M. and M. Lounsbury (2007), 'Introduction: the sociology of entrepreneurship', in M. Ruef and M. Lounsbury (eds), *The Sociology of Entrepreneurship*, Research in the Sociology of Organizations, vol. 25, Amsterdam and Oxford: Elsevier, pp. 1–32.

Schumpeter, J. (1975), *Capitalism, Socialism and Democracy*, New York: Harper.

Schumpeter, J. (2000), 'Entrepreneurship as innovation', in R. Swedberg (ed.), *Entrepreneurship. The Social Science View*, Oxford: Oxford University Press, pp. 51–75.

Snow, D. (2004), 'Social movements as challenges to authority. Resistance to an emerging conceptual hegemony', in D. Myers and D. Cress (eds), *Authority in Contention*, Research in Social Movements, Conflicts and Change, vol. 25, Amsterdam: Elsevier, pp. 3–27.

Snow, D. and R. Benford (1988), 'Ideology, frame resonance, and participant mobilization', *International Social Movement Research*, **1**, 197–217.

Solari, L. (2007), 'Entrepreneurship at the margins of society: founding dynamics in grey (sex shops) and black markets (Mafia)', in M. Ruef and M. Lounsbury (eds), *The Sociology of Entrepreneurship*, Research in the Sociology of Organizations, vol. 25, Amsterdam and Oxford: Elsevier, pp. 337–68.

Sorensen, J. (2007), 'Closure and exposure: mechanisms in the intergenerational transmission of self-employment', in M. Ruef and M. Lounsbury (eds), *The Sociology of Entrepreneurship*, Research in the Sociology of Organizations, vol. 25, Amsterdam and Oxford: Elsevier, pp. 83–124.

Swedberg, R. (ed.) (2000), *Entrepreneurship. The Social Science View*, Oxford: Oxford University Press.

Tarrow, S. (2001), 'Contentious politics in a composite polity', in D. Imig and S. Tarrow (eds), *Contentious Europeans: Protest and Politics in an Emerging Polity*, Boulder, CO: Rowman & Littlefield, pp. 233–51.

Thornton, P. (1999), 'The sociology of entrepreneurship', *Annual Review of Sociology*, **25**, 19–46.

Tilly, C. (1978), *From Mobilization to Revolution*, Reading, MA: Addison-Wesley.

Tilly, C. and S. Tarrow (2007), *Contentious Politics*, Boulder, CO: Paradigm.

Vries, K. de (1998), 'The entrepreneurial personality: a person at the crossroads', in S. Birley (ed.), *Entrepreneurship*, Aldershot: Ashgate, pp. 113–36.

10. Social entrepreneurship in the UK: from rhetoric to reality?

Paola Grenier

10.1 INTRODUCTION

> A growing band of social entrepreneurs, working at the grass roots of the welfare system in the space between the public and private sector, are developing innovative answers to many of Britain's most pressing social problems.
>
> Social entrepreneurs are leading innovation in the most dynamic parts of the voluntary sector and on the edge of the public sector, often with the help of private sector partners. They frequently use business methods to find new solutions to problems such as homelessness, drug dependency and joblessness. They create innovative services by taking under-utilised resources – particularly buildings and people – to address social needs left unmet by the public sector or the market. (Leadbeater, 1997: back cover)

In the mid to late 1990s, the idea that individual 'social entrepreneurs' were critical to the successful tackling of social problems started to be taken seriously in policy circles in the UK. Social entrepreneurs were presented as similar to business entrepreneurs – visionary individuals with the drive, passion and skills that are generally associated with the private sector. Social entrepreneurs, however, were credited with creating social value and public benefit rather than private wealth, most often through non-profit or voluntary action. They were presented as a new kind of innovative leader, transforming existing institutions and introducing much needed social change at all levels of society. They were promoted as central to the modernisation of welfare and the effective provision of social services, especially in tackling those social issues where the state and the market are said to have failed.

Social entrepreneurship suffers from a particularly bad case of terminological confusion, with multiple and often ambiguous definitions. The most helpful clarification on the multiple definitions that exist is the broad division drawn by Dees and Anderson (2006) between the 'social innovation' and the 'social enterprise' schools of thought. The 'social innovation' school of thought focuses on the role of innovative leaders, people who bring about transformatory social change; the 'social enterprise' school of thought focuses on the simultaneous pursuit of social and financial goals by organisations. More often than not, however, 'social entrepreneurship' is used either ambiguously or as an umbrella term, deliberating incorporating both schools of thought.

The late 1990s in the UK provided especially fertile ground for 'social entrepreneurship'. Social entrepreneurship inspired political rhetoric and policy proposals. It was the subject of numerous reports and publications, presented by left of centre think-tanks eager to contribute to and shape New Labour thinking and policy (Brickell, 2000; Leadbeater, 1997; Thake and Zadek, 1997). And the emergence of 'social entrepreneurship' within UK policy was closely associated with the election of New Labour into government in 1997. In his first speech as new Prime Minister, on the pressing topic of welfare reform, Tony Blair, commented: 'We will be backing thousands of social entrepreneurs – those people who bring to social problems the same enterprise and imagination that business entrepreneurs bring to wealth creation' (Blair 1997).

From its early association with the 'third way', social entrepreneurship rapidly came to attract unequivocal cross-party political support. As interest in social entrepreneurship grew and developed, the term acquired a cachet that attracted resources, policy debate, and media attention (Taylor et al., 2000).

In more practical terms, the enactment of social entrepreneurship in the UK has motivated the founding of several organisations that identify, support, train and fund 'social entrepreneurs'. Between 1997 and the end of 2006 hundreds, if not thousands, of social entrepreneurs were identified in the UK: the School for Social Entrepreneurs (SSE) trained more than 280 social entrepreneurs; Community Action Network (CAN) involved around 900 social entrepreneurs in its membership network; Senscot engaged with approximately 1500 people who either are social entrepreneurs or work with social enterprises; and UnLtd, the foundation for social entrepreneurs, supported more than 2000 budding social entrepreneurs. These social entrepreneurs have been supported and funded to help 'solve' a wide range of intractable social 'problems'.

Yet, amid all the enthusiasm for social entrepreneurship and all the hopes and claims associated with it, it remained unclear what the discourse of social entrepreneurship actually meant: to what extent was it merely a rhetorical device, a call for change and an inspirational assertion of what was possible; and in what ways did government support provided in the name of social entrepreneurship actually impact on communities, the voluntary sector and the specific practices of welfare provision?

This chapter traces the emergence of social entrepreneurship in the UK and how it was taken up as an idea and practice in UK social policy between 1980 and 2006. It explores the political and policy context within which social entrepreneurship developed, the changing ways in which the idea of social entrepreneurship was presented, and the range of practices and organisational enactments that were carried out in the name of social entrepreneurship. It argues for a more complex dynamic than a simple gap between policy rhetoric and the reality of policy interventions and organisational practices. It discusses the implications and effects of policy and the ways in which policy discourses created opportunities that were then manipulated and used to support different vested interests and practice based agendas (Mosse, 2004).

10.2 DISCOURSE AND MEANING

The language of social entrepreneurship is striking – the claims made on its behalf, the descriptions of social entrepreneurs, the sheer enthusiasm with which it was greeted. Its application in policy and practice belies its use as an analytical or descriptive term, and it can be better considered as a rhetorical device or a 'slogan' (Dey, 2006; Sutherland, 2001; Swedberg, 2006). 'One of the difficulties with the notion of social entrepreneurship is that is it not connected to a general theory of entrepreneurship, but is usually used as a slogan or inspiring phrase' (Swedberg, 2006: 21).

It is primarily through language that the contested nature, ambiguous definitions and claim-bearing nature of social entrepreneurship are apparent. Social entrepreneurship can seem as smoke and mirrors, and challenges us to think carefully about what is 'real', what is 'spin', and whose interests are being served and to what ends. But where Dees (2004) calls for a separation of the 'rhetoric from the reality', explicitly acknowledging the normative and often rhetorical nature of the literature, I would rather suggest that the rhetoric is itself part of the phenomenon under study. To consider social entrepreneurship without engaging with the rhetoric and the use of language is to miss something fundamental about its particular contemporary salience.

In his classic book *Keywords* Raymond Williams (1976) comments on the importance of the way in which words are used, and that their meaning and significance may have little to do with formal definitions. He points especially to words which 'involve ideas and values', words which circumscribe how an issue is discussed and approached, and which reflect our understanding of how we experience the world (Williams, 1976: 17). Social entrepreneurship may not warrant the status of a 'keyword', but it can be seen as a fashionable term, a 'buzzword' that is deliberately ambiguous at the same time as attracting policy attention, press coverage, money, and as inspiring people and organisations to take action. Such 'buzzwords' are said to frame issues and solutions, to influence how practitioners and policy-makers think, to imply possible futures and to constrain what is done in practice and policy (Cornwall and Brock, 2005). 'The way words come to be combined allows certain meanings to flourish, and others to become barely possible to think with' (Cornwall and Brock, 2005: iii).

The academic literature on social entrepreneurship is dominated by a managerialist approach, with much of the writing coming out of US business schools (Anderson and Dees, 2006; Austin, 2006). There has been a small amount of academic work on social entrepreneurship from a social constructionist perspective, and this has provided more critical and politically oriented examinations of social entrepreneurship (Amin et al., 2002; Cho, 2006; Dart, 2004; Dey, 2006; McDonald and Marston, 2001; Parkinson, 2005).

These more critical perspectives on social entrepreneurship do not make up a systematic or coherent critique, and there is little or no cross-referencing between them, but taken together they offer analyses with a number of implications for the basic conceptualisation of social entrepreneurship, for policy and practice, as well as for future research and theory development. The literature points to a tension between the rhetoric of social entrepreneurship as a necessary and radical new force for change, and analyses which argue that social entrepreneurship mimics the mainstream, is a way of gaining legitimacy and represents a continuation of the neo-liberal impulse to reduce the role of the state and propel welfare provision further towards the market. Based on the literature three main critiques of social entrepreneurship can be identified:

1. It focuses too much on the characteristics and role of exceptional individuals, thereby crediting individuals with more power and effect than they can realistically have. It individualises what are societal and structural problems, undermining the role and responsibilities of the state and fragmenting social welfare (Amin et al., 2002; Edwards, 2002; McDonald and Marston, 2001).
2. It mimics the mainstream by privileging business and crediting being business-like and market oriented with attributes and effects which extend inappropriately in the arenas of social and political action. This undermines the role of communities as sources of creative alternatives. (Amin, Cameron and Hudson, 2002; Dart, 2004).
3. It sidelines political and social issues and processes, including the place of social justice, the effects of power inequalities, the implications of economic inequality and the inherent nature of the social as contested (Cho, 2006; Dey, 2006; McDonald and Marston, 2001).

The main implication of these critiques is that social entrepreneurship is ineffective in practice in bringing about the kind of radical change with which it has been associated or in introducing alternatives to outdated institutions. It 'plasters over the cracks' rather than creates systemic change.

This chapter takes up the challenge and potential of adopting a social constructionist perspective to analysing social entrepreneurship, and seeks to contribute to the more critical literature by examining the specific case of the emergence of social entrepreneurship into UK social policy. Social constructionism provides a uniquely appropriate approach that enables this chapter to engage with the ambiguous and contested definitions that characterise social entrepreneurship, and to understand the resulting confusion as part of the field. Social entrepreneurship is understood here in terms of discourse, and discourse analysis is employed to unpack social entrepreneurship as both an idea and as a practice. This research explores what sort of conversations and debates 'social entrepreneurship' enables, who engages in the field and why, who benefits from social entrepreneurship and how, and what types of organised actions and practices social entrepreneurship has given rise to.

Research data was collected from a wide variety of sources, including interviews, media coverage, policy documents, speeches, 'grey' think-tank reports, promotional materials, books, organisational documents, websites, membership databases, newsletters and academic writing. In this way, the intention was to engage with the breadth of social entrepreneurship as a field of discourse, policy interest and organisational practice. It was also important that the data collected capture: the range of contextual influences; the variety of ideas, representations and images; and the diversity of organisational and individual practices and enactments. Data covered the period from 1980 to 2006, with interviews conducted between 2000 and 2003.[1]

10.3   SETTING THE SCENE

The shift from the 'enterprise culture' of Thatcherism to the 'third way' of New Labour between 1980 and 2000 formed the policy context into which social entrepreneurship emerged. In particular, it was the shift from the free market 'selfish' values promoted under Thatcher to a concern for community and civic values under Labour that created set the scene for social entrepreneurship. As one leading proponent of social entrepreneurship commented during a research interview: 'the political climate is important. Social entrepreneurs have been around forever but the idea of promoting a movement of social entrepreneurship – Thatcherism helped, the focus on the individual and the individual ability to change things, to achieve things, to take responsibility for themselves.'[2]

The term 'enterprise culture' came into common usage during the 1980s and 'emerged as a central motif in the political thought and practice of the Conservative government in Britain' (Keat, 1991: 1). The Conservative Prime Minister, Margaret Thatcher, was concerned that 'the British sense of enterprise and initiative would have been killed by socialism' (Keat, 1991: 1). She saw her role as aiming to reignite that spirit and give it free reign in a deregulated free market economy, and so 'to transform Britain into an "enterprise culture"' (Keat, 1991: 1). The private sector was privileged as an organisational form; and individuals were extolled to demonstrate 'initiative, energy, independence, boldness, self-reliance, a willingness to take risks and to accept responsibility for one's actions' (Keat, 1991: 3). Business entrepreneurs were presented as the heroes of the day, and welfare recipients as dependent. Challenging welfare 'dependency' became a major plank of policy discourse, and the battle lines were drawn as the market orientation of the 'enterprise culture' was pitted against the 'dependency culture' of the 'nanny' state.

The enterprise culture seemed to imbue almost all aspects of life, taking on different forms and prioritising different aspects (Hall, 1988; Keat, 1991). But despite its seeming pervasiveness, critics and commentators concur that Thatcherism did not wholly succeed in changing British culture (Hetzner, 1999; Phillips, 1998). Two reasons for this can be identified from the literature. First was the absence of a moral emphasis on decency, fair play and serving the public good (Heelas, 1991; Hetzner, 1999). Hertzner argues that such strongly expressed self-serving values did not serve the entrepreneur, who, while glamorous, was also a figure of avarice, opportunism and corruption, a figure who might be envied but was not admired or loved – 'the business-person-as-manager was still held in contempt' (Jenkins, quoted in Hetzner, 1999: 307).

The second shortcoming was the absence of 'community' from the enterprise discourse. Thatcher's famous statement that 'there is no such thing as society'[3] has come to represent the lack of concern for the social and the obsession with the market. Communities were fractured and became sites of unrest rather than sites of solidarity. Rising levels of poverty, inequality and unemployment meant that there were increasing numbers of people left out of the 'market society' and the drive towards consumerism (Slater and Tonkiss, 2002; Taylor, 2003). As local communities felt besieged, there were outbreaks of rioting and urban unrest, often sparked by racial tensions.

An energy for change and optimism for the future accompanied New Labour's landslide electoral victory in 1997. Contrary to what former

Prime Minister Margaret Thatcher had said, people again started to believe that there was such a thing as society: there was a sense that the 'me' generation was becoming the 'we' generation, rejecting the rampant individualism of the 1980s (Mulgan, 1997; 19). Mirroring Thatcher's concerns 18 years previously, where she had fretted that the naturally enterprising nature of the British people had been destroyed by socialism, New Labour were concerned that the essential civic nature of the British had been eroded by neo-liberalism. New Labour discourses emphasised 'community', 'partnership', 'participation' and 'inclusion', invoking an ethic of reciprocity as well as individual responsibility. 'The language of democracy, citizenship, society, community, social inclusion, partnership, public participation, central to new Labour's discursive repertoires, can be understood as an attempt to reinstall "the social" in public and social policy' (Newman, 2001: 6).

Labour promised to bring together the competing priorities of economic prosperity and social cohesion, under the banner of a new pragmatism that they described as the 'third way'. It sought to retain the progress achieved under consecutive Conservative governments, but to place social justice as central to policy in the tradition of social democratic politics (Blair, 1998; Blair and Schroeder, 1999; Giddens, 1998; 2000).

Enterprise and entrepreneurship remained strong themes in New Labour, both in terms of continuing to ensure an enterprising business culture (Brown, 2003), and in references to making the public services more enterprising and more entrepreneurial (du Gay, 2000; Hendry, 2004). 'We need more successful entrepreneurs, not fewer of them. But these life-chances should be for all the people. And I want a society in which ambition and compassion are seen as partners not opposites – where we value public service as well as material wealth' (Labour Party Manifesto, 1997).

New Labour brought with it a new language and a new accommodation between the 'social' and the 'market' (Fairclough, 2000). Business was reframed as a socially positive actor, and the 'social-ising' of business terms became increasingly common and familiar. Hybrid expressions which brought together a social term with a business term – such as 'social capital', 'social investment', 'venture philanthropy', 'social business', 'social enterprise', even 'fair-trade' – proliferated. These hybrid expressions mirrored the 'third way' discourse of creating a middle ground between the politics of right and left, between society and the individual, between the state and the market, and resonated with the communitarian edge that characterised much policy rhetoric at that time (Hale, 2004; Taylor, 2003).

'Social entrepreneurship' was one example of this hybridisation of business and the social. The term first appeared in the UK press in 1985.

In these early appearances, there was little sense of a coherent notion of social entrepreneurship, let alone a policy agenda around it. From 1994 social entrepreneurship started to be discussed as being relevant to UK social policy (Atkinson, 1994; Thake, 1995). The idea was picked up on and enthusiastically advocated for by a few individuals, several of whom had close links with the Labour Party and with the left of centre think tanks influencing the emerging political agenda. These included Lord Michael Young, Geoff Mulgan, Charles Leadbeater, Andrew Mawson and Dick Atkinson; all had a strong background in voluntary action and several of them identified themselves as social entrepreneurs. They were all outspoken, articulate and experienced, and were increasingly interested in this rather nebulous idea of social entrepreneurship and how it might translate into organisational action.

The election of the New Labour government in 1997 was the turning point for 'social entrepreneurship'. The Demos report *The Rise of the Social Entrepreneur* published in 1997 was especially influential (Leadbeater, 1997). And soon social enterprise and social entrepreneurship were consistently on the lips of those in New Labour and those influencing it (Field, 1994; Leadbeater, 1997; Mulgan, 1997). Overnight social entrepreneurship became 'flavour of the month' and had the attention of the 'boss' (White, 1999). '[I]f the concept of "social enterprise" didn't exist, Tony Blair would have invented it' (Taggert, 2002: 30).

This section has shown how enthusiasm for creating an 'enterprise culture' during the 1980s under the Conservative government of Prime Minister Thatcher, was followed by calls for an 'entrepreneurial culture' by the New Labour government. Dissatisfaction and disillusionment with the self-interest promoted during the 1980s gave way to a concern for the social, and a desire to bring back ideas of community into political discourses. The election of the New Labour government in 1997 and their 'third way' political framework provided the opportunity for 'social entrepreneurship' to be considered as a policy issue.

10.4 THE RHETORIC OF SOCIAL ENTREPRENEURSHIP

The opportunity presented by the election of the Labour government, and the concomitant interest in new policy ideas with a 'social' edge, was enthusiastically taken up by those promoting social entrepreneurship. They had two priorities. One was to influence government thinking and policy; the other was to raise funding to set their own ideas for supporting social entrepreneurs in motion and to established new organisations. For both purposes the idea of social entrepreneurship needed greater legitimacy, and its role and potential contribution in the UK needed to be spelt out more clearly and more persuasively. 'Over the last term New Labour has managed to free "entrepreneurship" from its Thatcherite connotations of individual greed by linking enterprise to issues of inclusion, regeneration and to personal aspiration' (Westall, 2001: 49).

A main way in which legitimacy was sought was through the left of centre think-tanks which were keen to influence the Labour government, for example Demos, the New Economics Foundation (NEF), and the Fabian Society.[4] In his research on think tanks, Blank (2003: 104) notes that 'social entrepreneurship has come via Demos'.

> Since 1997, and in the years running up to that election, there has hardly been a think-tank worth its salt – and certainly not a Labour-inclined think-tank – that has not been promoting the idea of social entrepreneurs and social enterprises: people and organisations that plug the gap between state-owned enterprises and organisations and the traditional private sector, for-profit model. (Timmins, 2001)

Such think-tanks and their numerous reports were important influences on New Labour. Equally, Denham and Garnett (1998) argue that think-tanks in the UK are more interested in media coverage and asserting a particular position than in detailed research or in contentious and difficult policy issues. They conclude that their influence on government has been 'more easily detected in its discourse or rhetoric than in the detail of policy' (Denham and Garnett, 1998: 185). The think-tanks depended on the advocates of social entrepreneurship for ideas and information, and they acted as a mechanism for aligning certain novel ideas or interesting practices with policy agendas, ensuring that they were politically relevant and would catch the attention of politicians. To this end, the language of the reports drew on the policy discourses of the day to reinforce the importance of social entrepreneurship to issues such as 'social capital' and 'community cohesion', thereby positioning social entrepreneurship as immediately relevant to government policy. It was largely through the think-tank reports that the rationale for social entrepreneurship and the different forms it could take started to be spelt out.

Discourse analysis draws attention to the nature of the 'problem' and the 'solution' as starting points for analysing how an argument or rationale is constructed discursively and made persuasive. This part therefore focuses on the ways in which social entrepreneurship was promoted, rationalised and justified, by reviewing first how the 'problem' was characterised and second how the 'solution' (social entrepreneurship) was located within existing policy discourses.

The 'problems' that social entrepreneurship was intended to 'solve' were presented as 'pressing', 'urgent', 'acute', 'intransigent', 'intractable' – all words that contribute to a sense of impending crisis and alarm.

[T]hose intransigent social and environmental problems the government is committed to addressing. (Thake and Zadek, 1997: 21)

We are at a major turning point in history, and that social and development models are in crisis and require immediate attention. (Favreau, 2000: 227)

I think that there is a desperation in our society to find some answers to very pressing social problems.[5]

The impression of crisis was reinforced by the portrayal of existing 'traditional' institutions and approaches as having completely failed.

The state, once the saviour, is regarded as just another of the problems. Some of the passion has drained out of general politics and been transferred to a thousand separate good causes. Successive governments have undermined their own civil service and the professionals in the public sector employed in teaching, local government and medicine. The domain of public service has been vacated ... (Young, 1997: 20)

The urgency of existing problems, the absolute failure of existing approaches, and the sense of historical changes requiring something new and immediate can be described as 'epochal' (du Gay, 2004): 'epochal accounts are those that seek to encapsulate the Zeitgeist in some sort of overarching designation' (du Gay, 2004: 43).

'Social entrepreneurship' was put forward as the answer to these 'problems'. In policy terms, social entrepreneurship was credited as having the potential as a force for good at *all* levels of society, and in all fields of action. For some, social entrepreneurship was a panacea that could cure *all* social ills (Nicholls, 2006). 'Social innovation holds the key to our social ills. Social entrepreneurs are the people most able to deliver that innovation' (Leadbeater, 1997: 19).

Social entrepreneurship can be understood as a claim-bearing term, and there were four main arenas within which it claimed to make a potentially critical impact:

1. Community renewal (Brickell, 2000; Moore, 2002; Thake and Zadek, 1997). Social entrepreneurship was said to enhance social capital and build community (Leadbeater, 1997; Thake and Zadek, 1997). In an overview of the field, Moore (2002) identified the impetus for social entrepreneurship in the UK as having its origins in community and

neighbourhood renewal, in particular urban regeneration, issues that had been policy priorities for many years: 'it is the impetus for local regeneration and renewal that has provided one of the major driving forces of the social entrepreneurship movement' (Moore, 2002: 3). 'Community leaders and "social entrepreneurs" were to become the catalysts for overcoming the problems of run-down neighbourhoods' (Newman, 2001: 145).

2. Voluntary sector professionalisation (Defourny, 2001; 2003; Leadbeater, 1997). Social entrepreneurship was identified in the UK context as essential to reform a sector that 'is slow moving, amateurish, under-resourced and relatively closed to new ideas' (Leadbeater, 1997: 50). Defourny argued that there is a 'new entrepreneurial spirit' reflecting an 'underlying movement' which is impacting and reshaping the non-profit sector (Defourny, 2003: 1). In these accounts, social entrepreneurship appeared as a kind of modernising force within the UK voluntary and community sector, providing an impetus for change, new forms of voluntary action, and a professional edge that would take the sector forward to further expand its role as a mainstream provider of social services.

3. Welfare reform (Leadbeater, 1997; Mort et al., 2003; Thompson et al., 2000). Yet others envisaged social entrepreneurship as a timely response to social welfare concerns of the day and as an answer to the 'crisis of our welfare systems' (Defourny, 2003; see also Dees, 1998; Leadbeater, 1997; Thake and Zadek, 1997). Social entrepreneurship was claimed to 'help empower disadvantaged people and encourage them to take greater responsibility for, and control over, their lives' (Thompson et al., 2000: 329), and to counter dependency on welfare systems and charity (Leadbeater, 1997; Mort et al., 2003).

4. Democratic renewal (Favreau, 2000; Moore, 2002; Mulgan, 2006). Moore (2002) argues that globalisation and the rapidly changing world had given rise to new philosophical debates, new notions of a more socially and environmentally responsible economics, and basic questions such as: what kind of society would we like to live in? 'Social entrepreneurs and the social enterprises they create are one kind of response to a renewed search for the public good' (Moore 2002). She argued that social entrepreneurship was 'producing a new form of citizenship, a new relationship between civil society and the state' (Moore 2002). Along similar lines Mulgan (2006) described social entrepreneurship as: 'part of the much broader story of democratization: of how people have begun to take control over their own lives, over the economy, and over society' (Mulgan, 2006: 94).

With such claims and promises associated with social entrepreneurship, who could doubt that supporting social entrepreneurs was not only a good thing but also an urgent policy priority?

Social entrepreneurship was not put forward as a 'new' solution to a 'new' policy problem. Rather it drew on existing policy discourses and ongoing concerns about 'the dependency culture', poverty, the 'welfare state crisis', 'bureaucracy' and government 'inefficiency'. This was brought together with the policy interests of New Labour in embracing the voluntary sector as an alternative and preferred provider of social welfare, with public sector reform agendas, and concerns about rebuilding 'community' and the 'social fabric' of society.

But what exactly was 'social entrepreneurship'? The assumed and unquestioning focus was on the figure of the individual 'social entrepreneur', and as such social entrepreneurship was invariably and exclusively identified with a type of person. 'Social innovation holds the key to our social ills. Social entrepreneurs are the people most able to deliver that innovation' (Leadbeater, 1997: 19). Three main representations of social entrepreneurs are identified and discussed below.

Charismatic Heroes

The social entrepreneur as 'charismatic hero' became the figure most immediately and commonly associated with social entrepreneurship in the UK. 'The early picture of social entrepreneurs as lone, charismatic heroes' (Bentley, 2001: 22).

The most influential representation of social entrepreneurs was put forward in the Demos report *The Rise of the Social Entrepreneur*:

> But what makes a social entrepreneur? Social entrepreneurs are:
> - entrepreneurial: they take under-utilised, discarded resources and spot ways of using them to satisfy unmet needs
> - innovative: they create new services and products, new ways of dealing with problems, often by bringing together approaches that have traditionally been kept separate
> - transformatory: they transform the institutions they are in charge of, taking moribund organisations and turning them into dynamic creative ones. Most importantly, they can transform the neighbourhoods and communities they serve by opening up possibilities for self-development. (Leadbeater, 1997: 77)

The social entrepreneur as 'charismatic hero' quickly took on a specifically British form. One person interviewed referred to social entrepreneurs in terms of the 'buccaneering' figure of Richard Branson, bringing

to mind a kind of adventurer and risk-taker, a modern-day Errol Flynn
who challenges the status quo, but is inherently good and romantic,
someone who overcomes all obstacles and pitfalls with charm and
determination.

'Social entrepreneurs are individualistic mavericks, the Dysons and
Bransons of community development' (MacGillivray et al., 2001: 31).
With Branson as its business counterpart, it is not surprising that the social
entrepreneur as 'charismatic hero' became the most clearly articulated and
popular image of social entrepreneurship.

Managerial Social Entrepreneurs

Social entrepreneurs were also presented as founders of new organisations,
as skilled, rational and strategic. These managerial social entrepreneurs
were not necessarily especially innovative or visionary, but rather acted
as facilitators or enablers, working through organisations to bring about
change. There were three ways in which social entrepreneurs came to be
represented in managerial terms: as leaders of large regeneration organisations, as leaders of successful mainstream voluntary sector organisations
and as leaders of social enterprise organisations.

First was the social entrepreneur as heading up community regeneration organisations, as presented by Thake (1995) in *Staying the Course*.
Community regeneration organisations were large, cross-sector partnerships, generally funded by government grants, and tasked with regenerat-
ing the economies of deprived areas. Even though Thake's (1995) report
devoted only two pages to describing social entrepreneurs, he painted a
compelling picture:

> At the centre of every successful community regeneration organisation is a new
> type of professional person: the social entrepreneur. In many ways they are
> similar to private sector entrepreneurs. They are able to see and develop the
> potential of under-utilised resources – human, financial and physical. They are
> personable, have energy and are able to motivate people. They have organisa-
> tional and persuasive skills and they are excited by the prospect of getting things
> done. They are adept at the administration and manipulation of grant regimes.
> They differ from their private sector counterparts in that the purpose of their
> involvement is to create assets, resources and surpluses which make the com-
> munity richer. They are part of an apolitical, ethical thread within society which
> has a concern for social justice. (Thake, 1995: 48)

Second was the idea of mainstream voluntary sector managers as social
entrepreneurs, bringing an entrepreneurial approach to the voluntary sector.
The School for Social Entrepreneurs encapsulated this idea with its aim
of creating a business school for the voluntary sector. 'The idea of social

entrepreneurs – extolled by the Demos think-tank and a new business school – is of individuals who lead risk-taking voluntary organizations' (Noble, 1997: 8).

Third was the idea of social entrepreneurs as heading up social enterprise organisations. The particular skill of the social entrepreneur was to balance 'social' and 'business' goals when running such hybrid organisations. The main emphasis on being 'entrepreneurial' was to be 'business-like', and there was a secondary emphasis on being 'innovative' in that social enterprise was a novel organisational form. It could also involve founding an organisation, though not necessarily. 'Social entrepreneurs are the people who make the Social Economy and Social Enterprises work' (Pearce, 1999). 'There is a growing interest in the contribution of "social entrepreneurs" who work for community objectives through a combination of commercial and non-commercial activities' (Deakin, 2001: 16).

The managerial social entrepreneur was especially appealing to policy-makers, as a type of professional person managing a range of welfare services at the same time as being 'community' focused. This fitted neatly with emerging policy discourses – the professionalism of the 'enterprise culture' coupled with a moral purpose and sense of the public good which were important to the Labour party and reflected public concerns about how to reconnect with 'society'.

Community-Based Entrepreneurs

The 'ordinary' person as entrepreneur also came through strongly in the discourse. There was an emphasis on local community-based action in Atkinson's 1994 report, and the centrality of 'community' was strongly emphasised by Thake and Zadek (1997) and Leadbeater (1997). 'Social entrepreneur: One of the new breed of local activists who believe that energy and organisation can improve a community. To be found organising street patrols to liberate red-light districts, or running local exchange-trading schemes' (Rowan, 1997: T67).

Social entrepreneurship became a way of re-imagining the role of individuals within communities, where a sense of community had been 'lost' following the embrace of the market and neo-liberalism during the 1980s (Taylor, 2003). It was also a way of highlighting the importance of community development and updating it with a more contemporary language, attracting policy attention. 'Community' quickly became a central and defining feature of many forms of social entrepreneurship in the UK. It even appeared in Leadbeater's (1997) account of 'heroic' social entrepreneurs – people who transform local communities. 'Community' was a legitimising badge for social entrepreneurship, fitting neatly with Labour party discourses which were incorporating ideas of 'localism' and 'community' into their policy agenda.

But social entrepreneurship as a solution to pressing social problems was not just about the figure of the individual social entrepreneur. It was also about a change in culture, about promoting a shift in the way of doing things, in attitudes and values. 'We are trying to put in place the foundation stones for a new, entrepreneurial culture in the public and voluntary sectors' (Mawson, quoted in Garrett, 2000: 142).

Invariably 'entrepreneurship' was equated with business, and social entrepreneurs were deemed the same as or 'equivalent' to business entrepreneurs. 'Social entrepreneurs are the equivalent of true business entrepreneurs but they operate in the social, not-for-profit sector' (CAN, 2001).

Social entrepreneurs were portrayed in the interviews as having 'the skills and values which are common to entrepreneurs in the business sector', and as using business-type tools and techniques such as planning, marketing and measurement. Social entrepreneurship was about 'competition', 'outputs', 'audit trails' and 'quality of service'; 'business plans' and 'accounting'; 'return on investment' and 'customer care'. It was also about 'seizing the moment, making connections, wheeling and dealing in ideas' and 'someone who actually gets things done'. It emphasised the role of the 'customer', 'the quality of service', and the importance of organisational growth and replication.

Taken together, this gives a sense that social change is more about meeting consumer needs (or wants and preferences) than a process of political empowerment or promoting human rights. And welfare becomes a business transaction rather than a democratic commitment to social justice. This is well illustrated by one of the leading proponents of social entrepreneurship in the quote below, advocating a more 'business-like' approach:

> Calling for a more businesslike approach to regeneration, he said 'inner city areas need managing properly by experienced players; the problem is not a democratic deficit but access to a greater range of quality services. Who provides services is not a political decision really but a business one' (Mawson, quoted in Butler, 2002).

The rhetoric of social entrepreneurship was powerful and the rationale and claims associated with social entrepreneurship became closely tied into specific UK policy discourses. This was an essential transition from the very generic claims that were being made in the previous period if social entrepreneurship was to become significant within policy. The effect was to frame social entrepreneurship as directly relevant to very contemporary policy concerns. Furthermore, social entrepreneurship became imbued with concepts and language that connected directly to the ways in which policy-makers were discussing issues. This helped to make social entrepreneurship familiar, easy to talk about and therefore an appealing and natural 'solution' to call on.

The swash-buckling charismatic social entrepreneur was the most obviously appealing construction of social entrepreneurship. However, the charismatic social entrepreneur was not so immediately or obviously relevant to policy-makers. The charismatic hero was popular in the media and with some organisations promoting social entrepreneurship, but did not become a part of political or policy discourse. There are two main reasons for this. First, policy agendas and were focused on 'reform' and 'modernisation' rather than radical transformation, and the epochal discourses supporting charismatic forms of social entrepreneurship were therefore at odds with dominant policy discourses. Second, charismatic heroic figures, who were characterised as being idiosyncratic and unpredictable, and who challenge existing institutional structures, were not easily accommodated within highly structured and systematised state programmes.

The managerial social entrepreneur, on the other hand, was more attractive to policy makers. This was a 'business-like' figure – professional and skilled, good at leading and managing organisations, focused on efficiency and effectiveness. The managerial social entrepreneur as flexible, and could put his or her talents to use in a variety of settings. First, as voluntary sector managers who were better able to deliver social welfare services for the right cost, at the right quality and at a large enough scale to warrant government interest. Second, as a new cadre of professional managers of hybrid social enterprise organisations, bringing together a business-like edge with an ethical focus, and with a particular capacity for providing cost-effective social welfare services. Third, as working within the public services, bringing about reform and leading change. In some ways this is a reformulation of the enterprising manager from the Thatcher period, the professional self-starter made decent and virtuous (Hetzner, 1999).

This was not a figure associated with radical transformation or epochal change, but fitted neatly into the New Labour government policy discourses of 'reform', 'modernisation' and professionalisation of both the voluntary and the public sectors. It was a representation that drew particularly on 'third way' discourses, providing a 'technical', pragmatic and ideologically neutral solution to the inevitable and unstoppable changes taking place (Bastow and Martin, 2003). It trod a middle path between left and right, between 'social' and 'market', reconciling long-standing antagonisms, without needing to account for how this reconciliation takes place in practice. The managerial social entrepreneur was identified almost solely with the practical task of social welfare service provision. And this had the effect of equating social change with an organisational level of action and with effective and financially sustainable organisational practices rather than with raising public consciousness or creating a new political vision around which to mobilise and inspire people.

The representation of the community-based social entrepreneur was also consistent with government policy interests and discourses, but in a different way. The community-based social entrepreneur represented initiative and self-reliance at the local level. There was little emphasis on the 'business-like' nature of community-based entrepreneurs. In policy terms the community-based entrepreneur reflected communitarian themes, and was about communities taking more responsibility for their own welfare. It was also an expression of government concerns with promoting active citizenship, and the role of citizens in rebuilding deprived communities both socially and economically. The community-based social entrepreneur was the moral face of society, the pro-social, responsible citizen, the opposite of those people subject to ASBOs (anti-social behaviour orders).

10.5   THE PRACTICE OF SOCIAL ENTREPRENEURSHIP

The two main ways in which social entrepreneurship was enacted in the UK was through organisational practices and policy interventions. There were multiple ways in which the policy discourses and rhetoric of social entrepreneurship were translated and realised in practice.

Policy Interventions

Social entrepreneurship was embraced enthusiastically in policy circles, and quickly became a serious policy consideration with the New Labour government. But it proved challenging in terms of concrete policy interventions and support, and translating the hopes and claims associated with social entrepreneurship into tangible structural and policy change was not straightforward (Mulgan, 2006).

There were three main ways in which social entrepreneurship came to be supported through government policy. First was that by 2001 support for social entrepreneur organisations had become a routine part of government funding for the voluntary sector infrastructure through the Active Communities Unit (ACU) in the Home Office. Social entrepreneurship was becoming incorporated into public policy; at the same time its impact was very limited: '4 years after Tony Blair's breathless paragraph, social entrepreneurship has become a well-established part of the social policy landscape, but has not yet had a decisive impact on the mainstream delivery of social policy through public services, even in the field of urban regeneration' (Bentley, 2001: 23).

Second was government funding targeting 'enterprising' individuals within communities. The Millennium Awards Scheme had been set up under the Conservative government in 1996, providing small grants of around £2000 to individuals with an idea to do something beneficial within their local community. Between 1996 and 2004 the Millennium Awards Scheme supported more than 32 000 'starpeople'. In 1999 the Department of Education piloted the Community Champions Fund which followed the same model as the Millennium Awards Scheme, but focused more specifically on educational initiatives. The pilot was deemed successful and it became an ongoing funding programme. This was then followed with the granting of an endowment of £100 million to UnLtd, the foundation for social entrepreneurs. UnLtd continued and extended the work of the Millennium Awards Scheme, but re-branded it as social entrepreneurship.

Third was that from 2000, social enterprise started to appear on the government agenda in a significant way. Even during the early stages of its emergence into social policy agendas, social enterprise was more easily amenable to government support and direct policy interventions than social entrepreneurship. Her Majesty's Treasury (HMT) set up the Social Investment Task Force (SITF) which reported to the Chancellor of the Exchequer in October 2000 with its report, 'Enterprising communities: wealth beyond welfare'.[6]

Five proposals were made which were all taken up by the Treasury, and were clearly carefully anticipated and previously negotiated. They included tax incentives to encourage financial investment in deprived areas and recommendations for two new legal forms of organisation. By 2001, social enterprise featured consistently in government policy and it became possible to identify a systematic policy framework to support its development. In 2001 the Social Enterprise Unit was set up within the Department of Trade and Industry (DTI), to act as a hub and reference point for the development of social enterprise. Barbara Philips, head of DTI Social Enterprise Unit was quoted in the *Observer* as saying: 'For a lot of ministers, it's a winning formula: business solutions to social problems' (Walsh, 2003: 12). There is no evidence of any government departments or other stakeholders who do not think that social enterprise has a role to play in policy delivery (Henry et al., 2006: iv).

Social enterprise featured in a significant way in several policy documents on the voluntary sector,[7] where the idea of social entrepreneurship as 'social innovation' was all but absent. And the government set out is agenda for social enterprise in 2002 with 'Social Enterprise. A strategy for success', which was followed up in 2006 with 'Social Enterprise action plan. Scaling new heights'.

In his account of the policy initiatives introduced to encourage social entrepreneurship, Mulgan (2006) listed a number of interventions that government undertook during his time in the Cabinet Office. These were initiatives aimed not so much at supporting social entrepreneurship directly, but at removing barriers and providing incentives in order to encourage the organic development of the field. He included the small grants given to individual social entrepreneurs through the Millennium Commission and UnLtd. But everything else listed concerned the mainstream voluntary sector or social enterprise, including: improving the tax treatment of donations; encouraging volunteering; licensing the Charity Bank; creating the Community Interest Company as a new legal form; setting up the Futurebuilders fund to support voluntary sector infrastructure; targeting advice to social enterprise through Business Links; funding voluntary sector participation in Local Strategic Partnerships; introducing the New Deal for Communities; and promoting social enterprise in public sector procurement.

None of these initiatives stand out as contributing to creating substantial support for the social innovation version of 'social entrepreneurship' as a clear-cut field of activity. Encouraging volunteering, promoting giving, and developing the organisational and management capacity of voluntary organisations, are aimed at furthering the government's agenda to expand the role of the voluntary sector in social service provision. None of these require a concept of social entrepreneurship or a distinct set of organisations supporting social entrepreneurs. It was social enterprise that captured the imagination and attention of policy-makers.

Organisational Practices

This section is about what has been done in the name of social entrepreneurship. It describes the organisational practices that were developed and how these shaped social entrepreneurship as a field of action.

By 2000 there were five key organisations specifically set up to support UK social entrepreneurs:

● Ashoka was a US-based non-profit organisation, generally credited with having pioneered the idea of social entrepreneurship in terms of the 'social innovation' school of thought (Bornstein, 2004; Dees and Anderson, 2006). Its main focus was to support individual 'social entrepreneurs' in developing countries, but in 1997 it started to talk about launching a UK programme.

- The School for Social Entrepreneurs (SSE) was set up by Lord Michael Young in 1997 offering a year-long training and development course for aspiring social entrepreneurs from all walks of life. Its expressed purpose was to create a business school for the voluntary sector.
- Community Action Network (CAN) was established in 1998 by Andrew Mawson, Adele Blakebrough and Helen Taylor-Thompson. It supported an Internet based network of social entrepreneurs, and ran a number of projects and programmes intended to foster entrepreneurial activity in different geographical locations and within different fields. It was established with the very specific aim of identifying 2000 social entrepreneurs by the year 2000, promoted under the slogan '2,000 by 2000'.
- Senscot was founded in 1999, a Scottish-based membership network of social entrepreneurs and people interested in social entrepreneurship. The co-founder and director of Senscot was not especially concerned with the terminology of social entrepreneurship, but with getting something off the ground that resonated and would attract support. He made the following comment during an interview for this research:

> It doesn't matter, community activists, community leaders. I intersperse the terms. It's nothing to me, more than that, its almost quite cynical, to attract money. I could equally have set up the social community leaders network . . . I am also an opportunist, so when the name seemed to attach energy I adopted that and managed to attract some funding. (Co-founder and Director of Senscot)

- UnLtd was created in 2000 as the vehicle for a £100 million endowment from the Millennium Commission. It was a collaborative effort that included SSE, CAN and Senscot and four other organisations. UnLtd was set up as a grant-making foundation, providing funding and support to social entrepreneurs throughout the UK. UnLtd was especially important in that it represented the permanent establishment of social entrepreneurship in the UK with the ambition that 'social entrepreneurship' pass into 'common usage'.

A small and specialist field working on social entrepreneurship was therefore starting to establish, supported financially by business donors, grantmaking trusts, and increasingly through government grants. Table 10.1 shows the progress of the organisations in attracting funding and also in identifying social entrepreneurs. It shows in particular the relatively large

*Table 10.1   Progress of social entrepreneur support organisations,
2000–2006*

Organisation	No. of UK soc entrepreneurs		UK income	
	2000	2006	2000	2006*
Ashoka	—	—	£0.3 million	—
CAN	400	909	£1.5 million	£3.2 million
Senscot	180	1500	£0.1 million	£0.4 million
SSE	51	276	£0.5 million	£0.4 million
UnLtd	—	2216	—	£9.2 million
Total	631	4901	£2.4 million	£13.2 million

Note: *Figures are taken from Charity Commission website for the financial year
2005/2006.

impact of UnLtd compared with the other organisations, contributing 70
per cent of the total income within the field of social entrepreneurship and
45 per cent of the social entrepreneurs in 2006.

The types of activities as well as the way these organisations arranged
their work served to structure the space within which social entrepreneurship developed, and therefore what forms social entrepreneurship took.
As the space for social entrepreneurship became more carefully structured,
defined and bounded, the nature of what was social entrepreneurship in the
UK also became clearer.

The infrastructure organisations acted as gatekeepers to the field of
social entrepreneurship. The 'charismatic hero' version failed to gain
purchase in the UK, and this was particularly evident in that Ashoka
struggled to find a position in the UK. This is clear from Table 10.1. The
SSE deliberately moved away from its original focus on voluntary sector
managers to locate its work within deprived communities; from the beginning Senscot positioned itself as close to the community sector, aiming
to empower people at the grassroots; and CAN drew on community
discourses to justify and position itself as tackling community depriva-
tion. These organisations determined who were (and who were not) the
social entrepreneurs and where social entrepreneurship was located. And
in practice there was a consensus locating social entrepreneurship and
social entrepreneurs as 'community based', carrying out small-scale local
activities to meet community needs.

Support was provided to individual social entrepreneurs in three main
ways: making small grants, providing expertise and consultancy, and facilitating peer networks. The nature of this support was in marked contrast

to more traditional forms of support for community development coming from government, which had tended to involve large-scale urban regeneration programmes implemented through large institutional partners. The structuring of social entrepreneurship targeted individuals within communities, and, rather than assuming that large amounts of money were necessary, worked to release the creativity and initiative of people to make a small difference. The assumption was that enough small-scale activities would make a large impact in deprived areas.

The social entrepreneurship organisations concentrated on making friends with the business sector, where a similarity of approach and interests was often cited as providing a positive basis for partnership. 'Business recognises that social entrepreneurs add value to depleted social resources, just as businesses seeks to add value to shareholders' investment . . . CAN has benefited enormously from the advice, encouragement and financial support of numerous companies' (CAN, 2007).

Community Action Network has been most successful in attracting business support and it has formed some novel partnerships with the private sector, finding ways to channel the expertise on offer in more structured and strategic ways than is often the case. In 2006 CAN and Permira entered a partnership to support the scaling up of social enterprises, creating the Breakthrough programme. For CAN, Permira offered the expertise and funding that social enterprises needed; and for Permira, CAN was an organisation it could relate to and that would provide it with a worthwhile and meaningful role in supporting social causes. The relationship was about transferring skill and expertise more than it was about transferring money.

However, the most striking development in the nature of the support provided by these organisations was their struggle with how to locate themselves in relation to 'social enterprise'. Policy was increasingly focused on social enterprise, and there were growing numbers of social enterprise organisations and organisations set up to support social enterprise, including Social Enterprise London (SEL) and the Social Enterprise Coalition (SEC).

All four organisations outlined here struggled in different ways with whether to or how to incorporate the growing policy and practitioner interest in 'social enterprise' into their work. Both CAN and Senscot developed a range of activities, and broadened their focus to include social enterprise. By the end of 2006, the work of both organisations centred on the 'social enterprise' school of thought and their original purpose of promoting social innovation was abandoned. The SSE and UnLtd, on the other hand, felt under pressure to incorporate social enterprise into their work, but in practice they remained focused on social entrepreneurship as a 'community-based' phenomenon, promoting initiative and innovation at the local level.

'Social entrepreneurship' in the UK developed into a substantive field, enacted in two main forms. First, the several thousand people who were labelled and supported as 'social entrepreneurs' and who carried out relatively small-scale local social action. In this form 'social entrepreneurship' was about community and community development, and was a way of targeting individuals while sustaining a commitment to 'community action'. At the same time, this form of social entrepreneurship did not have fundamental implications for social welfare, but was rather a specific organisational innovation as practised by UnLtd and the SSE. The second form of 'social entrepreneurship', however, was more pervasive, as social enterprise was promoted as a preferred way of 'doing business' in the private, public and voluntary sectors.

10.6   DISCUSSION AND CONCLUSIONS

The findings point to a disconnect between the extravagant claims made on behalf of social entrepreneurship and the ways in which it has been enacted. 'Social entrepreneurship' did not result in the radical transformation of sectors or society as had been claimed. 'Social entrepreneurship' was rather a means through which those seeking to influence policy and raise funds, in particular the social entrepreneur support organisations, have gained a policy profile by distinguishing themselves from 'traditional' approaches at the same time as adopting and adapting dominant policy discourse in order to appear familiar and relevant.

As an *idea*, there are several different understandings of social entrepreneurship. Yet, despite the different definitions in use and the distinctions between different versions of social entrepreneurship, the exact meaning of social entrepreneurship seems to matter less than what it is used to signify in general terms. For policy-makers the language of social entrepreneurship is more important than the organisational practices or specific policy interventions. The idea of social entrepreneurship frames a convenient discourse within which to emphasise policy priorities centred on further incorporating a market orientation to addressing social needs.

In policy debate, the terminology of social entrepreneurship is indicative of the coming together of 'business' with the 'social'. However, it is not used to signify an equal relationship, rather its usage indicates the application of business concepts, practices and approaches to the provision of social welfare. It equates the course of social change with a set of organisational processes – good management, strong leadership, effective governance, performance measurement, organisational expansion and growth. It also communicates the need for individuals to be enterprising and entrepreneurial – not only in their work lives, but also in taking responsibility for their own and their community's welfare. With this in mind, the discourse of social entrepreneurship is one aspect of 'enterprising-up' the arena of social welfare, a way of further extending what was known under Thatcherism as 'the enterprise culture' into the community and into the voluntary and public sectors.

The *practice* of social entrepreneurship contrasts with social entrepreneurship as an idea. The centrality of 'community' to the enactment social entrepreneurship in the UK has been clearly shown. Social entrepreneurship was manifested primarily at the community level, as directing support and attention to the thousands of local people who are taking the initiative in identifying and meeting social needs, generally through community and voluntary organisations. As such it was positioned as closer to the field of traditional community development than as originating innovation within the mainstream voluntary or public sectors and in bringing about societal-level transformation. As such, the practice of social entrepreneurship in the UK assumed that innovation, and even social transformation, was a collective phenomenon, rather than the result of the lone charismatic heroes that are typical of the popular imagination.

As a practice, it is suggested here that social entrepreneurship was a mechanism through which business and policy support and attention was directed into poor communities. It was an expression of the communitarian tendency in policy discourse, which was drawn on and adapted to gain legitimacy and facilitate relationships between the private sector and the field of community development.

Social entrepreneurship is therefore part of a complex dynamic within UK social policy. Its implications are neither entirely positive nor entirely problematic. Rather it has drawn on and been drawn into existing and emerging policy discourses as a way of creating space for the development of support for particular practice-based interests.

Social entrepreneurship is not so much a new movement or radical new approach, but can be more realistically considered a useful label and rhetorical devise which resonated in the political climate for those wanting to construct their support for social action in new ways – be they people in business, in the voluntary sector, in community development or in government. It was a way in which some people working in the voluntary and community sector have reframed their field in order to gain greater purchase on policy, and to attract resources and support from the private sector. Three roles are suggested below as the main ways in which social entrepreneurship has made an impact on UK social policy: renegotiating welfare responsibilities, creating a channel through which business can engage with community and enabling government policy to respond to the particularism of the local.

Renegotiating Welfare Relationships

Social entrepreneurship is associated with government interests in creating 'enterprising communities' where entrepreneurial responses to welfare needs are encouraged and enterprising individuals are credited with catalysing such action. Social entrepreneurship is used in policy discourses to signal the need for 'enterprise' and culture change in a variety of institutional settings. Social entrepreneurship was not a way of focusing or structuring policy interventions, but rather a way of signalling the need for a change in attitude, approach, behaviour and, ultimately, culture, in the voluntary sector, in the public sector and in community development. Social entrepreneurship represented the introduction of a new enterprising culture. By locating social entrepreneurs at the community level, the support organisations are reflecting policy discourses that exhort individuals to be self-reliant and responsible.

Engaging Business

Social entrepreneurship in the UK was about local community and small-scale voluntary action while it drew on managerial and enterprise discourses. The effect was to bring 'business' to the 'community'. Where the voluntary sector has been subject to many decades of influence and pressures to become more professional and more 'business-like', finding ways to make the dominant societal paradigm of 'business is best' relevant to small and often ad hoc community groups has been less straightforward. Social entrepreneurship has created a channel through which private sector approaches and resources can be filtered, adapted and directed into communities.

By adopting the language of business and asserting that business methods and processes are essential to tackling social problems, a space is created within which those in business can engage with social issues. Business and management become important, and business people are made to believe they can contribute and make a difference without needing to understand the complexity of social needs. Within that space, the practice of social entrepreneurship has introduced mechanisms that enable the exchange of ideas, money, expertise, energy, people and techniques between the sectors. Money has perhaps been the least significant aspect, as business support for social entrepreneurship in financial terms has been marginal. The transfer of skills and expertise has taken place through consultancy services, both formally and informally, whether targeted to the support organisations or to the social entrepreneurs.

Facilitating Community-Based Policy

On the one hand social entrepreneurship is a way in which individuals and individualism can gain recognition within community development, a field that has been otherwise dominated by notions of solidarity and collective action, and has often been reluctant to engage with issues of leadership and to respond to the growing individualism of society as a whole. On the other hand, government has struggled to find ways of supporting locally initiated action in deprived communities, where it has consistently tried and failed to achieve economic and social prosperity. Small-scale locally targeted support to individual social entrepreneurs offers a way of doing that. Social entrepreneurship infrastructure organisations have provided government with a mechanism through which they can support grassroots action without imposing centralised structures. A wide diversity of actions and types of people are supported through social entrepreneurship. As such, social entrepreneurship can be understood as a way for the universalist tendencies of the state to respond to the particularism of the local.

NOTES

1. The research was carried out as part of a PhD in social policy at the London School of Economics, entitled 'The role and significance of social entrepreneurship in UK social policy'.
2. Interview conducted confidentially by the author.
3. The much quoted comment by Thatcher, that 'there is no such thing as society', is indicative of the way in which the individualised nature of the enterprise culture as a political project was interpreted and understood. The intention was to refer to the abstraction of society, and attempt to ground it in where actual responsibility lay: 'And, you know, there is no such thing as society. There are individual men and women, and there are families. And no government can do anything except through people, and people must look to themselves first. It's our duty to look after ourselves and then, also to look after our neighbour. People have got the entitlements too much in mind, without the obligations. There's no such thing as entitlement, unless someone has first met an obligation' (Prime Minister Margaret Thatcher, talking to *Women's Own* magazine, 3 October 1987).
4. See the Appendix for a list of think-tank reports on social entrepreneurship and social enterprise.
5. Interview conducted confidentially by the author.
6. The commission of this report was one of the recommendations that came out of the Policy Action Team Report 16 (PAT 16, 1999). '4. Commission a feasibility study into options for providing easier access to social capital funding and low-cost loans for community-based organisations. This should be co-ordinated by HMT with a report completed by autumn 2000' (PAT 16 1999, 33).
7. The 'Role of the voluntary and community sector in service delivery: a cross cutting review' by HM Treasury, September 2002, identified social enterprises as potentially

important service delivery organisations that could contribute to economic development and public sector reform. And 'Private action, public benefit. A review of charities and the wider not-for-profit sector' by the Cabinet Office and Strategy Unit, September 2002, sought to 'encourage entrepreneurialism' by which was meant 'entrepreneurial ways to secure a sustainable income'.

REFERENCES

Amin, A., A. Cameron and R. Hudson (2002), *Placing the Social Economy*, London: Routledge.

Anderson, B.B. and G.J. Dees (2006), 'Rhetoric, reality, and research: building a solid foundation for the practice of social entrepreneurship', in A. Nicholls (ed.), *Social Entrepreneurship: New Models of Sustainable Social Change*, Oxford: Oxford University Press, pp. 144–68.

Atkinson, D. (1994), *The Common Sense of Community*, London: Demos.

Atkinson, D. (2000), *Urban Renaissance: A Strategy for Neighbourhood Renewal and the Welfare Society*, Studley: Brewin Books.

Austin, J.E. (2006), 'Three avenues for social entrepreneurship research', in J. Mair, J. Robinson and K. Hockerts (eds), *Social Entrepreneurship*, London: Palgrave Macmillan, pp. 22–33.

Baderman, J. and J. Law (2006), *Everyday Legends*. The Ordinary People Changing the World – Stories of *20 Great UK Social Entrepreneurs*, London: UnLtd.

Bastow, S. and J. Martin (2003), *Third Way Discourse: European Ideologies in the Twentieth Century*, Edinburgh: Edinburgh University Press.

Bentley, T. (2001), 'Creative tension? Social entrepreneurs, public policy and the new social economy', unpublished report, September, Demos.

Blair, T. (1997), 'Speech given by the Prime Minister at the Aylesbury Estate, June 1997', available from www.cabinet-office.gov.uk/seu/index/more.html, accessed 29 October 1999.

Blair, T. (1998), *The Third Way: New Politics for the New Century*, Fabian Pamphlet, No. 588, London: Fabian Society.

Blair, T. and G. Schroeder (1999), 'Europe: the third way/Die Neue Mitte', a speech given by the Prime Minster to the Labour Party, London, 8 June.

Blank, R.C. (2003), *From Thatcher to the Third Way. Think-Tanks, Intellectuals and the Blair Project*, Stuttgart: ibidem-Verlag.

Bornstein, D. (2004), *How to Change the World*, Oxford and New York: Oxford University Press.

Brickell, P. (2000), *People before Structures: Engaging Communities Effectively in Regeneration*, London: Demos.

Brown, G. (2003), 'A modern agenda for prosperity and social reform', speech by the Chancellor of the Exchequer to the Social Market Foundation, Cass Business School, London, 3 February.

Butler, P. (2002) 'Voluntary sector needs to adopt entrepreneurial spirit', *Guardian*, Guardian Society, 7 November, available at: http://guardian.co.UK/society/2002/nov/07/5, accessed 3 May 2003.

Cho, A.H. (2006), 'Politics, values and social entrepreneurship: a critical appraisal', in J. Mair, J. Robinson and K. Hockerts (eds), *Social Entrepreneurship*, London: Palgrave Macmillan, pp. 34–56.

Community Action Network (CAN) (2001), available using 'internet archive: wayback machine' from www.archive.org/web/web.php by inputting www.can-online.org, dated February 2001, accessed on 5 March 2004.

Community Action Network (CAN) (2007), 'About us, the CAN story', available from www.can-online.org, last accessed 16 September 2007.

Christie, I. and C. Leadbeater (1999), *To our Mutual Advantage*, London: Demos.

Cornwall, A. and K. Brock (2005), *Beyond Buzzwords. 'Poverty Reduction', 'Participation' and 'Empowerment' in Development Policy*, Overarching Concerns, (Programme Paper Number 10), United Nations Research Institute for Social Development.

Crabtree, T. and A. Roberts (1992), Towards a New Sector: Macro-policies for Community Enterprise, London: New Economics Foundation.

Dart, R. (2004), 'The legitimacy of social enterprise', *Nonprofit Management & Leadership*, **14** (4), 411–24.

Deakin, N. (2001), 'Five years after: a brief commentary', in W. Plowden (ed.), *Next Steps in Voluntary Action*, London: NCVO, pp. 3–54.

Dees, G.J. (1998), 'The meaning of social entrepreneurship', available from http://www.the-ef.org/resources-Dees103198.html, accessed 1 May 2000.

Dees, G.J. (2004), 'Keynote speech', Skoll World Forum on Social Entrepreneurship, Skoll Centre for Social Entrepreneurship, Said Business School, Oxford, 29–31 March.

Dees, G.J. and B.B. Anderson (2006), 'Framing a theory of social entrepreneurship: building on two schools of practice and thought', in R. Mosher-Williams (ed.), *Research on Social Entrepreneurship: Understanding and Contributing to an Emerging Field*, ARNOVA Occasional Paper Series, vol. 1, No. 2, Indianapolis: ARNOVA, pp. 39–65.

Defourny, J. (2001), 'Introduction. From third sector to social enterprise', in C. Borzaga and J. Defourny (eds), *The Emergence of Social Enterprise*, London: Routledge.

Defourny, J. (2003), 'A new entrepreneurship in the social economy', available from www.emes.net/en/recherche/emes/analyse.php, accessed on 21 August 2000.

Denham, A. and M. Garnett (1998), *British Think Tanks and the Climate of Opinion*, London: UCL Press.

Dey, P. (2006), 'The rhetoric of social entrepreneurship: paralogy and new language games in academic discourse', in C. Steyaert and D. Hjorth (eds), *Entrepreneurship as Social Change: A Third Movements in Entrepreneurship Book*, Cheltenham, UK and Northampton, MA, USA: Edward Elgar, pp. 121–42.

Edwards, S. (2002), 'Social enterprise: changing the landscape of welfare provision in the United Kingdom and Ontario, Canada', paper presented at ISTR Conference, Cape Town, South Africa, July.

Fairclough, N. (2000), *New Labour, New Language*, London: Routledge.

Favreau, L. (2000), 'The social economy and globalisation: an overview', in J. Defourny, P. Develtere and B. Foneneau (eds), *Social Economy North and South*, Belgium: Katholieke Universiteit Leuven and Universite de Liege.

Field, F. (1994), 'Book review. Map readings and extracurricular activities: *Radical Urban Solutions* by Dick Atkinson', *The Independent*, 18 April, p. 15.

Garrett, A. (2000), 'Dynamic leaders with a social conscience', *Management Today*, 1 November, 138–43.

Gay, P. du (2000), 'Enterprise and its futures: a response to Fournier and Grey', *Organization*, **7** (1), 165–83.

Gay, P. du (2004), 'Against "Enterprise" (but not against "enterprise", for that would make no sense)', *Organization*, **11** (1), 37–57.

Gibson, A. (1996), *The Power in Our Hands: Neighbourhood-based World Shaking*, Chipping Norton: Jon Carpenter Publishing.

Giddens, A. (1998), *The Third Way. The Renewal of Social Democracy*, Cambridge: Polity Press.

Giddens, A. (2000), *The Third Way and its Critics*, Cambridge: Polity Press.

Hale, S. (2004), 'Community by contract? New Labour, the rhetoric of community, and the language of the social contract', paper prepared to the Political Studies Association Conference, University of Lincoln, 6–8 April.

Hall, S. (1988), *The Hard Road To Renewal: Thatcherism and the Crisis of the Left*, London: Verso.

Heelas, P. (1991), 'Reforming the self', in R. Keat and N. Abercrombie (eds), *Enterprise Culture*, London: Routledge, pp. 72–92.

Hendry, J. (2004), 'Cultural confusions of enterprise and the myth of the bureaucratized entrepreneur', *Entrepreneurship and Innovation*, February, 53–7.

Henry, N., J. Medhurst and J. Lyttle, (2006), 'Review of the social enterprise strategy. Small business service', a full report submitted by GHK, Job No. J1837.

Hetzner, C. (1999), *The Unfinished Business of Thatcherism: The Value of the Enterprise*, New York: P. Lang.

Keat, R. (1991), 'Introduction', in R. Keat and N. Abercrombie (eds), *Enterprise Culture*, London: Routledge.

Labour Party Manifesto (1997), 'Labour Party Manifesto', available from www. labour-party.org.uk/manifestos/1997/1997-labour-manifesto.shtml, accessed 5 March 2007.

Landry, C. and G. Mulgan (1995), *The Other Invisible Hand: Remaking Charity for the 21st Century*, London: Demos.

Leadbeater, C. (1997), *The Rise of the Social Entrepreneur*, London: Demos.

MacGillivray, A., C. Wadhams and P. Conaty (2001), *Low Flying Heroes: Micro-social Enterprise below the Radar Screen*, London New Economics Foundation.

Mayo, E. and H. Moore (2001), *The Mutual State: How Local Communities can run Public Services*, London: New Economics Foundation.

McDonald, C. and G. Marston (2001), 'Fixing the niche? Rhetorics of the community sector in the neo-liberal welfare regime', paper presented at workshop 'Social entrepreneurship: whose responsibility it is anyway?', Centre of Full Employment and Equity (CofEE) and the Department of Social Work.

Moore, H. (2002), 'Building the social economy', available from www.fathom.com/feature/35515/, accessed 23 September 2004.

Mort, G., J. Weerawardena and K. Carnegie (2003), 'Social entrepreneurship: towards conceptualisation', *Nonprofit and Voluntary Sector Marketing*, **8** (1), 76–88.

Mosse, D. (2004), 'Is good policy unimplementable? Reflections on the ethnography of aid policy and practice', *Development and Change*, **35** (4), 639–71.

Mulgan, G. (1997), 'On the brink of a real society', *Guardian*, Features Page, 1 February, p. 19.

Mulgan, G. (2006), 'Cultivating the other invisible hand of social entrepreneurship: comparative advantage, public policy, and future research priorities', in

A. Nicholls (ed.), *Social Entrepreneurship: New Models of Sustainable Social Change*, Oxford: Oxford University Press, pp. 74–95.

Newman, J. (2001), *Modernising Governance: New Labour, Policy and Society*, London: Sage.

Nicholls, A. (2006), 'Endnote', in A. Nicholls (ed.), *Social Entrepreneurship: New Models of Sustainable Social Change*, Oxford: Oxford University Press, pp. 407–12.

Noble, L. (1997), 'Partners 2000: the price of social enterprise', *Guardian*, Guardian Society, 5 November, p. 8.

Parkinson, C. (2005), 'Meanings behind the language of social entrepreneurship', Lancaster University Management School Working Paper, 072, Institute for Entrepreneurship and Enterprise Development, Lancaster University Management School.

PAT 16 (1999), 'Learning lessons. National strategy for neighbourhood renewal: report of Policy Action Team 16, HM Treasury, March.

Pearce, J. (1999), 'Individual and collective models of social entrepreneurship', available from www.sse.org.uk/conference/speakers/pearce_paper1.html, accessed 15 June 2000.

Phillips, L. (1998), 'Hegemony and political discourse: the lasting impact of Thatcherism', *Sociology*, **32** (4), 847–67.

Pike, M. (2003), *Can-do Citizens: Rebuilding Marginalised Communities*, London: Scarman Trust.

Plater-Zyberk, H. (2005), *Working from the Heart: An Exploration of What Propels 12 Quality Social Entrepreneurs*, London: UnLtd.

Rowan, D. (1997), 'Lastword: glossary for the 90s', *Guardian*, Guardian Weekend, 15 February, p. T67.

Scott, D., P. Alcock, L. Russell and R. Macmillan (2000), Moving Pictures: Realities of Voluntary Action, York: Joseph Rowntree Foundation.

Slater, D. and F. Tonkiss (2002), *Market Society: Markets and Modern Social Theory*, Malden, MA: Polity Press.

Sutherland, J. (2001), 'How the potent language of civic life was undermined', *Guardian*, Guardian Society, 20 March, p. 10.

Swedberg, R. (2006), 'Social entrepreneurship: the view of the young Schumpeter', in C. Steyaert and D. Hjorth (eds), *Entrepreneurship as Social Change: A Third Movements in Entrepreneurship Book*, Cheltenham, UK and Northampton, MA, USA: Edward Elgar, pp. 21–34.

Taggert (2002), 'Britain: the third way in action; social enterprise', *The Economist*, **364** (8285), 30.

Taylor, M. (2003), *Public Policy in the Community*, Basingstoke and New York: Palgrave Macmillan.

Taylor, N., R. Hobbs, F. Nilsonn, K. O'Halloran and C. Preisser (2000), 'The rise of the term social entrepreneur in print publications', in P.D. Reynolds, E. Autio, C.G. Brush, W.D. Bygrave, S. Manigart, H.J. Sapienza and K.G. Shaver (eds), *Frontiers of Entrepreneurship Research*, Wellesley, MA: Babson College.

Thake, S. (1995), *Staying the Course: The Role and Structure of Community Regeneration Organisations*, York: Joseph Rowntree Foundation, York Publishing Services.

Thake, S. (1999), 'The training and education needs of social entrepreneurs', available from www.sse.org.uk/conference/speakers/thake_paper1.html, accessed 15 June 2000.

Thake, S. and S. Zadek (1997), *Practical People, Noble Causes: How to Support Community-based Social Entrepreneurs*, London: New Economics Foundation.

Thompson, J., G. Alvy and A. Lees (2000), 'Social entrepreneurship – a new look at the people and potential', *Management Decision*, **38** (5), 338–48.

Timmins, N. (2001), 'When not-for-profit outgrows its usefulness', *Financial Times*, 19 November, Comment and Analysis, p. 23.

Walsh, C. (2003), 'The underpinning: essential elements that make social enterprise work', *Observer*, 2 November, p. 12.

Welch, P. and M. Coles (1994), *Towards a Social Economy – Trading for a Social Purpose*, London: Fabian Society.

Westall, A. (2001), *Value Led Market Driven: Social Enterprise Solutions to Public Policy Goals*, London: IPPR.

Westall, A., P. Ramsden and J. Foley (2000), *Micro-entrepreneurs: Creating, Enterprising, Communities*, London: New Economics Foundation and IPPR.

White, M. (1999), 'Whitehall warfare', *Guardian*, 12 August, p. 17.

Williams, R. (1976), *Keywords: A Vocabulary of Culture and Society*, London: Fontana.

Wilson, J. (ed.) (2000), *The New Entrepreneurs: Seminar 3   Social Entrepreneurship*, London: Smith Institute.

Young, M. (1997), 'Do-gooders with savvy', *New Statesman*, **126** (4322), 20.

APPENDIX: UK REPORTS AND PUBLICATIONS ON SOCIAL ENTREPRENEURSHIP

Table 10A.1   UK think-tank reports on social entrepreneurship

Date	Title	Author(s)	Published by
1994	*The Common Sense of Community*	Dick Atkinson	Demos
1995	*The Other Invisible Hand: Remaking Charity for the 21st Century*	Charles Landry and Geoff Mulgan	Demos
1995	*Staying the Course: The Role and Structure of Community Regeneration Organisations*	Stephen Thake	Joseph Rowntree Foundation
1997	*The Rise of the Social Entrepreneur*	Charles Leadbeater	Demos
1997	*Practical People, Noble Causes: How to Support Community-based Social Entrepreneurs*	Stephen Thake and Simon Zadek	NEF
2000	*The New Entrepreneurs: Seminar 3 – Social Entrepreneurship*	John Wilson (ed.)	Smith Institute
2000	*People before Structures: Engaging Communities Effectively in Regeneration*	Paul Brickell	Demos
2000	*Moving Pictures: Realities of Voluntary Action*	Duncan Scott, Pete Alcock, Lynne Russell and Rob Macmillan	Joseph Rowntree Foundation
2001	*Low Flying Heroes: Micro-social Enterprise below the Radar Screen*	Alex McGillivray, Chris Wadhams and Pat Conaty	NEF
2001 (unpublished)	*'Creative tension? Social entrepreneurs public policy and the new social economy'*	Tom Bentley	Demos

'Social Innovation' School of Thought

Table 10A.2   Other UK books and publications on social entrepreneurship

Date	Title	Author(s)	Published by
1996	The Power in Our Hands: Neighbourhood Based World Shaking	Tony Gibson	Jon Carpenter Publishing
2000	Urban Renaissance: A Strategy for Neighbourhood Renewal and the Welfare Society	Dr Dick Atkinson	Brewin Books
2003	Can-do Citizens: Re-building Marginalised Communities	Matthew Pike	Scarman Trust
2005	Working from the Heart: An Exploration of What Propels 12 Quality Social Entrepreneurs	Helena Plater-Zyberk	UnLtd
2006	Everyday Legends: The Ordinary People Changing the World – Stories of 20 Great UK Social Entrepreneurs	James Baderman and Justine Law	UnLtd

'Social Enterprise' School of Thought

Table 10A.3   UK think-tank reports on social enterprise

Date	Publication	Author	Think tank
1992	Towards a New Sector: Macro-policies for Community Enterprise	Tim Crabtree and Andy Roberts	NEF
1994	Towards a Social Economy – Trading for a Social Purpose	Peter Welch and Malcolm Coles	Fabian Society
1999	To our Mutual Advantage	Ian Christie and Charles Leadbeater	Demos
2000	Micro-entrepreneurs: Creating Enterprising Communities	Andrea Westall, Peter Ramsden and Julie Foley	NEF/IPPR
2001	Value Led Market Driven: Social Enterprise Solutions to Public Policy Goals	Andrea Westall	IPPR
2001	The Mutual State: How Local Communities can run Public Services	Ed Mayo and Henrietta Moore	NEF

11. Entrepreneurship, sociality and art: re-imagining the public

Daniel Hjorth

That for [Adam] Smith capitalism is only one of the forms of all men's activity to improve their condition means also that capitalism is only legitimate if it increases productivity for the benefit of all. (Meuret, 1993: 67–8)

11.1 INTRODUCTION

Maybe we have lost the social. At least we have lost sight of the social. Protesters in the streets of Paris in the autumn of 2007 provided an emblematic example of this analysis, carrying placards with the wordings: 'Sarkozy détruit le social'. In slight modification of this perspective, I believe it is rather the 'public sphere' that is at stake. We urgently need new ideas and tactics for imagining what the public should be today, and for exploring how we can act as citizens in order to enhance individuals' quality of life. My ambition is to contribute to this by elaborating on what I will call a public form of entrepreneurship which can create a new form of sociality in the public realm. The purpose pursued by such a development is to re-establish the social as a force different from the economic rather than encompassed by it. Its basis is a revised understanding of entrepreneurship (Hjorth, 2003). Entrepreneurship is then re-conceptualized as a sociality-creating force, belonging to society and not primarily to business. I also make use of an analysis of entrepreneurship as distinct from management, the latter being focused on efficient stewardship of existing resources and social control, while the former is animated primarily by creativity, desire, playfulness and the passion for actualising what could come into being. Public entrepreneurship is a term thus meant to emphasise the creative and playful as central to entrepreneurial activity. This is all the more necessary as the 1980s and 1990s saw an embrace of entrepreneurship by management literature and society more generally – the emergence of the 'enterprise discourse' (du Gay, 1997). Such a tendency promoted a tamed, controllable version of entrepreneurship. I insist on calling this 'managerial entrepreneurship', and describe it as a product of the enterprise discourse.

The recent (1980s in the US/UK societies and in the 1990s mainly in Scandinavia and Northern Europe) proliferation of an enterprise discourse is primarily driven by a *managerial* interest in the enterprising employee and citizen. Enterprise discourse produces the *managerial* entrepreneur, a role that squeezes the citizen off the stage of everyday life as it installs the entrepreneur-as-consumer as a total category. The establishment of such a consumer/employee allows for a shrinking welfare state, replaced by markets or quasi-markets for service offerings, and a self-organising employee. That is, it allows for cost-savings and its related delegation of full responsibility to the individual. This managerial form of entrepreneurship – enterprise – is a tamed version of the phenomenon, in which creative and desiring elements are bleached out for the purposes of securing control and efficiency. 'Social entrepreneurship', launched in the wake of this 'enterprise discoursed society' is therefore highly problematic, representing a managerialisation of society predicated on its economisation. 'Social entrepreneurship' proliferates via promises to solve social problems by re-describing the social as a form of the economic, and thereby subjecting them to the dominant expert-regime of our time: management knowledge. It makes sense that the history-writing of 'social entrepreneurship' players, for example, Ashoka's William Drayton, also situate the 'rise of the social entrepreneur' at this time (Drayton, 2006).

I seek to set free an entrepreneurial (creative/playful) form of entrepreneurship, which, when operating as a socially creative force, is described here as 'public entrepreneurship'. To the neo-liberal programme of 'social entrepreneurship' I thus present an alternative – 'public entrepreneurship'. Whereas the former is based on an enterprise discourse (on managerial entrepreneurship), the latter is based on an understanding of entrepreneurship in which the creative and desiring elements are intensified. This chapter seeks to clarify how the citizen (rather than the customer) can operate as an entrepreneur in the public (rather than the social) to create sociality. However, I am interested in a particular question regarding the actualisation of such entrepreneurial forms of entrepreneurship in the public, that is, I am interested in how 'public entrepreneurship' can be actualised. For this I turn to art as a form for creating aesthetic experiences (affect or intensities), understood as generating disorientation and interruption, through which the introduction of new configurations are subsequently made possible.

I should emphasise that I am not trying to reconnect to society as a state-regulated apparatus by promoting a unitary concept such as the 'public' or the 'citizen'. Rather I am interested in destabilising the presently dominant order in which the coding and recoding of desire is regulated by capitalist production. Precisely because this represents a limiting constraint on the socius and constantly imposes a unitary form, it prevents the emergence of experimental assemblages, of events. I relate this – experimentation and event – to entrepreneurial entrepreneurship, contrasted with managerial entrepreneurship as introduced above, and ask what role art could have in consolidating the relationship between entrepreneurship and experimentation/event. Thus, beyond a performative interest in destabilising the dominant order of thinking the relationship between entrepreneurship and society, that is, enterprise discourse and its codings and re-codings of desire, I am also interested in analysing what role art could have in such destabilisations. That is, how could art support the entrepreneurial creation of sociality in the public? How could the citizen become a public entrepreneur with the help of art? In view of this introduction I would state the purpose of this chapter as providing a perspective that allows us to imagine a future space for citizen-entrepreneurs, creators of new forms of sociality enhancing the fellow-citizens' quality of life.

This chapter strives towards this purpose with the help of the following structure. Section 11.2 provides a background and elaborates on central concepts. Section 11.3 discusses 'social entrepreneurship' as a received managerialist notion of the entrepreneurship – society relationship. Section 11.4 elaborates on the role of art in transforming the social and Section 11.5 develops 'public entrepreneurship' as an alternative image of entrepreneurship's role in society, where I rely on 'entrepreneurial entrepreneurship' and the way art can provide means for actualising this, what I call, 'public entrepreneurship'.

11.2 BACKGROUND AND CENTRAL CONCEPTS

The recent and ongoing entrepreneurialisation of society – via enterprise discourse's productivity in the economy – is performed in the name of dealing with the problems of the welfare state. What was once thought by Adam Smith to be a framework for the social *administration of capitalism* – economics in the sense of a political economy – has gradually become a framework for the *management of society*. It is enterprise discourse that makes this substitution of administration for management and society for economy pass unnoticed, as if neutral and natural. We have lost sight of the social: rather than being constituted by the relational ethics of the public, of *abundantia* (the idea that there is enough food and prosperity to cover all of the populace) and *aequitas* (the idea that the means should be equally shared among citizens; the governing ones as well as the governed ones), it is now understood as an epiphenomenon of the economy. Maybe the social is lost to the economy. This would in turn mean that 'the public' has gradually become synonymous with 'audience' or 'consumers in general'. If this is the case, the role of manager has acquired preferential right of interpretation beyond its 'home-domain' of the company, as the most successful way of handling the economisation of society since the second world war, as Gordon has pointed out, has been to managerialise one's identity (Gordon, 1991).

The current dominant form of political economy – enterprise discourse-powered neo-liberalism – disguises itself as non-political and addresses individuals not as citizens but as 'entrepreneurs' (at work) or enterprising consumers (in the experience economy). Responding to such pressures is rewarded not only with status and financial means, but also with the ability to speak truth and be right (as we learned from Foucault). The weight of 'rationality' is bestowed upon the argument of those speaking consistently with the dominant discourse, which in turn stigmatises the opposing view as irrational or abnormal.

If 'social entrepreneurship' only leads to a managerialised society, how could 'public entrepreneurship' be different? The point is that the coding and recoding of desire to produce (or social production), which happens in the 'socius' (Deleuze and Guattari, 1983), consolidates the social as a form of the economic precisely as this coding is dominated by capitalism. The coding and recoding of desire prepares subjects for social roles and functions. The socius is where desiring production is territorialised on organisations, companies or societies after which subjects become targets of discourses setting up formations where, in turn, certain rationalities exercise control and ensure the governability of subjects. The problem is that this coding of desire in capitalism, when dominated by managerial-governmental rationality, makes the roles of the consumer and enterprising employee into privileged subject-positions. Our desire to create is channelled into consumption and into being in business for oneself within the company (cf. Kanter, 1990).

Enterprise discourse achieves its productive function not simply as it is prepared by and prepares the ground for neo-liberal economy of the 1980s and 1990s version. It summons its force by reactivating a citizen-as-economic-man present already in Adam Smith's conception of the individual qualifying *as citizen* to the extent that he or she contributes to the production of wealth (Meuret, 1993: 71). Gordon has described neo-liberalism as recycling the economic man by simultaneously re-activating and inverting its central premise (Gordon, 1991). The autonomy of classical (Smith's) liberalist conception of 'economic man' is lost in the neo-liberalist managerialist conception which aims, as do all forms of management, at the governable subject. Smith's citizen is an individual whose autonomy safeguards him/her from the long arm of the state. The individual, in the economist conception articulated by Smith, qualifies *economically* as citizen. Classical liberalism imagines that the freedom of the individual is secured through autonomy vis-à-vis state rule. The individual is, however, dependent upon the institutions guaranteeing this autonomy. At the same time, government is dependent upon the 'free individual' for the exercise of government. 'Liberty is the circumambient medium of governmental action: disrespect of liberty is not simply an illegitimate violation of rights, but an ignorance of how to govern' (Gordon, 1991: 20).

The move towards neo-liberalism represents a novel way of securing the governable citizen. Classical liberalism, according to neo-liberalist critique, provides too few means for control. Neo-liberalism changes this by reactivating a *homo oeconomicus* that – having learned the success of the managerial revolution in US corporations (1950s and onwards; Chandler, 1977) – combines economic rationality with behaviourism. Liberalism's problem of integrating free individuals into a political order is solved during the Welfare State era by developing collective schemes of security – multiplication of the socialisation of risk – through which 'freedom' is collectively guaranteed. Unemployment support makes the individual independent of any particular employer, and relies instead on a socialised risk, the guarantor in the end being the state.

Neo-liberalism moves government into the sphere of individual shaping of conduct by imagining a *homo oeconomicus* that is free to realise its potential, presented as opportunities for exploitation. This is the call upon the enterprising individual, misrepresented in management as simply 'the entrepreneur'. The neo-liberal promotion of a governable *homo oeconomicus* makes it easier to *manage* individuals as their freedom depends on their willingness to participate in a new opportunity-freedom system. They shape their conduct according to a certain way of performing the self and exercising freedom. This ordering of one's self, this mode of shaping conduct, is what is stimulated by a certain governmental rationality (Foucault, 1991). Neo-liberalism developed a critique of inefficiencies attributed to the excessively bureaucratised welfare state. Collective schemes of socialised risk took away incentives to work and made individual efforts insignificant. The cure was the return of the entrepreneur, but in a governable form. Management provided the example of how to control the structuring and distribution of opportunities and thus the exercise of freedom as enterpriser. The welfare state was pushed back in order to set free the potential of new markets or quasi-markets where services could be offered to enterprising consumers. New public management entered public organisations in the name of ending the bureaucratic era. Society was to be entrepreneurialised, but was in effect managerialised.

The construction of the individual as enterprising, not only defined as such in economic terms but also normalised/individualised along the disciplinary regimes stipulated by new 'entrepreneurial management' and new public management, reactivates also the citizen as an economic agent. At work or at home, we are exposed to opportunities the exploitation of which belongs to the responsibility of the enterprising individual. The initiative-taking and self-organising consumer/employee is the one that obtains the deals. In between Smith's citizen-as-wealth-producer and the enterprising citizen of the present day we have witnessed a gradual enlargement of the domain of the market. This also means a gradual expansion of the domain proper to management knowledge as expertise. Our possibilities of imagining entrepreneurship exercised in the role of citizen thus depends upon our ability to diagnose the citizen-enterpriser in the managerially defined role/function made governable and useful (in economic senses) in the enterprising society, as in 'social entrepreneurship'. 'Social entrepreneurship' is thus not so much an oxymoron as an attempt to promote the 'citizen-as-managerial-entrepreneur' answering to the governmental rationality of neo-liberalism, intensified in enterprise management, seeking to forge an initiative-taking and self-organising individual: we are not unemployed but job-seeking; not homeless but rough-sleeping. That is, we are consumers in a new opportunity structure, provided by operators on new markets made possible by a crumbling societal responsibility.

The expansion of the market is simultaneously an expansion of the domain of the consumer. We may speculate as to what extent the inclusion of the social in the economic, of society in the economy, is also represented by an absorption of the citizen into the role of consumer. It seems that the establishment of economy as a particular form of reality, as a level of intervention, taking place according to Foucault (1991), during the eighteenth century (Smith's *The Wealth of Nations* was published in 1776) has gradually eroded the status of the citizen by waves after waves of addressing the consumer through the operation of the market. It is here that the public becomes important as a way of diffusing the social, pluralising its forms beyond the economic and providing virtual space for the citizen as relationally defined by an ethics of responsibility for the creation and re-creation of the public. Accomplishing such a differentiation of the social, opening a space for public citizens, decentring the citizen-consumer, is of course a political project. Art has an important role to play in such processes.

Art, creating affects, has the power to provoke conceptions of what the social could become, beyond the limits of the necessary as confirmed by today's dominant institutions. Politics, Rancière asserts, is the interruption of the distribution of the sensible so as to provide those with no or a very small part in the community with a new role, a say (Rancière, 2004).

In Deleuze's terms this would be the setting free of a people to come, the missing people (Deleuze, 1998). If I believe today that the public is at stake, I also believe that the missing people are the citizens beyond their role as performed within the gallery of the consumer. I turn to art as a force in the creation and re-creation of society that can supplement the dominant interpolation of individuals as citizen-consumers in the social-as-economy with constructing citizens of a more entrepreneurial kind in the public.

Thus, central to my discussion, to be developed below, are the relationships between citizens, consumers, entrepreneurs, the social, the public and art. I use these central concepts in working toward the purpose previously stated, that is, that of providing a perspective that allows us to imagine a future space for citizen-entrepreneurs. In addition, the discussion of concepts above have indicated my interest in investigating the role of art in accomplishing an intervention in the distribution of the sensible so as to create the presently missing role of citizen beyond the horizon of the consumer. This will require a short genealogy of the entrepreneurialised society, and the distinction between the managerial and the entrepreneurial entrepreneur (Hjorth, 2003). Why would such an inquiry be necessary? It is important, and perhaps necessary, if we acknowledge that entrepreneurship is a society-creating force that enhances citizens' quality of life, that is, if we can see entrepreneurship as primarily belonging to society and not simply to the economy (Hjorth and Steyaert, 2003; Steyaert and Katz, 2004). The potential of entrepreneurship as a force in creating new forms of sociality is arrested at present by being normalised in its tamed, managerial version. The same understanding is operative in the term 'social entrepreneurship', fit for a government of 'enterprising citizens, employees'. The attempted move could be pictured as in Figure 11.1.

11.3   VALUE, CITIZENS, AND 'SOCIAL ENTREPRENEURSHIP'

Entrepreneurial Value

The post-industrial society alters the economic order sedimented in the industrial society. Reflections on the normalities of the industrial society therefore helps us understand the scope of the present changes. Toffler is one of those who have shown how high-modern societies changed from hosting economies where value was primarily based on land, gradually transforming into economies of what Marx called the holy trinity of land–labour–capital (Toffler, 1984). The industrial revolution places a strong emphasis on the labour-capital relationship and this is prioritised

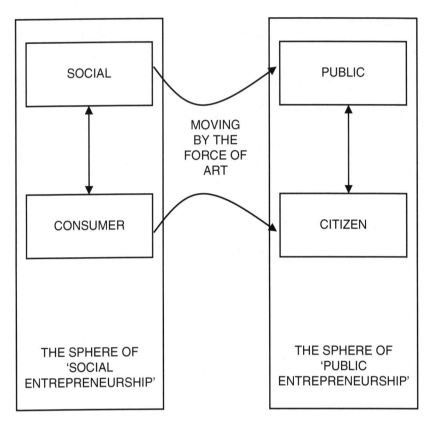

*Figure 11.1   Spheres of social entrepreneurship and public
entrepreneurship*

by political economy. The laissez-faire policy vis-à-vis the economy, as
argued for by the physiocrats in the late eighteenth century, is based on
their identification of 'natural tendencies' in the economy (cf. Hirschman,
1977). By the end of the eighteenth century, the discussion moves from
the physiocrats' fixation on land as the basis of value (together with
labour) to more clearly include capital. Emerging industrialisation of
course drives this development. Marx, Mill and Ricardo refine these
discussions:

> The produce of the earth – all that is derived from its surface by the united
> application of labour, machinery and capital, is divided among three classes of
> the community, namely, the proprietor of the land, the owner of the stock or
> capital necessary for its cultivation, and the labourers by whose industry it is
> cultivated. (Ricardo, 1817: 3)

Marx protests against the tendency to see land, labour, and capital as equally important for economic value, and Jones and Spicer report how he ironises this:

> They have about the same relation to each other as lawyers fees, red beets and music' (Marx 1894, 814). . . . Marx asks how anything other than the products of human labour can be attributed with value, and finds appeals to the self-valorising character of capital to be a shabby case of self-interested presumption. (Jones and Spicer, 2005: 186)

The 'trilogy' land–labour–capital remained more or less intact throughout the welfare state era, strongly animated by the way in which Keynesian economics successfully outflanked the Austrian school's (Friedrich Hayek, Ludwig von Mises and, partly within this school, Joseph Schumpeter) ideas in criticising and questioning economic orthodoxy in the 1920s. Keynes successfully argued that classical economic theory lacked a working macroeconomic theory, and his own *General Theory* (1936) was well-timed in providing for governments an active role in preventing the kind of macroeconomic problems experienced in the late 1920s and 1930s. The buildup of the welfare state model leaned heavily on a Keynesian line of thinking.

Starting with the Thatcherism and Reaganism of the 1980s, which applied the theories emerging out of Friedman's interpretations of (for example) Hayek's theories, the land–labour–capital trilogy is slowly altered by an emphasis on entrepreneurial profit as a fourth source of economic value. This is the essence of neo-liberal enterprise discourse (du Gay, 1997; Hjorth, 2003) that becomes highly productive as it resonates with the views of important stakeholders in society:

1. Politicians realise (by the help of David Birch's studies of job-creation in the economy (1979; 1984) that it is rather new and rapidly growing companies, not the big ones, which generate new jobs (more precisely 70 per cent of all new jobs). Politicians' primary concern is of course – then as now – to stimulate the creation of new jobs, wherefore policies for stimulating entrepreneurship are launched on a grand scale throughout the so-called Western economies;
2. Managers find that they have exhausted concepts of total quality management and business process re-engineering, and sense that competitiveness in the 1990s is spelled speed, innovativeness and flexibility. All of a sudden they turn towards entrepreneurship to find a solution. For the first time in history we see the job advertisements asking for entrepreneurs. The call for the enterprising employee is fuelled by emblematic management writers talking about 'being in business for

oneself within the company' (Kanter, 1990; Peters and Waterman; 1982).

3. Academia explodes with courses, conferences, new journals and chairs within the field of entrepreneurship. This is one of the most, perhaps the most, rapidly growing areas in 1990s academia, first in the USA (Katz 2003) and later in Europe, primarily in Scandinavia (Hjorth, 2008).

Value, in the context of an economised society, is almost automatically understood as *economic* value. The public is of course also economic, but it is precisely this that it is *also* economic that differentiates it, and makes it impossible to inscribe as a sub-category of the economic (Polanyi, 1944). This view is opposed by neo-liberalism that precisely represents such a re-description as natural and neutral. I define the public as that in-between, the set of relations, constituted by the social places – being neither public nor private – that are regulated by state structures as well as civil society (White and Hunt, 2000). Enterprise discourse, through which neo-liberalist economy efficiently operates, has pushed 'social entrepreneurship' as a new form of freedom. The consumer's domain is enlarged while the citizen's is shrunk as we are all buyers of services on markets. This is done to get at the efficient exchange of information that the price-mechanism provides. To the extent that 'social entrepreneurship' is successful, the domain of management as expert knowledge is increased, something that has provided chief executive officers (CEOs) moving into retirement with the possibility of establishing organisations for the application of managerial knowledge on social problems redefined as economic.

But entrepreneurship cannot be co-opted by management and survive as a creative force. The point of entrepreneurship as a societal force (Hjorth and Steyaert, 2003; Steyaert and Hjorth, 2006) is to be found in its capacity to create new forms of sociality in the public. This is how the possibilities for living are enhanced for citizens. *Sociality* is then understood as a collective engagement (affective relation) that generates an assemblage (a project, a group of people). Such an assemblage/project is a heterogeneous multiplicity bound together by its function vis-à-vis other socialities in the public, and by the needs of engaged citizens.

Citizens

The concept of the citizen has a complicated history of its own. Thomas Hobbes's critique of Aristotle's conception of the citizen becomes influential during the end of the seventeenth and eighteenth centuries. Aristotle said man was born fit for society, whereas Hobbes emphasised: 'Man is made fit for society not by nature, but by education' (1651 [1983]: 44). Character, and developing a character, was deemed important and it oriented the individual towards the public, towards the kind of responsibility one has to the public. We here find connections attaching this discussion to the Roman virtues we have mentioned above – *abundantia* and *aequitas* – which stipulate a social relatedness to the populace, to the public, for which one shares a responsibility. From the twentieth century, however, a shift in emphasis appears: personality rather than character becomes important (cf. Greenblatt's 1980 study of self-fashioning in sixteenth century England). This shift from character to personality corresponds to a shift from responsibility for others to a typical high-modern responsibility towards oneself. One is responsible for realising *one's* potential: 'The quest for personality resonates with an expanding individualization that is marked by the rise of a consumer market which encourages the expression of individuality through the structured choices of the market' (White and Hunt, 2000: 105).

The role as consumer pushes back the role as citizen, and this corresponds to a simultaneous shrinking of the 'public' and an enlargement of the market. Participation in public affairs, famously analysed by Albert O. Hirschman's theory of exit, voice and loyalty (Hirschman, 1970), is more and more regulated by a cost-calculus. The 'free choice' of the customer is equated with freedom. Not even the choice is of course free, as it is prepared and structured by the offerings on a market. (One should, however, be careful not to totalise the domination of such structures. Foucault has shown us that no power is total, and that it emerges as response to freedom. De Certeau (1984) elaborates this tactical 'making-use' of dominant strategies to create space for play.) This gradual individualisation has most probably resulted in a view of citizenship today that is dominated by a self-image including the conscious, freely choosing individual who decides whether to engage in public matters on the basis of a cost-calculus. This image is, in various degrees, mixed up with a sense of belonging to an imagined community.

Social Entrepreneurship

A precondition for the proliferation of the 'new public management' discourse (Osborne and Gaebler, 1992) is of course the gradual redefinition of the social as part of the economic, which in turn makes possible the re-description of social problems as economic problems. This is possible in the context of neo-liberalist economic policies and part of how this is operating via enterprise discourse (du Gay, 1997; Gordon, 1991; Hjorth, 2003). New public management, the central branch of enterprise discourse that operates on public organisations specifically for the purpose of managerial-ising them, has of course created lots of necessary organisational changes. It has, however, been primarily about moving 'entrepreneurial governance' (Osborne and Gaebler, 1992) into these organisations. It means leaving to the market what it is not absolutely necessary to keep within the organi-sation, and relying on enterprising employees' orientation towards the customer (with demands) rather than the citizen (with rights).

We all know that hospitals, railway operations, telecommunications and so on are part of histories heavily burdened by the downsides of bureauc-racy. What is significant, though, is new public management's success in turning attention away from the efficiencies and generally good sides of bureaucracy (cf. du Gay, 2000; Kallinikos, 2004), as are well developed in Weber's concept of the bureau (Weber, 1947), and instead refer to bureaucracy as a 'composite term for the defects of large organizations', as du Gay puts it (du Gay, 2000: 106). New public management's critique of 'bureaucratic rationality' – that bureaucracy slows down the allocation of resources to the extent that it makes organisations suffer unnecessary costs – re-thinks the ethical from an emphasis on the relational and values, to an attention to calculable rules. Bauman's *Modernity and the Holocaust* (1989) is perhaps the strongest critique of the ethical effects of bureaucratic ration-ality. This is, of course, important and valid critique. What I speak about here is the ethics of equality and fair, skills-based treatment, disregarding personal preferences. That is, the functions of the bureau that most of us rely on everyday, on the way to and at work: documentation, skills-based recruitment. What Bauman correctly warns us against is the tendency of bureaucracy to 'undermine the possibility of individuals exercising a capacity for moral action' (du Gay, 1999: 575), by its hyper-rationalism, appalling impersonalism and destruction of moral personality. Bauman points out: 'the bureaucratic culture which prompts us to view society as an object of administration . . . was the very atmosphere in which the idea of the Holocaust could be conceived, slowly, yet consistently developed, and brought to its conclusion' (ibid.: 576). But, as du Gay (1999) is equally right in pointing out, Bauman bases his critique of bureaucracy on a differ-ent reading than suggested by Weber's own: 'For Weber, bureaucracy is a particular instituted style of ethical life or *Lebensführung*. In his account, the impersonal, procedural, expert and hierarchical character of the bureau is not treated as a symptom of moral deficiency; instead the bureau is represented as a specific 'order of life' subject to its own particular *modus operandi*' (du Gay, 1999: 581). Bauman's warning, however correct as such, is thus based upon something else than bureaucracy as conceptualised by Weber. Indeed, it would instead more precisely direct us towards neo-liberalism's transformation of political economy from an administration of capitalism (as suggested by Adam Smith) into a more general management of society. It is management's prioritisation of the calculable that brings along a rule-based ethics consistent with such a line of thinking. This is what prevents the exercise of moral action that Bauman speaks about.

The key point here is my conclusion that when the managerial critique of public organisations targets bureaucracy it simultaneously legitimises the enlargement of the market and a corresponding transformation from a relational ethics to a rule-based calculable ethics. New public management and enterprise management have had the unfortunate effect of critiquing bureaucracy in the name of entrepreneurship without leaving further space for anything else than the economic human. Certainly a more cost conscious and customer-oriented human qua employee, but not a more fully human in terms of ethically consciousness and relational orientation. In perspective of the history of management, this is not strange or unexpected (Hoskin, 1998; 2006; Hoskin and Macve, 1988). But entrepreneurship, in the context of the public, in society, operating in the social, is of course about something else. It is about the passionate engagement, based upon a relational ethics of shared responsibility for the public, driving the creation of new forms of sociality that enhance the possibilities for living. The question is: how art can function in such processes, in accomplishing the move from 'social entrepreneurship' towards what I in section 11.5 will elaborate upon as 'public entrepreneurship'?

11.4 ART AND THE RELATIONAL CONSTITUTION OF THE PUBLIC

When *homo oeconomicus* gradually (during the sixteenth to the eighteenth centuries) crowded out alternative regulative ideals for understanding Western life (Hirschman, 1977; Huizinga, 1955), art was simultaneously assigned a marginal place. Modernity, characterised by scientific reason joining (and sometimes replacing) God as a ruling force, simultaneously prescribed for art a place within Sunday culture (Huizinga, 1950 [1962]). The continuity of a hierarchy between lent and carnival secured the subsequent hierarchy between seriousness and play (see Umberto Eco's, 1994, *The Name of the Rose*). The sciences started to lock human knowledge into neat boxes used for building disciplines at universities (first established in the twelfth century), where analysis qua Galileo and Descartes (detachment from nature or object and from one's passions, law based, context free) could become practiced. The 'art' of knowing was still familiar to Erasmus and Copernicus, though, who made use of aesthetics and the fantastic-fabulous to tell stories of how things could become thought, knowing that these stories could also be told differently (Findlen, 1998). This openness of knowledge, the possibility of telling stories differently, manifests an acceptance of multiplicity to the extent that the wit of personal narratives and an aesthetics of beautifully composed stories were mingled with the rationality of scientific discourse. Enlightenment definitely instigated a hierarchy between the two (narrative wit vs. scientific rationality), reactivating the hierarchies between seriousness and play and between Lent and Carnival.

Art was, for a long time, considered to have the purpose of representing life in various beautiful forms. Thus, it seemed destined for a more marginal place within modern life, which was being increasingly monitored scientifically. Its function, instead, was to entertain and cultivate a disinterested relation to an ornament. In the struggle to get out of this prescribed function, art has moved through a series of leaps, following the moves of science. From having been an admixture in the cultural blend of life, it achieved a position where it struggles mainly with the heritage of representation and ornamentation. Art, like science, has become locked into its corner, from where it enviously observes life, leaving a great distance between itself and everyday women and men. As long as art maintains a place outside everyday life, the expressive form that remains for it in the struggl to find a way back into life is shock (Vattimo, 1992), something easily validated by today's exhibition visitors.

With inspirations from Gilles Deleuze's concept of art and Jacques Ranciére's elaborations on the politics of aesthetics, we can argue against modernity's assignment of a marginal place for art, and instead intensify what we find to be crucial forms of creativity already inventing new places for art in contemporary society. This chapter's emphasis on entrepreneurship as the desire to create (novelty), which in turn is seen as what sets it apart from management's focus on utilising resources efficiently, relates it to art as a practice sharing this effect upon the social, that is, the creation of the new. Resonant with Ranciére's idea of the aesthetic regime, we would say that entrepreneurship and art both affect the dominant distribution of the sensible in society. Art as well as entrepreneurship affect the sensible order that determines how we perceive things and which forms we use for engaging with it in various places (Ranciére, 2006). Why there would still be a point suggesting that art can function as a way to enlarge the public entrepreneurially, and hence enhance the possibilities for living, is to be found in the force of art as identified by Deleuze: art creates affects and percepts. It thus has the power of providing us with the possibility to think anew through the infinite ways in which affects and percepts can become affections and perceptions in concrete experiences and situations.

I will try to intensify our relationship to a function of art as constituting the aesthetic experience, which is at the same time impossible to cling on to. It is there, but vanishes as we have identified it. That is, we cannot make an essential distinction between art and other social practices on the basis of an aesthetic regime (Ranciére, 2006). Deleuze, however, is clear on the affect he sees distinctly produced by art. This is its ephemeral effect, a rupture that has no other core than its force of immediacy. Taken together we may conclude that Ranciére and Deleuze allow us to say that art is the context in which the aesthetic experience is intensified; an experience that leaves us with an affect as its trace of emergence, and this affect locates us in an infinitive, in a potentialised context, from which new reflections, experiences and situations can emerge.

The aesthetic element of the experience is crucial for the emergence of a space for creating new social practices. I am not targeting the experience of art in the traditional sense of visiting a gallery or walking around a museum. Even if this distinction of certain places for art is both obsolete *and* relevant, it is rather aesthetic experiences occurring in everyday life that interest me here. These experiences, these events, to the extent that they are desired today, form the entrepreneurial rather than the enterprising subject, which is why I have suggested entrepreneurship and art are united in that they affect the sensible order that determines how we perceive and engage with things and people. What this subject desires, I argue, is the openness, the poetic of the aesthetic experience. At the same time, it is the aesthetic element in the experience that forms the desiring subject. The question is, how does the aesthetic experience work? I suggest working with a conception of experience well described by Massumi, who has stated that: 'Every experience, as it happens, carries a "fringe" of active indetermination. Experience under way is a constitutionally vague *"something doing"* in the world' (Massumi, 2002: 197; emphasis in original). This emphasises what traditionally would be described as the aesthetic quality of experience, but which is characteristic of experience as such. It is this indeterminacy that constitutes its openness which in turn is why it is the stuff that both entrepreneurship and art can creatively use. It constitutes the in-between, the entre- of entrepreneurship. But also the generative indeterminacy of art.

What is the context in which we may locate this experience? It relates to Heidegger's aesthetic experience discussed as the experience of an event, not reducible to, or controllable by, a subject. The event is characterised by participation and disorientation. A subject position is the possible effect of such an event and not the condition for its appearance. In his famous essay 'The origin of the work of art' (1971) Heidegger states that the aesthetic experience is characterized by participating in a clearing of openness where truth happens. People that become part of such an experience are 'standing within' this truth as it happens in the work (of art). Such participation is further characterised as 'taking us beyond ourselves and our subjective standpoint' (Scheibler, 2001). Participating in the event means a discontinuity from the everyday ongoingness of life. We find this emphasised also in Vattimo's (1992) and in Benjamin's (1999) discussions of aesthetic experience, where the blow, the (German) *Stoß*, or shock, marks this discontinuity that leaves us in a state of disorientation, indeterminacy, openness, play.

Together with Derrida, we here affirm the impossibility of founding or grounding knowledge either on phenomenological 'pure experience' (without subject) or on the structuralists' signs and chains of concepts (in language), noting as well that relativism is equally impossible. To make sense at all is always already to make use of concepts that make us understood. Deleuze regards this as an opportunity and asks us to grasp this (entrepreneurially, we would add) as a challenge to transform life, to create in this in-between (in the impossible necessity, as Derrida called it). Deleuze, instead, refers us to difference and becoming. These are concepts of the in-between (entre-concepts), and of movement, and they deny us the possibility of thinking in terms of ground and closure. What does this mean for the aesthetic experience as a rupture or disorientation?

The aesthetic experience would work in the following way: through producing affects, we are taken back from composites of experience that we have imagined and invested in, to the affects whence those composites have emerged. 'Affect, as presented in art, disrupts the everyday and opinionated links we make between words and experience' (Colebrook, 2002: 23).

> Affections are what happens to us (disgust, or the recoil of the nostrils at the smell of cheese); perceptions are what we receive (odour, or the smell itself). Affects and percepts, in art, free these forces from the particular observers or bodies who experience them. . . . Affects are sensible experiences in their *singularity*, liberated from organising systems of representation. (Ibid.: 21–2; emphasis in original).

Skilfully staged aesthetic experiences play with the sensation- as much as the perception-side of experience.[1] It is of course in our 'organised systems of representation' that we feel comfortable and oriented. 'Destroying' this sense of homeliness, the aesthetic experience relocates us into a space of becoming – of becoming reoriented. This provokes either pleasure or disgust in that we are offered to make sense of our experience, to enjoy a moment of 'being lost', or to flee such feelings of void and confrontation.

Art as a primary (although not unique) context for the aesthetic experience represent an intensification of the sensing of the possible. As such it shares an agenda with entrepreneurship. Learning from art as a method for creating assemblages, projects, groups, engagements for a world-to-come, seems to hold great promise for altering the distribution of consumers and citizens in society. We are, of course, always balancing these roles – together with several others – in conducting ourselves in public, at work, at home. If 'social entrepreneurship' should intensify and radicalise the social, it cannot stay within the limits of managerial entrepreneurship as promoted in enterprise discourse. It would have to operate in the public, as that which remains more open and undetermined, and through the role of the citizen. 'Social entrepreneurship' stages the social as an epiphenomenon to the economic and offers the enterprising consumer as role. This is how neo-liberalist capitalism decodes and then re-codes the subject on the templates for action it benefits from. If we seek entrepreneurship as a creative force – capable of generating sociality – we need to resist this tendency, and art provides a promising form for organising disruptive experiences in the public, providing possibilities for entrepreneurial intervention. I suggest we call this creation of new forms of sociality by the engagements of citizens 'public entrepreneurship'. Art as the context for an intensified aesthetic experience can function as a most forceful method for interrupting consumers and address them as citizens. Let me elaborate on this 'public entrepreneurship' and its promise of creating space for a people to come.

11.5   PUBLIC ENTREPRENEURSHIP: THE ART OF CREATING SOCIALITY

When, in the name of management-entrepreneurship (for example, new public management or 'social entrepreneurship'), one tries to instigate market mechanisms as a solution to problems attributed to bureaucracy, the effect is that of a further economisation of the social and a subsequent pushing back of the citizen and an enlargement of the domain of the customer.

I see 'public entrepreneurship' as an attempt to channel the creative force of entrepreneurship into the building of a society with greater possibilities for living for citizens. Stressing the relational ethics of a responsibility for the public, I have opted for 'public entrepreneurship' as better describing how new forms of sociality can be created. Such creation is driven by citizenship, constituted by a relational ethics of *abundantia* and *aequita*. From this conception of the role of entrepreneurship in society, we can ask the central question: 'What's the social in social entrepreneurship?' (cf.

Steyaert and Hjorth, 2006). 'Social entrepreneurship' needs to be seduced by 'the other', by the social as a strange attractor, as a virtuality to be actualised (ibid.: 7). 'Public entrepreneurship' is my answer to how such an intensification of the social can be thought and practised.

Public entrepreneurship, like all entrepreneurial entrepreneurship, functions by bringing fodder to the desiring production that actualises the virtual in assemblages – projects, groups, teams, networks. This is a process – entrepreneurial creation – that primarily uses passionate speech, improvisation and convincing resonance to articulate images of 'what could become'. In several scenes of Shakespeare's *Othello*, Iago brilliantly performs to achieve this function. He becomes a director in the socius, steering the coding of desire so as to serve people the social roles his scheme needs. Coding and re-coding of desire prepares subjects for the social roles and functions. Desiring production is territorialised on the project of 'getting rid of the Moor', which, of course, is a horrible plot. It is by playing on the openness of the social that Iago subtly steers the coding of people into roles. Once established in these roles, they are targets for discourses – moral, racist, sexual – that become highly productive. Iago figures here as example precisely because the play in which he operates more clearly than most stories demonstrates the power of desire. Thus it also demonstrates the need for a relationally constituted ethics to be part of creations of sociality, for it is in the open, in the indeterminate, in undecidability that Bauman's 'moral action' is both possible and necessary. This is where Iago utterly fails.

Central to how Iago (or Don Quixote for that matter, see Hjorth, 2003) accomplishes the creation of sociality is, so I suggest, how he creates affect. It is the aesthetic forming of the speech, of the gestures, of the role that 'is involved in this partition of the visible and the sayable, in this intertwining of being, doing and saying that frames a polemical common world' (Ranciére, 2004: 10). This is the politics of aesthetics in processes of actualising the virtual. The virtual, in our case, is the creation of new forms of sociality in the public; sociality that will enhance the possibilities for living for citizens. It is by intervening in the relationships between the sayable and the visible that 'public entrepreneurs' can reach the doable by providing a tactical goal that focuses the social production. To the extent that art can be made to work as that force that keeps the public – as determined here by *abundantia* and *aequitas* – open, by calling on the citizen, it also maintains that radical democratic force that addresses anyone. This is also how art can have a disrupting effect; how it can stop us in our tracks and make us 're-boot' as thinkers. Our habitual consumer-script is marginalised and we therefore have to start thinking rather than use someone else's thoughts. Art is used in this chapter as a name for this method of staging, arranging, preparing and potentialising the social in order to increase the probability for an assemblage to form. But this is not the basis for a rule or a general strategy. There is nothing preventing art from becoming re-coded on the subject of the consumer. When art, however, creates aesthetic experiences, creates affects, there is an immanent resistance to this comfortable sliding into consumption-convention. We are thrown into the openly relational, the realm of ethics, where we have to make choices. From there it becomes more obvious that those choices that are prepared for us also limit our freedom. We sense that freedom is not reducible to freedom of choice, that is, the consumer's freedom.

With this idea of 'public entrepreneurship' and the role of art in making it actual, I have tried not so much to put forth an image of an illness as to formulate a critical diagnosis of health, as Deleuze puts this (Deleuze, 1998). I have approached the responsibility of a clinician of health, where health is associated with the multiple dynamics of the socius, beyond the singularity of capital as coding of desire for production. The image of 'public entrepreneurship' and the citizen, to which it is related, represent the liberation of a people to come. This is the missing people of public entrepreneurs, tactically making use of the strength of the discourse of 'social entrepreneurship' but poaching it, creating surprises. At most it hopes to become a transformative insinuation in the important discussion of how we may imagine new (sustainable) forms of sociality.

NOTE

1. '. . . "perception" is used to refer to object-oriented experience, and "sensation" for "the perception of perception", or self-referential experience. Perception pertains to the stoppage- and stasis-tending dimension of reality . . . Sensation pertains to the dimension of passage, or the continuity of immediate experience (and thus to a direct registering of potential)' (Massumi, 2002: 258–9).

REFERENCES

Bauman, Z. (1989), *Modernity and the Holocaust*, Ithaca, NY: Cornell University Press.
Benjamin, W. (1999), *The Arcades Project / Walter Benjamin; Translated by Howard Eiland and Kevin McLaughlin; Prepared on the Basis of the German Volume Edited by Rolf Tiedemann*, Cambridge, MA and London: Belknap Press.
Birch, D.L. (1979), *The Job Generation Process*, Cambridge, MA: MIT.
Birch, D.L. (1984), *The Role Played by High Technology Firms in Job Creation*, Cambridge, MA: MIT.
Certeau, M. de (1984), *The Practice of Everyday Life*, Berekley, CA: University of California Press.

Chandler, A.D. (1977), *The Visible Hand: The Managerial Revolution in American Business*, Cambridge, MA: Harvard Belknap.

Colebrook, C. (2002), *Gilles Deleuze*, London: Routledge.

Deleuze, G. (1998), *Essays Critical and Clinical. Translated by Daniel W. Smith and Michael A. Greco*, London: Verso.

Deleuze, G. and F. Guattari (1983), *Anti-Oedipus: Capitalism and Schizophrenia; Preface by Michel Foucault*, Minneapolis, MN: University of Minnesota Press.

Drayton, W. (2006), 'Everyone an change maker – social entrepreneurship's ultimate goal', *Innovation – Technology, Governance, Globalization*, **1** (1), 1–32.

Eco, U. (1994), *The Name of the Rose / Umberto Eco; Translated from the Italian by William Weaver*, San Diego, CA: Harcourt Brace.

Findlen, P. (1998), 'Between Carnival and Lent: the scientific revolution at the margins of culture', *Configurations*, **6** (2), 243–67.

Foucault, M. (1991), 'Governmentality', in G. Burchell, C. Gordon and P. Miller (eds), *The Foucault Effect: Studies in Governmentality*, Chicago, IL: University of Chicago Press, pp. 87–104.

Gay, P. du (1997), *Production of Culture/Cultures of Production*, London: Sage.

Gay, P. du (1999), 'Is Bauman's bureau Weber's bureau? A comment', *British Journal of Sociology*, **50** (4), 575–87.

Gay, P. du (2000), *In Praise of Bureaucracy*, London: Sage.

Gordon, C. (1991), 'Governmentality – an introduction', in G. Burchell, C. Gordon and P. Miller (eds), *The Foucault Effect: Studies in Governmentality*, Chicago, IL: University of Chicago Press, pp. 1–52.

Greenblatt, S. (1980), *Renaissance Self-fashioning: From More to Shakespeare*, Chicago, IL: University of Chicago Press.

Heidegger, M. (1971), 'The origin of the work of art', in M. Heidegger, *Poetry, Language, Thought*, New York: Harper & Row, pp. 15–86.

Hirschman, A.O. (1970), *Exit, Voice, and Loyalty: Responses to Decline in Firms, Organizations, and States*, Cambridge, MA: Harvard University Press.

Hirschman, A.O. (1977), *The Passions and the Interests: Political Arguments for Capitalism before its Triumph*, Princeton, NJ: Princeton University Press.

Hjorth, D. (2003), *Rewriting Entrepreneurship – for a New Perspective on Organisational Creativity*, Malmö/Copenhagen: Liber/CBS Press.

Hjorth, D. (2008), 'Nordic entrepreneurship research', *Entrepreneurship, Theory & Practice*, **32** (2), 313–38.

Hjorth, D. and C. Steyaert (2003), 'Entrepreneurship beyond (a new) economy: creative swarms and pathological zones', in C. Steyaert and D. Hjorth (eds), *New Movements in Entrepreneurship*, Cheltenham, UK and Northampton, MA, USA: Edward Elgar, pp. 286–303.

Hobbes, T. (1651 [1983]), *De cive, (Philosophicall rudiments concerning government and society, title of first English translation), Critical ed. by Howard Warrender*, Oxford: Clarendon Press.

Hoskin, K. (1998), 'Examining accounts and accounting for management: inverting understanding of "the economic"', in A. McKinlay and K. Starkey (eds), *Foucault, Management and Organization Theory*, London: Sage, pp. 93–110.

Hoskin, K. (2006), 'Management as product of the European knowledge tradition: a modern form of ancient paideia?', in P. Gagliardi and B. Czarniawska (eds), *Management Education and Humanities*, Cheltenham, UK and Northampton, MA, USA: Edward Elgar, pp. 159–73.

Hoskin, K. and R. Macve (1988), 'The genesis of accountability: the West Point connection', *Accounting, Organiation and Society*, **13** (1), 37–73.

Huizinga, J. (1950 [1962]), Homo Ludens – A Study of the *Play Element in Culture*, 3rd edn, Boston, MA: Beacon Press.

Huizinga, J. (1955), *Homo Ludens: A Study of the Play-element in Culture*, Boston, MA: Beacon Press.

Jones, C. and A. Spicer (2005), 'Outline of a genealogy of the value of the entrepreneur', in G. Erreygers and G. Jacobs (eds), *Language, Communication and the Economy*, Amsterdam: Benjamin, pp. 179–97.

Kallinikos, J. (2004), 'The social foundations of the bureaucratic order', *Organization*, **11** (1), 13–36.

Kanter, R.M. (1990), *When Giants Learn to Dance*, London: Unwin Hyman.

Katz, J.A. (2003), 'The chronology and intellectual trajectory of American entrepreneurship education 1876–1999', *Journal of Business Venturing*, **18**, 283–300.

Keynes, J.M. (1936), *The General Theory of Employment, Interest and Money*, Cambridge: Palgrave Macmillan.

Marx, K. (1894 [1974]), *Capital*, vol. 3, London: Lawrence & Wishart.

Massumi, B. (2002), *Parables for the Virtual: Movement, Affect, Sensation*, Durham, NC: Duke University Press.

Meuret, D. (1993), 'A political genealogy of political economy', in M. Gane and T. Johnson (eds), *Foucault's New Domains*, London: Routledge, pp. 49–74.

Osborne, D. and T. Gaebler (1992), *Reinventing Government: How the Entrepreneurial Spirit Is Transforming the Public Sector*, Reading, MA: Addison-Wesley.

Peters, T.J. and R.H. Waterman (1982), *In Search of Excellence: Lessons from America's Best-run Companies*, New York: Harper & Row.

Polanyi, K. (1944), *The Great Transformation*, Boston, MA: Beacon Press.

Ranciére, J. (2004), 'The politics of literature', *SubStance*, **33** (1), 10–24.

Ranciére, J. (2006), *The Politics of Aesthetics*, New York: Continuum.

Ricardo, D. (1817), *On the Principles of Political Economy and Taxation*, London: J. Murray.

Scheibler, I. (2001), 'Art as festival in Heidegger and Gadamer', *International Journal of Philosophical Studies*, **9** (2), 151–75.

Smith, A. (1776), *An Inquiry into the Nature and Causes of the Wealth of Nations*, 1st edn, London: printed for W. Strahan and T. Cadell.

Steyaert, C. and D. Hjorth (2006), 'Introduction: what is social in social entrepreneurship', in C. Steyaert and D. Hjorth (eds), *Entrepreneurship as Social Change*, Cheltenham, UK and Northampton, MA, USA: Edward Elgar, pp. 1–18.

Steyaert, C. and J. Katz (2004), 'Reclaiming the space of entrepreneurship in society: geographical, discursive, and social dimensions', *Entrepreneurship and Regional Development*, **16** (3), 179–96.

Toffler, A. (1984), *Previews and Premises: An Interview with the Author of Future Shock and the Third Wave*, London: Pan.

Vattimo, G. (1992), *The Transparent Society*, Baltimore, MD: Johns Hopkins University Press.

Weber, M. (1947), *The Theory of Social and Economic Organization*, London: Free Press.

White, M. and A. Hunt (2000), 'Citizenship: care of the self, character and personality', *Citizenship Studies*, **4** (2), 93–116.

12. Hope for sustainable development: how social entrepreneurs make it happen

Christian Seelos and Johanna Mair

12.1 INTRODUCTION

> The massive scale on which social problems are conceived precludes innovative action because bounded rationality is exceeded and dysfunctional levels of arousal are induced. (Weick, 1984: 40)

Well into the first decade of the new millennium, we still cannot escape being confronted with social, environmental, political and economic problems on a scale that seems overwhelming in the sense of Karl Weick's statement. The emotional drama caused by pictures of war, terrorism, natural catastrophes that caught their victims unprepared, the hungry and the diseased – pictures that refuse to disappear from our daily newspapers and television screens – may indeed promote resignation, a feeling of hopelessness and powerlessness. At the same time, important decisions need to be made about how to address socio-economic challenges at a global level. This includes issues such as global warming, elimination of poverty, and allocation of funds to education, economic development and technological innovation. The aim is to balance economic growth and social development for all with the ability of the natural environment to sustain human life on this planet. To achieve this, international organisations are striving to define frameworks that enable local actions to result in a form of global *sustainable development*. Corporations are expected to identify and develop future growth markets and to allocate resources to the creation of new business models able to serve the needs of billions of low-income customers. Citizens are asked to support national policies that increase the spending of tax money for development efforts, and at the same time policies that reduce public debts so as to lower the constraints on future generations.

Unfortunately, the current level of uncertainty about the future and about political, economic and ecological development does not facilitate decision-making for public institutions, businesses or private individuals. This is exacerbated by the failure of decades of effort to define what sustainable development might mean and how to achieve it. A way of acting without knowing all the answers might be to purposely shift our focus to those areas where possible solutions emerge. This chapter introduces and examines such solutions and presents reasons for hope that the idea of more sustainable development and the global goal of eradicating poverty are not empty words or dreams. We propose that so-called *social entrepreneurs* are transforming social dilemmas in *developing countries* into manageable problems, which they solve in innovative and entrepreneurial ways. These entrepreneurs therefore build hope and optimism from the ground up by focusing on what is achievable locally, rather than trying to implement global best practices as development organisations have attempted for several decades. Through sensible experimentation and discovery, social entrepreneurs often grow their initiatives to unexpected scale and scope, and change our concept of what is possible along the way. Our analysis is based on the initiatives whose founders were recognised as outstanding social entrepreneurs by the Schwab Foundation established by Klaus Schwab, executive director of the World Economic Forum. We have produced in-depth case studies using interviews and field-based research on a number of initiatives.

We start by describing Sekem, an organisation in Egypt, to give the reader an idea of the type of scope and scale that social entrepreneurs create. This is followed by our main arguments: why there is a need for innovative and entrepreneurial solutions to complement or even replace some of the more traditional efforts to achieve sustainable development. In a next step, building on in-depth field research, we contextualise the notion of sustainable development using a richer description of a social enterprise in Bangladesh, BRAC. The case highlights the processes as well as the ingredients we believe are necessary to achieve sustainable economic and social development in the poorest of countries. Additional cases are used to augment and further illustrate the frame that we use to evaluate the impact of social entrepreneurs on recognised sustainable development goals.[1]

12.2   SEKEM: A CASE STUDY

On 15 December 2003, Dr Ibrahim Abouleish was the first social entrepreneur to receive the Right Livelihood Award, which has honoured many great people and organisations since its inception in 1980 (Seelos and Mair, 2004). Widely known as the Alternative Nobel Prize, it is traditionally awarded in Stockholm the day before the Nobel Prize ceremony. From the 2003 press release:

Sekem (Egypt) shows how a modern business can combine profitability and engagement in world markets with a humane and spiritual approach to people and respect for the natural environment. The Jury sees in Sekem a business model for the 21st century in which commercial success is integrated with and promotes the social and cultural development of society through the 'economics of love'. (Right Livelihood Awards, 2003)

The award honoured the fruits of the 26-year mission of Abouleish and his family to build hope for the poor masses of his home country, Egypt. Abouleish had visited Egypt in 1975, after many years abroad, to show his Austrian wife and their two children the beauty of his home country. However, the picture was grim. The many social problems, widespread poverty and lack of hope left him in shock about the sad fate of his countrymen. Abouleish decided to find solutions for many of these problems and to contribute to the holistic development of Egypt's society. In 1977, Abouleish said goodbye to many friends, a secure and comfortable life, the senior position he held in a pharmaceutical company, and many memories from two decades studying and working in Austria. To give his vision structure, he started an initiative and named it Sekem – meaning 'vitality from the sun'. He wanted to prove that development was not necessarily dependent on donations, abundant resources, strategic plans or the application of sophisticated economic models. Abouleish's determination, coupled with a healthy element of stubbornness, led him to prove his point in a drastic way. He bought a piece of desert land in the poorest of surroundings as the starting point of his initiative. Using imagination and creativity and the support of people he had inspired with his vision, he built and acquired the resources that he needed in order to succeed – for example, a water source, buildings, roads, electricity – and transformed the desert soil into fertile land with the help of organic dung from cows that he had received as a donation from Germany. Throughout the 1980s and 1990s, Sekem developed into a modern business conglomerate based on organic agriculture and bio-pharmaceuticals. It also runs a modern and well-equipped medical centre, a kindergarten, primary and secondary schools, an academy, an orchestra and a university. Furthermore, Sekem has established many partner organisations and a network of many thousands of farmers to enable a wide variety of commercial, social and cultural activities that embrace the poorest sectors of Egyptian society.

12.3 SUSTAINABLE DEVELOPMENT AND THE MILLENNIUM DEVELOPMENT GOALS

In 1987, Gro Harlem Brundtland put forward the global objective of achieving sustainable development (SD). She had been tasked by the United Nations General Assembly with writing 'a report on environment and the global problématique to the year 2000 and beyond, including proposed strategies for sustainable development' (United Nations General Assembly, 1983: 132). Brundtland identified finding a path of balanced social and economic development compatible with a notion of social equity across space and time as the main goal for the proposed global efforts (United Nations General Assembly, 1987). At a minimum, SD should offer people a basic level of subsistence necessary to live in dignity, and an overall level of consumption and use of resources that does not limit the options available to future generations. The report left open the question of how such balanced development is to be achieved:

> No single blueprint of sustainability can be found, as economic and social systems and ecological conditions differ widely among countries. Each nation will have to work out its own concrete policy implications. Yet irrespective of these differences, sustainable development should be seen as a global objective. (United Nations General Assembly, 1987: 51)

To instil new momentum in efforts to achieve SD, the UN Millennium Declaration was adopted in 2000 at the largest-ever gathering of international heads of state. It committed countries – rich and poor – to do all they can to eradicate poverty, promote human dignity and equality, and achieve peace, democracy and environmental sustainability. To operationalise the notion of SD, the United Nations defined a set of Millennium Development Goals (MDGs), based on a resolution adopted by the General Assembly in September 2000. The MDGs comprise eight specific, quantifiable and monitorable goals (with 18 targets and 48 specific indicators) for development and poverty eradication by 2015 (United Nations General Assembly, 2000). Goals included human rights, health, education and environmental issues. However, by 2002 it had already become clear that in many countries the targets might not be reached. The participants at the International Conference on Financing for Development held in Monterrey noted with concern 'current estimates of dramatic shortfalls in resources required to achieve the internationally agreed development goals, including those contained in the United Nations Millennium Declaration' (United Nations, 2002: 10). This concern was confirmed by other institutions that are monitoring progress against the MDGs (UNDP, 2003).

12.4   A NEED FOR INNOVATIVE ACTION

Reducing income poverty and many of the associated symptoms of poverty has become the overarching goal of sustainable development efforts. Economic development is considered essential to reduce poverty and to meet the MDGs (World Bank, 2004). However, three decades of experience with aid, foreign investment and policy reforms to kick-start economic growth have produced more stories of failure than of success (Stiglitz, 2002). For many decades, economic theory assumed that the relative backwardness of poor countries would drive them to 'catch-up' with richer ones. Unfortunately, that did not happen for many of the poorest countries (Pritchett, 1997). Aid and investment, in diverse forms ranging from general capital investment, adjustment loans and provision of fully equipped factories, to direct efforts towards large-scale education or birth control, did not achieve much in many poor countries.

Equally, within such countries the poor often remain stuck in poverty traps, unable to catch up. Both between countries as well as within countries, developed and underdeveloped, the distribution of wealth and resources is highly unequal (Gottschalk and Smeeding, 1997). Analysing positive and negative effects of the economic development in Brazil, Richard Trotter notes that 'income inequality in Brazil remains one of the most extreme in the world' and has resulted in dividing Brazil into a 'first world and a third world country', where an aggregate growth in income during the 1980s translated into the top 1 per cent earning as much as the bottom 50 per cent together (Trotter, 2004: 178–83).

Why Traditional Models Have Failed

Development is a complex process and cannot be programmed through linear interventions (Easterly, 2001). More than 20 years ago, Dennis Rondinelli pointed to the problem of false assumptions in development projects, noting that 'delays, cost overruns, changes in objectives, and other deviations are usually attributed to inadequate design, analysis, and administrative control' (Rondinelli, 1982: 47). He emphasised the inherent unpredictability of many of the problems and the fact that rigid designs, rational analysis, and planning procedures may themselves be the source of many problems.

The realisation that decades of experimentation and large-scale efforts of multilateral development organisations have not revealed any replicable designs that would enable sustainable economic development on a truly global scale reflects Brundtland's concerns for the lack of a blueprint for sustainability. Furthermore, we clearly have not achieved the original goal of social equity – neither for today's society nor for tomorrow's. While consumption levels for the poorest are insufficient to yield decent living standards, consumption levels of the wealthy may increase the overall risk of sudden changes in the planet's life-support systems. This is reflected in concerns over our level of usage of natural resources and production of waste that are a result of this process (Arrow et al., 2004). Because we have no agreed formulas or reference points that would guide decisions to balance today's spending with saving for tomorrow, SD remains a learning process in dire need of innovative solutions and models for the creation of socio-economic development.

More Aid Alone Is Unlikely to Do the Trick

The call for significantly more aid by leaders such as Tony Blair at the 2005 World Economic Forum in Davos highlights the fact that priority is still being given to continued attempts to finance achievement of the MDGs. How more aid is supposed to lead to positive outcomes for the poor, however, remains unclear. During the last decade, as development projects grew more sophisticated and complex, many poor countries were already overwhelmed by the need to administer an increasing number of development projects. Thus, the main argument of many observers critical to traditional development efforts is that SD cannot be designed or achieved merely through supply and central administration of resources. What might be needed is a fresh approach of finding solutions and changing the very systems that produced the problems in the first place – an approach that does not emphasise aggregate or average positive outcomes but is driven by the ownership of positive outcomes by individuals. This is at the heart of the phenomenon of social entrepreneurship – to change the lives of real people and to change the systems that create and sustain poverty.

12.5 THE PHENOMENON OF SOCIAL ENTREPRENEURSHIP

In June 2006, an Internet search with the Google search-engine for the term *social entrepreneurship* (SE) produced more than 1 million hits. While SE as a practice seems to have taken off, academic research on the phenomenon is still scarce. Only in the last five to ten years, a number of business schools have established research centres for SE and offer MBA-level courses on the subject. However, research seems still preoccupied with terminology and defining the boundaries of the phenomenon. In his essay on 'The meaning of social entrepreneurship', J. Gregory Dees remarks:

> Though the concept of 'social entrepreneurship' is gaining popularity, it means different things to different people. This can be confusing. Many associate social entrepreneurship exclusively with not-for-profit organisations starting for-profit or earned-income ventures. Others use it to describe anyone who starts a not-for-profit organisation. Still others use it to refer to business owners who integrate social responsibility into their operations. What does 'social entrepreneurship' really mean? What does it take to be a social entrepreneur? (Dees, 1998: 1)

Neither of the terms *entrepreneurship* nor *social* lend themselves to clear definitions. The development of social entrepreneurship as an area for research closely resembles the development of research on entrepreneurship itself. Geoff Williams argued that interest in entrepreneurship as a practice and a field of study was crucially stimulated by community leaders' belief that entrepreneurship was a defining trend of the twenty-first century (Williams, 1999). Similarly, we observe that the rise of scholarly interest in social entrepreneurship goes hand in hand with an increasing interest in the phenomenon among elites. Over the last few years, a number of successful business entrepreneurs have dedicated substantial resources to supporting social entrepreneurship. For example, Jeff Skoll, co-founder of eBay, created a foundation and donated £4.4 million to establish a research centre for social entrepreneurship. Jeff Bezos, founder of Amazon, recently announced a US$1 million award for innovative approaches and breakthrough solutions to effectively improve communities or the world at large.

Sekem is among the first organisations whose founders were recognised as Outstanding Social Entrepreneurs by the Schwab Foundation. Klaus Schwab, founder and executive chairman of the World Economic Forum, endowed the Schwab Foundation for social entrepreneurship in 1998. The Schwab Foundation uses a number of criteria for awarding membership to the network. The successful social enterprise must demonstrate innovation, reach and scope, replicability, sustainability and direct positive social impact; it must also be a role model and add mutual value (for both the Schwab network and the social entrepreneur). Using these criteria, since its inception, the Schwab Foundation has selected an average of 10 Outstanding Social Entrepreneurs each year. In 2004, 15 were added to the network and in 2005 the Schwab network consisted of a total of 84 social entrepreneurs, who managed 74 social enterprises. Typically, the Schwab Foundation elects members to its network when their enterprise is in its growth and expansion phase, giving them the opportunity to network with members of the World Economic Forum and among each other, rather than offering cash grants.

A fruitful approach to understand the phenomenon of SE may be to study its importance for the achievement of desired social or economic outcomes

(Seelos and Mair, 2005a). To give meaning to the term social entrepreneurship we chose to examine its role for the overall goal of achieving sustainable development. Especially in the poorest countries, acting in a vacuum of effective government and market structures, we find that social entrepreneurs discover and create local opportunities and contribute to social, human and economic development. The dramatic need for development in these countries may explain how some small entrepreneurial initiatives were able to grow to an impressive scale and expand their scope to cover a wide range of human, social, cultural and economic activities. BRAC in Bangladesh, an organisation that has grown over 30 years and today is thought to be the world's largest social venture, exemplifies this dynamic.

BRAC: Social and Economic Development in Action

After a bloody liberation war with Pakistan, Bangladesh became independent in 1971. Millions of refugees returned, mainly from India, only to find destruction, violence and human misery. A Bangladeshi account executive working for Shell in London, Fazle Hasan Abed, decided to do something about the situation. In 1972, he founded the Bangladesh Rehabilitation Assistance Committee (BRAC) with a small grant from Oxfam, an international non-governmental organisation (NGO), as a temporary relief project with a regional focus. However, by 1974 the name had been changed to the Bangladesh Rural Advancement Committee, reflecting a new vision for dealing with a multitude of social problems on a national scale and the failure of government agencies to provide sufficient relief. Experiences in the early 1970s demonstrated that relief measures failed to impact the poor and that different solutions needed to be found through experimentation and learning. BRAC set up a research and monitoring division to support systematic prototyping, evaluation and learning in order to roll out programmes that work and limit the risk of failures. Innovation and learning was thus an integral part of BRAC's culture and organisational set-up from the beginning. The operation switched from relief projects to building an organisation for the holistic development of the poor. It combined skills transfer, improvement of health and educational status, provision of capital and the opportunistic creation of income-generating activities. By charging small (sometimes symbolic) fees, the idea was to become economically self-sufficient as much as possible and to instil a feeling of ownership that creates positive incentives in the participants. Over the years BRAC became more sophisticated in segmenting the poor into several levels that have unique needs. It has established customised programmes for all levels of poverty and abilities, which have enabled even the poorest to climb a development path that integrates them into

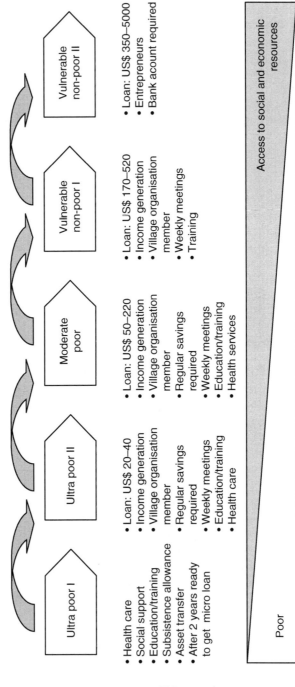

Ultra poor I
- Health care
- Social support
- Education/training
- Subsistence allowance
- Asset transfer
- After 2 years ready to get micro loan

Ultra poor II
- Loan: US$ 20–40
- Income generation
- Village organisation member
- Regular savings required
- Weekly meetings
- Education/training
- Health care

Moderate poor
- Loan: US$ 50–220
- Income generation
- Village organisation member
- Regular savings required
- Weekly meetings
- Education/training
- Health services

Vulnerable non-poor I
- Loan: US$ 170–520
- Income generation
- Village organisation member
- Weekly meetings
- Training

Vulnerable non-poor II
- Loan: US$ 350–5000
- Entrepreneurs
- Bank acount required

Access to social and economic resources

Poor

Figure 12.1 Poverty levels decline with access to social and economic resources

social and economic life. See Figure 12.1 for an illustration of the BRAC approach to segmented programmes for different levels of poverty.

BRAC coupled its microcredit provision with an elaborate economic development programme that ventured into various industries and helped people to find employment. It now also runs a commercial bank and a large dairy plant, shops selling the products of rural artists and other commercial ventures. The profits from these ventures enable BRAC to provide basic health services, to set up schools, adult education and training centres, and even a university. BRAC's ability to operate a large network of people in rural areas was recently acknowledged by the government, which increasingly seeks BRAC's support or even outsources to BRAC the implementation of large-scale health and education programmes (including a road safety programme). BRAC is now 80 per cent self-financed despite its many social and health-related activities for which costs cannot be fully recovered. Recently, BRAC began to transfer its model to Afghanistan to build a holistic development initiative based on insights from Bangladesh but adapted to the local context of Afghanistan.

Social Entrepreneurs and Sustainable Development

BRAC's strategy and activities clearly exemplify many of the issues implicit in Brundtland's definition of SD as development that 'meets the needs of the present without compromising the ability of future generations to meet their own needs' (United Nations General Assembly, 1987: 24). Using the cases of BRAC and Sekem, and providing details on a social enterprise called WasteConcern, allows us to operationalise the abstract notion of SD. Specifically, we propose to decompose the notion of SD into three distinct sets of activities that aim at: (1) satisfying basic human needs; (2) creating communities that establish norms, rights and collaborative behaviour as a prerequisite for participating in social and economic development; and (3) translating the more abstract needs of future generations into action today (Figure 12.2).

Catering to Basic Human Needs

In her report, Brundtland explicitly asked that priority be given to satisfying the essential needs of the poor (United Nations General Assembly, 1987). Given women's central position in the household, BRAC concentrates its efforts on poor women. Women are key to health, nutrition and family planning, and they are reliable savers and borrowers. Providing health services and educating women in how to prepare safe food for their families directly caters to basic human needs. To achieve this on a large

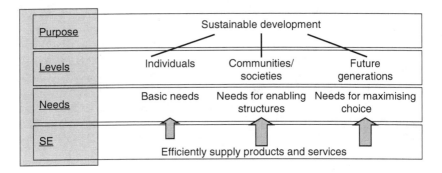

*Figure 12.2   An operational model of the contribution of social
entrepreneurship (SE) to sustainable development*

scale, BRAC trained a cadre of village health volunteers to provide a
comprehensive set of interventions to poor villagers, including preventive,
promotive, curative and rehabilitative health services. The many vegetable,
fish, poultry and dairy farms that BRAC operates are important sources
of food for the poor. BRAC also provides small loans to repair or build
houses and, as far as possible, also provides the means to repay the loans.

Sekem, the initiative briefly described in the introduction, opened a
medical centre in 1996 to provide health care for the neighbouring community. The medical centre soon developed a high demand for its services. As a
Sekem manager explained, 'everyone in the area was sick' (personal communication, 2004). When the medical staff visited the neighbouring community,
it turned out that almost everyone had illnesses such as parasite infections or
allergies. Soon the medical centre was providing treatment to around 30 000
people yearly, with comprehensive basic health-care services. The organic
agriculture that Sekem introduced within its network of farmers protected
thousands of people from the health damages of long-term pesticide exposure. Sekem also introduced a fair trade system that spreads risk along the
value chain and provides a form of insurance to vulnerable farmers against
becoming victims of famines caused by natural disasters.

Changing Norms and Behaviour to Create Opportunities

A second crucial development aspect was emphasised by Brundtland
when she called to provide the poor with 'the opportunity to satisfy their
aspirations for a better life' (United Nations General Assembly, 1987: 25).
Health and social issues needed to be taken care of before people could
be economically productive. Consequently, BRAC provided services in

all the areas that prevent poor people from participating in economic life. Women were the most vulnerable group and had the least rights. Thus, changing the roles and perception of women in Bangladeshi society was key to reducing inequality and promoting learning and development. Education about rights and the provision of legal services was important to enable women to participate in economic life. This also meant a constant fight against fundamental religious tendencies, but BRAC management believe that they were successful in breaking many of the old norms that discriminated against people due to race, gender or hierarchy. BRAC used effective group processes to engage the poor in a structure called the 'Village Organisation'. This was usually a closed group of women who relied on each other for support and for monitoring progress. In weekly meetings with BRAC workers, the groups discussed ideas and problems and repaid their loans in small regular amounts. This instilled discipline, mutual support and individual as well as communal responsibility. The need to develop new norms for how people relate to each other, as well as to change the outlook on life for individuals, was always an important objective for BRAC's schools and education programmes. On a recent field trip, the authors of this chapter visited one of BRAC's schools. The 10- to 12-year-old children expressed their own expectations when asked what their future dream jobs would be (personal communication, 2005). They clearly did not want to become rickshaw drivers or housewives but, rather, wanted to be teachers, doctors or managers – expectations that also created a responsibility to provide these opportunities. It became clear to BRAC management very early on that the absence of markets and opportunities limited people's ability to use micro-loans productively and make use of their education. BRAC has built a finance industry for the poor in Bangladesh that ranges from microcredit for different levels of poverty to venture capital for micro-entrepreneurs to full-fledged commercial banks. Furthermore, it has ventured into six sectors to productively employ large numbers of poor people: poultry, fishery, livestock, sericulture, agriculture and agro-forestry. The absence of efficient markets to provide reliable inputs and the lack of infrastructure made it necessary for BRAC to manage the whole value chain, from training and organising the supply chain, to production, quality control, marketing and sales. A negative side-effect was that BRAC's growth and speed of development has thus far left little space for collaborations with the private sector. Rare examples include a joint venture with Renata Limited, a local pharmaceutical company that was founded and later divested by Pfizer. BRAC-Renata expanded poultry breeding capacity to one of the largest in Bangladesh. However, the joint venture has been dissolved at the request of Renata because it felt that BRAC was too large and diversified to consider their joint venture of sufficient strategic importance. BRAC sold its stake at a significant profit to Renata.

BRAC today increasingly tries to connect the rural poor to existing markets in urban areas or international markets. Many other social entrepreneurs have succeeded in connecting the poor with markets. For example, Sekem pioneered organic agriculture in Egypt and sells its products in the local and international markets. A part of the profits of the Sekem Holding of companies provides financial support for its various non-economic activities.

Catering to the Needs of Future Generations

The third aspect emphasised by Brundtland was that satisfying the needs of current generations must be achieved 'without compromising the ability of future generations to meet their own needs' (United Nations General Assembly, 1987: 24). Future generations have a current – albeit abstract – need for us to act on their behalf and in their interest as well. We do not know the exact nature of future needs, but certainly, future generations have a need to make their own choices. The concept of sustainable development thus implies that we should act in ways that do not increase constraints and thus lower the choices available to future generations. Inheriting a set of serious environmental and social problems will not support this goal. The costs of environmental degradation as a side-effect, or even a result of economic growth and modern lifestyles, accrue over long time periods and are spread over many stakeholders. The environment as a social asset is a shared common property; this characteristic of the environment does not maximise the incentives for individuals to best maintain it. In many poor countries, priorities understandably focus on current problems and the value of future benefits is heavily discounted. BRAC focuses on water and sanitation issues. Among other efforts of awareness building, it uses local entrepreneurs to build slab latrines – over 180 000 were installed in 2003 alone. In collaboration with the government and other NGOs, BRAC wants to achieve 100 per cent national sanitation by 2010. But BRAC is also concerned about the increasing disappearance of local culture and handicrafts. It considers this an important public asset that should be maintained for future generations. Connecting artists with the markets in the capital through BRAC-managed stores led to a revival of local arts because of the possibility of generating an income from this activity. It now involves over 35 000 artists. In Egypt, Sekem, as part of its mission to heal the land, targeted an important environmental problem. Cotton was Egypt's most important cash crop. Unfortunately, it is also a magnet for countless insidious pests and has been known worldwide as one of the most pesticide-intensive crops. Sekem developed a biodynamic concept for organic cotton cultivation based on the use of pheromones to control cotton insects. The results were so convincing that the Egyptian authorities officially promoted the methodology and implemented strict legislation that limited the use of pesticides. Over the following years, the total use of pesticides in Egyptian cotton fields was reduced to less than 10 per cent of the previous amount on nearly the same cultivation area, thus saving about 30 000 tons of pesticides per year. By 1999, these methods had been applied to nearly 80 per cent of the entire Egyptian cotton-growing areas.

Waste and pollution are common side-effects of early industrialisation and urbanisation that create costs for future generations. Dhaka, the capital of Bangladesh, produces more than 3000 tons of solid waste daily. For the government, this created an insurmountable problem – it had to spend almost 20 per cent of its total budget to transport less than half of the waste to a limited number of available open disposal sites. Woman and children from city slums put themselves at great risk searching the disposal sites for items that could be sold, such as broken glass, metal, cloth or containers. The sites contain hazardous waste, are breeding grounds for disease vectors, pollute the ground water, constitute fire hazards and produce odour and significant amounts of methane – one of the greenhouse gases. Two entrepreneurs, Iftekhar Enayetullah and Maqsood Sinha, started an initiative called WasteConcern to address this problem in an entrepreneurial manner (Thurner et al., 2006). They recognised that the waste contained up to 80 per cent organic matter and that this could be composted to produce an organic fertiliser. WasteConcern also identified farmers as potential users of the compost. Farmland in Bangladesh was threatened by an overuse of chemical fertilisers that lowered organic matter in the soil to unsustainable levels. WasteConcern thus set up a marketing channel for their organic fertiliser by partnering with a local agrochemicals company. The demand from farmers for the product exceeded all expectations and the agrochemicals company then signed a contract stating that they would buy all the compost WasteConcern could possibly produce. It mobilised communities and orchestrated a simple but efficient waste collection mechanism that provided new jobs for several thousand poor people from city slums. The project is financially viable and is ready to be scaled up significantly. It also relieves the government of a huge social problem and saves tax money for other purposes.

Social Entrepreneurs Are Making an Impact

The scale of the impact on social and economic development that many social entrepreneurs are having is significant. BRAC has distributed more than US$2 billion in micro loans, with a pay-back ratio of more than 97 per cent. It has built over 40 000 mainly one-room schools and operates a network of 70 million people in 65 000 villages all over Bangladesh. Between 1980 and 1990, about 2000 BRAC health workers trained 13 million women in the use of oral rehydration therapy, a cost-effective means of treating most instances of diarrhoea. This success story hugely improved the standing of BRAC vis-à-vis the government of Bangladesh. The recent drop in infant and child mortality is attributed largely to this effort. Its economic development activities have generated more than 5 million jobs and in 2003 alone it provided the government with tax revenue of US$1.3 million.

Another example of social entrepreneurship, from Brazil, is the Committee for the Democratisation of Information Technology (CDI). Within 10 years of its founding, CDI has built a large network of schools that teach computer skills to the poorest children in the favelas of Rio, other disadvantaged areas in Brazil and many other countries in Latin America. In 2004, CDI had more than 500 000 alumni, many of whom found simple jobs for the first time after attending CDI schools.

In Kenya, an initiative called ApproTec was the idea of two entrepreneurs who started building simple technology using local resources that enabled poor people to start businesses. The income generated by these businesses amounted to 0.5 per cent of Kenya's gross domestic product (GDP) in 2004 and ApproTec created over 35 000 small businesses (Seelos and Mair, 2005a).

Social Entrepreneurs Contribute to Meeting Millennium Development Goals

Using a more formal framework for SD, we mapped all enterprises constituting the Schwab Foundation network according to their contribution to the MDGs. Figure 12.3 shows the results of our impact analysis of the models, products and services of the current population of 74 social enterprises.

We considered 48 initiatives to directly contribute to targets defined by the MDGs (Seelos et al., 2005). From the information available, the remaining initiatives may not directly affect the specific MDGs, although many of them fulfil other UN goals that were, in fact, also outlined in the Millennium Declaration of 2000, such as human rights issues, landmine clearance and others. Thus, a majority of the Schwab Foundation social entrepreneurs have a direct and positive impact on achieving the MDGs. These social entrepreneurs are able to operate in some of the least developed countries (LDCs) as defined by the United Nations (UN), including

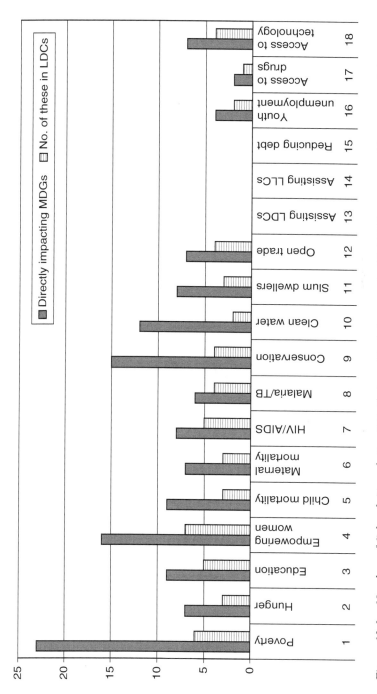

Figure 12.3   Number of Schwab Foundation SEs that positively impact the 18 MDG targets, and how many of these are operating in the least developed countries (LDCs)

Afghanistan, Angola, Benin, Chad, Congo, Ethiopia, Gambia, Lesotho, Malawi, Mozambique, Niger, Tanzania, Bangladesh, Cambodia, Laos and Nepal. Interestingly, we have no indication that any of the social entrepreneurs actually made a conscious attempt to directly contribute to the MDGs, especially as most of them were founded long before the MDGs were defined. Yet many of the models social entrepreneurs build through experimentation, trial and error are in line with the targets set by the development community. We therefore suggest that, by examining the models of successful social entrepreneurs, we will be able to generate a better understanding of how to address the MDGs and to achieve SD than by just focusing on the more traditional development projects undertaken by large multilateral institutions, local governments and non-governmental organisations.

12.6 CONCLUSION

Sustainable development goes beyond merely trying to achieve the Millennium Development Goals. It is about creating and discovering the many conditions necessary for the achievement of goals as an outcome. The social entrepreneurs we describe in this chapter are inspiring role models when it comes to devising innovative organisational models able to cater to the needs of the poor. The best models are profitable and continually expand in scale and scope. BRAC shows how economic development can be made possible by first investing in human needs in order to free people from a mere fight for survival. At the same time, BRAC invested in changing norms and rules in order to create communities that were consistent with productive economic activities. Several researchers have shown that social capabilities, in the form of individual education and skill sets as well as collective norms of cooperation and trust, are important prerequisites for economic development (Abramovitz, 1995; Chanda and Putterman, 2004; Temple and Johnson, 1998). After many years of investment in building these social prerequisites, BRAC now focuses more on economic development and builds commercial enterprises as an important driver to move the poor in Bangladesh out of poverty on a larger scale. So far this has happened with little involvement of the private sector.

However, the case of Telenor's joint venture with the Grameen Bank highlights how companies can leverage these dynamics to produce significant shareholder value and create large-scale positive social outcomes as well. Telenor, the incumbent telecommunications company in Norway, invested in a joint venture with the Grameen Bank to operate a mobile phone licence in Bangladesh in 1997. It now has two organisational structures with different but mutually reinforcing strategic objectives: one maximises shareholder value by providing mobile services to the growing middle class; the other sells mobile phones to poor women in villages, who create their own small businesses selling phone calls to other villagers. The for-profit side now has a 60 per cent market share in a market of 150 million people. It is hugely profitable and growing rapidly, with a long way to go (3 per cent penetration so far). The non-profit side of the joint structure has created more than 100 000 jobs for poor women and already generates revenues equal to 10 per cent of the total revenues of the for-profit side (Seelos and Mair, 2005b).

A great deal of the work done by social entrepreneurship initiatives, such as BRAC or Sekem, focuses on changing the context that influences how people perceive the world. As a BRAC manager said: 'As soon as poor people understand that poverty is not a normal state but a symptom of things missing, their perception of life changes. All of a sudden there is hope of a different future' (personal communication, 2005).

NOTE

1. The information in this study on Sekem, BRAC and WasteConcern is derived from interviews by the authors with the founders and managers of each organisation and from various secondary sources.

REFERENCES

Abramovitz, M. (1995), 'The elements of social capability', in B.H. Koo and D.H. Perkins (eds), *Social Capability and Long-Term Economic Growth*, New York: St. Martin's Press, pp. 19–47.

Arrow, K.J., P. Dasgupta, L.H. Goulder, G.C. Daily, P. Ehrlich, G. Heal, S. Levin, K.-G. Mäler, S.H. Schneider, D. Starrett and B. Walker (2004), 'Are we consuming too much?', *Journal of Economic Perspectives*, **18** (3), 147–72.

Chanda, A. and L. Putterman (2004), 'The quest for development. What role does history play?', *World Economics*, **5** (2), 1–31.

Dees, J.G. (1998), 'The meaning of social entrepreneurship', Occasional Paper, CASE (Centre for the Advancement of Social Entrepreneurship), Fuqua School of Business, Duke University, Durham, NC.

Easterly, W.R. (2001), *The Elusive Quest for Growth: Economists' Adventures and Misadventures in the Tropics*, Cambridge, MA: MIT Press.

Gottschalk, P. and T.M. Smeeding (1997), 'Cross-national comparisons of earnings and income inequality', *Journal of Economic Literature*, **35** (2), 663–87.

Pritchett, L. (1997), 'Divergence, big time', *Journal of Economic Perspectives*, **11** (3), 3–17.

Right Livelihood Awards (2003), Press release, retrieved 23 September 2005 from www.rightlivelihood.org/news/event03.htm.

Rondinelli, D.A. (1982), 'The dilemma of development administration: complexity and uncertainty in control-oriented bureaucracies', *World Politics*, **35** (1), 43–72.

Seelos, C. and J. Mair (2004), *The Sekem Initiative*, case study, DG-146-E, IESE Business School, University of Navarra, Barcelona.

Seelos, C. and J. Mair (2005a), 'Social entrepreneurship: creating new business models to serve the poor', *Business Horizons*, **48** (3), 247–52.

Seelos, C. and J. Mair (2005b), 'Sustainable development, sustainable profits', *European Business Forum*, **30**, 49–53.

Seelos, C., K. Ganly and J. Mair (2005), 'Social entrepreneurs directly contribute to global development goals', IESE Business School, University of Navarra, Barcelona.

Stiglitz, J.E. (2002), *Globalization and its discontents*, New York: W.W. Norton.

Temple, J. and P.A. Johnson (1998), 'Social capability and economic growth', *Quarterly Journal of Economics*, **113** (3), 965–90.

Thurner, C., C. Seelos and J. Mair (2006), *Waste Concern*, IESE Study, 33, IESE Business School, University of Navarra, Barcelona.

Trotter, R. (2004), 'The new economic and social model – a third stage of economic and social development in Brazil in the millennium: One Brazil – shared humanity – wealth creation and social justice', *The Journal of American Academy of Business*, **4**, 178–83.

United Nations (2002), 'Report of the International Conference on Financing for Development, A/CONF.198/11', Monterrey, Mexico, March.

United Nations Development Programme (UNDP) (2003), *Human Development Report 2003. Millennium Development Goals: A Compact among Nations to End Human Poverty*, New York, Oxford: Oxford University Press.

United Nations General Assembly (1983), 'Process of preparation of the environmental perspective to the year 2000 and beyond', Resolution 38/161, 19 December.

United Nations General Assembly (1987), 'Development and international economic co-operation: environment', Report of the World Commission on Environment and Development, Resolution 42/427, 4 August.

United Nations General Assembly (2000), 'United Nations Millennium Declaration', Resolution 55/2, 18 September.

Weick, K.E. (1984), 'Small wins. Redefining the scale of social problems', *American Psychologist*, **39**, 40–49.

Williams, G. (1999), 'An entrepreneurial odyssey: why the next century will belong to entrepreneurs', *Entrepreneur*, April, 106–13.

World Bank (2004), *World Development Report 2004: Making Services Work for Poor People*, Washington, DC: Oxford University Press.

Index